THIS BOOK IS FOR YOU IF:

- You're trying to cut down on added sugar and eat more vegetables

- You have a general sense that you could feel better, for example, you often feel bloated, stressed out, or exhausted

- You're "gut curious": You've seen articles about gut health and want to know what the fuss is about; or you know the gut is important but don't know how to go about keeping it healthy

- You value feeling good in your body and like keeping up with new health research

- You have a diagnosed modern chronic illness like type-2 diabetes, autoimmune disease, leaky gut, or allergies

- You have joint pain and inflammation

- You're already on board with eating for gut health and want some new, delicious recipes

HELP YOURSELF

HELP YOURSELF

A GUIDE TO GUT HEALTH

FOR PEOPLE WHO Love DELICIOUS FOOD

LINDSAY MAITLAND HUNT

PHOTOGRAPHY BY
LINDA PUGLIESE

HOUGHTON MIFFLIN HARCOURT
BOSTON NEW YORK 2020

Special-Occasion Short Ribs 274

Copyright © 2020 by Lindsay Maitland Hunt

Photography © 2020 by Linda Pugliese

Illustrations © 2020 by Mélanie Johnsson

Black and white patterns © Curly_Pat via Creative Market

One pot icon © Rashad Ashur / Shutterstock.com

Quick and easy icon © elnur SS / Shutterstock.com

Plant-based icon © NeMaria / Shutterstock.com

Gut icon © Arcady / Shutterstock.com

For information about permission to reproduce selections from this book, write to trade.permissions@hmhco.com or to Permissions, Houghton Mifflin Harcourt Publishing Company, 3 Park Avenue, 19th Floor, New York, New York 10016.

www.hmhco.com

Library of Congress Cataloging-in-Publication Data is available.

ISBN 978-0-358-00839-2 (POB); ISBN 978-0-358-00838-5 (ebook)

Book design and hand lettering by Laura Palese

Food styling by Monica Pierini

Prop styling by Lindsay Maitland Hunt

Printed in China

C&C 10 9 8 7 6 5 4 3 2 1

This book presents, among other things, the research and ideas of its author. It is not intended to be a substitute for consultation with a professional healthcare practitioner. Consult with your healthcare practitioner before starting any diet regimen. The publisher and the author disclaim responsibility for any adverse effects resulting directly or indirectly from information contained in this book.

Tell me what you eat, and I will tell you what you are.
—JEAN ANTHELME BRILLAT-SAVARIN, *The Physiology of Taste*

Sometimes I feel like I am living on a different
star from the one I am used to calling home. It has not been a
steady progression. I had to examine, in my dreams
as well as in my immune-function tests, the devastating effects
of overextension. Overextending myself is not stretching
myself. I had to accept how difficult it is to
monitor the difference. Necessary for me as cutting down
on sugar. Crucial. Physically. Psychically. Caring
for myself is not self-indulgence, it is self-preservation,
and that is an act of political warfare.
—AUDRE LORDE, *A Burst of Light: and Other Essays*

TO MY PARENTS.
For their love and support,
and for hosting me as a symbiont.

CONTENTS

INTRO

ALL ABOUT THE **1**

GUT MICRO-BIOTA

2 EAT GOOD TO FEEL GOOD

3 THE RECIPES

INTRO

Food has always been a defining feature of my life.
Whether it's work (developing recipes and writing about cooking for
magazines and websites) or personal (regularly hosting
dinner parties and showing my love through freshly baked cookies),
I deeply identify as a cook and food lover, and for a long time I had
no qualms about my life and career blending seamlessly.

That is, until I started collecting a grab bag of painful and debilitating symptoms like heartburn, migraines, itching, sudden and severe weight gain, joint pain, recurring yeast infections, stomach aches, and fatigue. Does that sound like a healthy, active, then twenty-nine-year-old woman? Not so much.

So, frustrated from years of sickness, I did something radical. I decided to cut almost every food out of my day-to-day diet. Goodbye sugar, not even fruit. No more gluten, dairy, soy, eggs, or any foods that the internet—where I was looking for answers at the time—considered "high carb" like whole grains. Just about every food I truly loved was off the list (and you're talking to someone who co-founded the Cheese Club in high school). If this sounds extreme, that's because it was. And don't

worry, that kind of restriction is decidedly *not* the way of eating I share in this book, nor—as I know now—is it supported by science. But my essentially scorched-earth approach of trying to get better through food speaks to where so many people are now: desperately mining the world of internet advice for what turns out to be fool's gold.

By the time I attempted my drastic food-based approach to feeling better, I had been amorphously sick for three-and-a-half years, finding no cure or even an overarching explanation, but rather accumulating distinct diagnoses accompanied by pills and more pills. Traditional medicine had not just failed me, it had wiped out my bank account and left me so depressed I no longer remembered who I was or why I cared about anything at all. Changing my diet was the last resort.

While you (or someone you love) might not have collected all the same symptoms in the same order or even the same patterns, you might also be enduring any number of chronic issues such as allergies, joint pain, headaches, fatigue, or unexplained weight gain. Or, you might be right at the cusp of tipping from health to sickness without realizing it. And at the extreme end, a steady ramping up of symptoms, depletion of money from doctor visits and medications, and suffocating sense of helplessness are a combination many people know all too well. For me, there was a light at the end of the tunnel: After everything fell apart, I finally turned to food to get better, and in the process, I learned about the invisible community of microbes that lives in our guts and informs how we feel both physically and emotionally. Once I started eating with my microbes in mind—a way of eating that is abundant and delicious, not restrictive—it was as though I waved a magic wand across my body, erasing years of pain, misery, and confusion.

In spring 2017, after years of snowballing symptoms, my health had reached a tipping point, and I set about to change the way I ate. I'd been a food writer and recipe developer for almost a decade, and saying goodbye to the foods I loved (and potentially changing part of my career) felt painful and lonely. Not to mention, I was, and still am, a true believer in "everything in moderation." I mean, I *literally* wrote the book on eating "healthyish." But, in the spirit of honesty, I admit that just because I wrote about balanced eating, it

didn't mean that I lived it all the time. Sure, I ate whole grains topped with vegetables and knew my way around a kale salad, but I also used food and alcohol to cope with loneliness, anxiety, and stress.

What I'm going to tell you is my honest story of going from being a child obsessed with food to an adult plagued by invisible symptoms, chronic pain, and a feeling of being lost in her own body. I learned while writing *Help Yourself* that truth often lies in the hyper-personal, and my hope is that if you read my story and recognize yourself in it, you'll feel hope and be inspired to take your health into your own hands.

The Situation

My love for food has often borderlined on obsession. I was lucky to grow up in a household where the kitchen was as much a playground as it was a place to get sustenance. My mom was a caterer in early-eighties San Francisco, and she met my dad when she catered a holiday party for him and his ex-wife. Yeah, it sounds more salacious and exciting than it was, but my point is that food was more than just, well, *food*. It was a way to bring people together, to find love, and to create and experiment. I was encouraged to explore in the kitchen, so, naturally, I turned to what tasted best—baking! I loved the feeling of handing someone a chocolate chip cookie and seeing the excitement in their eyes. It wasn't long before an equation became clear to me: To feed someone is to get their affection. Simple. As a summer job after my sophomore year of high school, I started my own baking company, naming it Loulou's Baked Goods after the nickname my parents use for me. I set up at the local farmers' market and sold my sugar-laden treats: banana bread (with nut and no-nut options), chocolate chip cookies, peanut butter cookies, sour cream coffee cake, and brownies. My baking stand was a hit, and I even got some clients on the side for extra baking jobs.

After graduating from college, I got my bartender's license and started working at an Austrian restaurant in Tribeca, serving drinks for the sixty-seat restaurant and closing up at 2 a.m. (And sometimes even sneaking in my boyfriend for a nightcap or three. Lesson: Don't let a twenty-one-year-old run your bar.) I left the restaurant for culinary school, where I learned the basics of savory cooking, having until then only loved baking. It was quickly obvious to me that a restaurant career wasn't the right fit—too stressful and the late hours weren't doable for me. Instead, through an internship working for author Sarah Copeland as she wrote her first cookbook, I learned that writing about food and creating recipes was a job. Over that summer I worked five days a week at a specialty food shop and two days working for Sarah. I looked forward to those two days as much as I would a weekend off. I ran between her apartment and the grocery store for fear of wasting a precious minute learning by her side. The work was challenging, creative, and best of all combined the three things I loved most: writing, cooking, and photography.

Following my internship, I left the specialty food shop, worked for a celebrity chef's website, and then landed my next dream-come-true job as the food editorial assistant at *Real Simple* magazine. There, I perfected getting in early and staying late—not realizing that an all-hours assault doesn't increase productivity, but it certainly does decrease well-being. I was so ambitious and focused on my work that the

stakes felt like life-or-death even when I was simply developing a recipe or curating the perfect selection of holiday gifts for food lovers. What I didn't know was that the stakes really *were* life-or-death, but not in terms of whether I'd get a promotion. What I should have noticed was that after two promotions in three years, I was only getting sicker. The stress and lack of self-care played out on the scale of my body, steadily eroding my physical health and mental well-being.

Throughout my entire life to that point, I had chronic stomachaches, pretty low self-esteem when it came to body image, and would experiment with all sorts of manic eating approaches, from functionally starving myself on three Lean Cuisines a day to eating every dessert I came across. After I left *Real Simple,* through a year freelancing and then a job at BuzzFeed, things continued to break down: I had recurring bouts of yeast infections, UTIs, and BV (bacterial vaginosis), which meant I had to take repeated, multiday treatments of antifungal and antibiotic drugs. Rather than talking to me about the root cause of these infections (an overly sugary diet devoid of whole plant foods, combined with chronic stress), doctors shrugged off the recurrence.

Why, you might be wondering, am I talking about my vagina in a book about gut health? The answer is that they're related: Our bodies are complex matrices of bidirectional communication. (You're already familiar with this in the form of a common drug like Advil. When you have a headache, somehow a pill you swallow is dissolved in your digestive tract and your head stops hurting.)

I developed these issues because of a steady flow of sugar into my body without eating enough whole plant foods like vegetables, whole grains, and beans. And despite being interested in self-help and psychology books, and seeing a therapist, I was only beginning to view the chronic, unchecked stress in my life as a whole-body problem, which not only affects the good microbes in the gut, but also mental health, cardiovascular functioning, and more. Were I to have addressed these root causes, I might have averted years of pain, expensive doctor visits, and depression. (But then you wouldn't be holding this book in your hands, and I wouldn't have the honor of helping you. Silver lining?)

I dutifully swallowed pills in the hopes that I would get better, because—like many Americans with a faith in drugs that borders on the religious—I didn't question what these medications might be doing beyond "helping" me. And, since the doctor never said, "This antibiotic will wipe out a swath of important microbes in your gut," I followed the dosage instructions and waited it out. The thing is, though, had one of those doctors said plainly that my gut microbiota and therefore my health would be affected by the antibiotics (which kill bacteria, both pathogenic and beneficial alike) or antifungals (which kill fungi like the candida that causes a yeast infection, but also other necessary fungi in our bodies), it probably wouldn't have changed my decision to take the pills. This is because, while microbiota science was on the rise, it wasn't mainstream. And it takes time for emerging

science to reach clinicians and for them to translate that into advice for patients.

So I took each successive prescription and over-the-counter medication and likely wiped out many species of microbes from my gut.

I started having migraines and vertigo. Pills. Then joint pain, chronic acid reflux, and a fifteen-pound weight gain. More pills. Next, a diagnosis of hypothyroidism. That needed pills, too. Depression started to kick up, which was to be expected when I continued to feel sick and accumulate more symptoms. In March 2016, I had an onset of such terrible itching and hives, I had to go to the hospital twice in one week. The answer? Three new types of pills. Not once did any doctor ask if I was experiencing other symptoms. When I tried to tell them, they dismissed the possibility of any connection.

By the end of 2016, three years into this saga, I had gained so much weight that I had to buy an entirely new wardrobe. The amount of time and money I was spending on trying to find answers with new doctors was already extreme, but on top of that, I was having to buy more and more clothes. Also, I didn't feel good! It was insult added to injury in the most literal way.

Soon after finishing the manuscript for my first book, *Healthyish*, I started reading a book by a functional medicine practitioner about the connection between the thyroid and diet. She talked about the importance of what we eat and how we feel. Ultimately, the overly restrictive elimination diet that she and similar authors recommend wasn't the answer—it isn't plausible for real life, and it isn't supported by the leading research on the gut microbiota. But this was the first time I saw clearly that what I chose to eat or not eat was an important lever that I could pull,

and it didn't require going to the doctor, taking a pill, or dealing with insurance claims.

The truth is, at that time, I was more stressed than ever. I was planning the photo shoot for *Healthyish*, editing the manuscript, and on top of that, feeling sick. I say *feeling sick* so often because it truly was the entire way I lived. I was spending my whole life working and trying to get better. Being sick all the time and the way it was usurping my jovial, life-of-the-party identity made me feel ashamed. I hid how badly I felt from everyone I could—my editors had no idea how much pain I was in. I resisted being open about what I was going through because I didn't want it to define who I was. And yet, managing my symptoms, going to doctors, and submitting insurance claims took up all my time outside of work, not to mention my money.

The pain was no longer invisible at this point. I looked swollen, my skin stretched taut across my face and fingers, which creaked painfully as I bent them. I felt mocked each time I looked in the mirror, that all this work I was doing to get better only resulted in someone who I recognized less and less. I couldn't go to any more doctors who told me that I was crazy to ask about diet.

It felt like there was only one option left, and I made the heartbreaking decision to leave New York. I told myself I'd failed, wondering what it meant that I was moving home to live with my parents.

Finding My Path to Health

While I was staying with my parents, I decided to see a local functional medicine practitioner. After having so little luck with traditional Western doctors, I was willing to try anything—in this case, an MD who used a systems-based approach to find and treat the root cause of disease. His office, decorated with Tibetan prayer flags, felt like a world away from the harsh doctors of New York, who often seemed bothered that I was in their office at all.

Before my appointment, I'd had to fill out an incredibly long online survey. It asked questions about everything in my personal history, including things like how frequently I'd taken antibiotics, whether I was breastfed as a kid, and when all my various symptoms started. When I got to the office, the doctor had plotted my symptoms on a chart that showed what looked like the swell of a big wave in the ocean. Some symptoms started together, others at unique points, and over time they grew exponentially into a huge peak.

I told him my story, leaving out no details, even the ones I was embarrassed by, like my thirty-five-pound weight gain and frequent yeast infections. It felt weird to list so many issues at once, and I was worried he'd tell me I was a hypochondriac or that he had no idea what was going on. Instead, he said the exact thing I needed to hear: "This is a completely normal story. I can help you."

Every time I remember that moment, I pause and repeat to myself what he said: "This is a completely normal story. I can help you." Hearing that my suffering didn't make me an unsolvable freak case, but rather it was something understandable and treatable, was the first step in the path toward healing.

He heard me, and he let me know it. I realized when he said those words that I'd been sitting rigidly upright in the chair, hands gripping each other tightly, my voice tight with the fear that tears would break up my tale. I relaxed into the chair and a sense of calm flooded my body in a way I can only liken to sinking into warm honey.

The doctor explained that the gut was at the root of my issues. He posited that I had a condition called leaky gut, which is a casual-sounding name for a very serious state of imbalance where the lining of the gut becomes more permeable than normal, which leaks toxins, microbes, and other food particles into the bloodstream, wreaking havoc on the body in ways that are just beginning to be understood. (You can read more about leaky gut on page 43.) Based on my symptoms and history, he said, it seemed likely that something was off in my gut, causing a reaction to common foods. His suggestion was to make dietary modifications to heal my gut and bring my health back into balance.

Bolstered by the hope that this was the answer to my issues, I dutifully followed my doctor's recommendations for changing what I ate: his guidelines were to avoid gluten, dairy, and eggs. Not fun, and worse, after two months, I found that despite making these sacrifices, I felt as bad as ever. Yikes. How could this happen? Looking back now, I have an idea of why. First, I was still eating excessive amounts of sugar (notice that no one had mentioned to me how detrimental it was to my health), and second, I wasn't focusing on vegetables and other fiber-rich plant foods, which health-promoting gut microbes thrive on. Point being—cutting out gluten, dairy, and eggs wasn't a successful path to anything other than being unhappy. And that, I was already an expert in.

His three-pronged elimination approach also didn't work well because the focus was primarily on what I *couldn't* eat, rather than emphasizing what could support a balance of diverse beneficial microbes in my gut. Also, our brains resist being told no, not unlike a stubborn toddler. When someone says "don't eat gluten, dairy, and eggs," it makes you want exactly those three things.

The books I'd bought to learn about my various symptoms all cited research showing that these conditions were connected. However, each author focused on a single symptom or disorder—thyroid, inflammation, or candida overgrowth (that's basically a yeast infection, which turns out can happen in your gut, too). Despite each resource noting that these conditions coexist—I was living proof!—they didn't dig down to the reasons why and how these problems were connected.

I started reading specifically about eating for the gut microbiota and "healing your gut." The good news was that there was a groundswell happening around gut health. But the execution left much to be desired: There were convoluted

Leaky gut is not the only type of gut imbalance that can cause the symptoms I was experiencing. An imbalance of microbes known as *dysbiosis* can be associated with the same symptoms. For the full rundown on the connections between the gut and feeling sick, see page 43.

meal plans by doctors or nutritionists that were indecipherable even to me, a professional cook! Or, the recipes were created with only the facts and no flavor. I'm sorry, but I'm just never going to want to eat a cinnamon-spiced ground beef and sweet potato scramble for breakfast. Yuck! Many of the books led with overwhelming amounts of information, which ended up making me feel more stressed. When you're feeling sick and without any answers, the last thing you need is convoluted jargon adding to the confusion about what's wrong. I didn't like that almost every book required a strict elimination diet and used fearmongering language that made me feel becoming healthy was a tradeoff between feeling better and having a life.

Surely, I thought, there must be a way to eat that addressed my underlying gut issues, and that didn't negate flavor or require expensive specialty ingredients like tiger nuts or maca powder?

Creating the *Help Yourself* Way of Eating

Clearly, no one was going to give me the answers I needed in a useful (and delicious) way. It was time to take things into my own hands. I decided to focus exclusively on books written by experts in the field of gut microbiota science as I shifted how I ate.

I learned about what the microbes in our gut need to produce chemical byproducts that influence health. It's not just about cutting foods out, in fact, it's most important to eat enough of the foods good microbes love, to heal the gut lining and restore the balance of microbes. This requires eating a diverse array of whole plant foods for their dietary fiber, which is the preferred food of microbes that have a beneficial effect on health.

I also learned that the combination of drug after drug, chronic stress, and—here's the key—too much sugar was a toxic cocktail for my gut and, by extension, my entire body.

Sugary foods were out the window (at least for now), and more plants was the name of the game, it seemed. I focused on eating more vegetables, whole grains, and other plants like nuts and seeds, beans and legumes. Equally importantly, I completely removed added sugar from my diet. I no longer worried about cutting out dairy and eggs, since I learned that there was scant evidence that they needed to be eschewed entirely for gut health. (I did learn through blood testing that I had a wheat allergy, which meant I continued to eat gluten-free, but importantly, I didn't cut out whole grains entirely.)

This is when everything started to change.

Within one week of cutting out sugar, I had lost eight pounds. I should say that *Help Yourself* isn't about weight loss; however, I had felt so physically uncomfortable in my body, and my weight gain was a constant reminder of how out of control my health felt. It was as though I waved a magic wand over my body—symptoms like itching, swelling, joint pain, and depression lifted in a matter of days.

At first, I thought changing how I ate was the worst thing that could happen to me—that my career and my personal identity would suffer. The reality is that years in the food media industry had infected me with a pervasive sentiment that healthful food isn't cool. Thankfully, by the time I got to this research, I was ready to throw such a silly misconception away for good. From the perspective of my microbes and my health, all that mattered was feeling like myself again.

I was the best person this onslaught of illness could have happened to. Sure, I was sick, but I was also the one who could create a solution. As a recipe developer, I had the skills to come up with a new way to eat that would not just heal my gut, but would also be delicious, use regular ingredients, and not take up all my time with complicated preparations. It would be a taste-first approach that I could maintain while still having a life.

Slowly, I started sharing posts on Instagram and opening up about what I had been going through. The new food was versatile and beautiful—and in addition to getting questions about how exactly I was eating to feel better, I learned how many people were going through some of the same things: chronic candida, inflammation, hypothyroidism, and more. Many people—if they even knew diet could help—also shared that they didn't know how to go about eating in a realistic (and flavorful) way to address these issues. Most importantly, I wanted to create a friendly resource without the all-too-common intimidating medical jargon, rigid eating plans, and elimination diet approach. Not only am I not a fan of extremes, neither is your gut.

A clear theme emerged as I discussed my health issues with more people: the hunger for this way of eating is stronger than ever.

~~~~~~

When you consider the wide spectrum of diseases known to be linked to gut microbiota, it's staggering to imagine the implications of changing what we eat. Imbalance in gut microbiota is correlated with allergic diseases, metabolic disorders, cancer, inflammatory bowel disease, and many, many other conditions.

There is also a proven connection between the gut, its microbes, and the brain that runs in both directions. Through chemical messengers, direct nerve connections, and more, the gut is in constant communication with the brain. The mind-body connection is more than just the opening monologue in a yoga class, it's real. This means that food alone isn't the only thing at play; stress is also a big contributing factor to dysbiosis and leaky gut.

As I changed the way I ate, I also recalibrated how I approach life to wrest control from anxiety and stress. Practices like meditation, regular exercise, and positive self-talk are important tools for healing our bodies. I got better at listening to my body, valuing my own needs, and setting boundaries. The happier I felt, the easier it was to treat myself kindly, including eating food that was good for me (and my microbes).

I followed my plan religiously for three months—cooking, documenting what I ate, and making an effort to keep my stress in check. In that short period, under the supervision of my doctor, I tapered down from seventeen to just two pills a day (a massive financial savings) and no longer experienced chronic symptoms like itching, inflammation, ovarian cysts, yeast infections, and joint pain. Now, as you hold this book in your hands, I take no medications at all.

As I delved deeper into the research for this book, I learned what it means to live and eat with your gut microbiota in mind. I don't recommend what is known as an elimination diet, in which you strictly cut out a particular food (like tomatoes) or an entire food group (like grains). Rather, I focus on the abundance of ways to enjoy whole plant foods (what I call plant-focused eating), and reduce or eliminate added sugar, while offering ways to incorporate animal products like dairy, eggs, meat, and fish. This is not a plant-based (aka vegan) cookbook, however you will find about half the recipes are entirely made of plants.

The process of writing this book was a boot

camp in more than just how to eat. I spent an entire year quite literally living by the book. I cooked these recipes more times than I have ever cooked any recipe I'd ever developed because I wanted them to be truly delicious.

I am beyond privileged to have incubated these philosophies, recipes, and strategies with the love and support of my community. My parents even got on board and cooked and ate the food, and this book is all the better for their participation as semi-willing guinea pigs. If you're wondering why it matters to mention their cooperation, it's because they proved to me that this book is not some esoteric plan that only a health-conscious millennial like me could stick to. Not only did they love the vegetable-forward meals, both told me how much better they felt when they ate the food from *Help Yourself.* As baby boomers who are entering the latter years of their lives, people my

parents' age are finding that microbial diversity is of essential importance, too. Decline in number and variety of microbes correlates with decline in health. Basically, as long as we harbor a party of friends in our guts, we are also alive.

When I do have a flare-up in symptoms—from stress or going too far down the sugar train, as I am often tempted to do—I remember how freeing it was to feel good again, whether I want to eat broccoli rabe and beets or not. If I eat pizza, I make sure it's the best damned pizza I can get, and I don't engage in guilty feelings. What a waste it is to taint delicious food with shame and judgment. I make sure to follow it with gut-friendly food to keep my microbes happy.

I'd be lying to you if I pretended that it's always easy, but I am telling you the truth when I say it is quite *simple* to eat with your microbes in mind: Eat a variety of vegetables and other whole plant foods every day. Limit added sugar, ultraprocessed foods, and refined grains (such as wheat flours and products made with them, like pasta). That's it.

When I look back, I sometimes envy the girl loading up on birthday cake, not realizing it's only making inflammation rage harder in her body. Ignorance was easier in lots of ways, but it hurt, too. These days, I have completely recalibrated how I view the connection between food and health. If you don't have a diagnosed chronic illness, pain, or obvious inflammation, it can seem like the connection between food and our health stops at only what is visible on the outside. But it's not just about maintaining your jean size—this relationship goes much further than just how our body looks. The gut influences our mood, how our bodies feel, and how well they function. It can have long-term implications for serious diseases. Put simply, the stakes are critical—neglect the essential community of bacteria that lives in your gut and you're handing yourself a ticking time bomb, healthwise.

While I can't promise results, I *can* promise that you will eat great food that opens your eyes to how delicious and doable eating a variety of vegetables and other whole plant foods can be.

It took years of an Alice-in-Wonderland-like fall, tumbling backward down a dimly lit, confusing cavern until I found a way to feel good again. I want better for you and for all of us who desire to feel good in our bodies. It is crucial to maintain a happy partnership with our beneficial microbes, even if you think of yourself as healthy. Whatever stage of life you are in, this way of eating is a roadmap to feeling good that tastes good, too. No matter where you are on the spectrum from sick to healthy, I wrote this book in the hopes that I can help you help yourself.

A Personal Note

I'm aware that a multitude of factors beyond just "what I ate" were a part of my ability to heal. However, it was beyond the scope of the book to chronicle unequal access to health care, food, and the equally important resources of time and emotional support, all of which I had provided to me from my first breath. As an upper middle-class person, I could afford the food I wanted and to dedicate my time to finding answers. Modern chronic illnesses like the ones I mention here disproportionately affect women (specifically women of color), low-income populations, and minorities. Access to healthful ingredients isn't just the only problem: Time is as much an ingredient in cooking as onions, oil, and salt. I highly recommend Kristin Lawless's *Formerly Known as Food* for a comprehensive look at the problems around processed food, politics, and even how they extend to affect the gut microbiota.

A Note about My Methods

Microbiota science is a relatively new and exciting area of research that will continue to rapidly evolve in the coming years and decades. My goal was to both cover what is known about what microbes are there, what they do, and how they're connected to the body, but also to respect the developing discoveries of "known unknowns" and even species or chemical byproducts we can't even begin to imagine yet. To that end, I decided to set about researching the science and developing the recipes with an eye toward what is widely accepted, leaving out speculation and spurious conclusions.

I gathered my information from books written by experts (not by laypeople), scientific papers, and interviews with gut microbiota researchers.

First, I read books by the researchers who are studying how the gut microbiota works and what food is best to eat. I wanted to hear it from the people who loved microbes, who spent as much time studying these tiny creatures as I did learning how to perfect the chocolate chip cookie.

The first book I read, *The Good Gut* by husband-and-wife researchers Justin and Erica Sonnenburg, was a revelation because they wrote about food from a microbes-first perspective. Finally, I understood that "digestion" was more than just about calories and the "gut" was more than just a metaphor for feelings. I learned about the trillions of tiny creatures that live inside my large intestine, how they do their jobs, and what they like to eat. Most important, I gained perspective on how vital it was to keep my microbes in mind when I ate.

I moved steadily through all the other books on the market written by well-respected researchers on the cutting edge of gut microbiota science. This gave me context for why eating plants was so important and also explained that an omnivorous approach can be fine—gluten, dairy, and meat aren't inherently problematic for our microbial friends, but rather problems arise when they're overly refined (as in the case of white flour), aggressively sweetened (like sugary yogurts or ice cream), and/or eaten to excess (as in a burger every day rather than occasionally). Once I got the lay of the land, I had context to read scientific papers, studies, and reviews.

The guidelines I drew up for the *Help Yourself* way of eating are based on this research. After creating them, I realized my guidelines are essentially an amalgam of the Blue Zones diet, a term coined by Dan Buettner to describe the ways that the world's longest-lived populations eat, and the Mediterranean Diet, a pattern of eating that has been scientifically lauded for its anti-inflammatory effects. Given that the microbes we house train and are influenced by our immune system, it's no surprise that an anti-inflammatory way of eating would so largely overlap with what is good for the microbes in the gut.

I also enlisted two registered dietitians to gut check (har har) my process. Colleen Webb, MS, RDN, acted as a sounding board for questions about nutrition, serving sizes, and whether my statements were aligned with what gut-focused practitioners like her believe. Jenny Passione, RD, ran the recipes through the ESHA database (a tool for nutritional analysis). While I don't recommend relying on nutritional data as your guidelines for eating (as everyone differs in how they absorb calories and nutrients) I did want you to have the option to look at those traditional metrics.

If you are going to look at the nutritional info (whether in the back of this book for these recipes or on a package of food), I recommend looking at only the grams of fiber and the added sugar (which I've highlighted in the nutritional index). You want the fiber to be high and the added sugar to be low. If you watch your sodium intake, you can look at that number, too. Foods are complex matrices of ingredients that add up to a dietary pattern. To isolate individual nutrients without considering where the ingredient came from, how it was processed, and the way it is prepared is to ignore several factors that determine the food quality and how it affects your body.

I was already skeptical of nutritional numbers, but reading Gyorgy Scrinis's book *Nutritionism* and speaking with him helped me refine my thinking further. His concept of nutritionism defines and dismisses a way of looking at food for its individual parts rather than the whole. In other words, it's a mistake to look at a carrot and see it as a combination of beta-carotene, fiber, and calories, and to overly value how those nutrients contribute to (or detract from) our health, rather than valuing the carrot as a whole. This reductive focus causes one to see the beta-carotene, for example, above all other factors, like how that carrot was grown or the level of processing it was subjected to.

Other effects of nutritionism have included the simplification of entire categories of macronutrients, at times vilifying all fats, at other times all carbs. It's likely that you or someone you know has talked about how they need "tons of protein." To speak of protein in this way is to reduce food to a nutrient level, obscuring the food source of that protein (e.g., animal vs. plant-based), how it was grown or raised (e.g., grass-fed vs. conventional), and the level to which it was processed (e.g., a steak vs. sausage).

Scrinis's book has deeply informed my approach to the food guidelines in this book. For instance, instead of recommending "high-fiber" foods for gut health, I have reworked the advice to "a variety of plants, including vegetables, whole grains, and beans and legumes." Not only does this make it clear what you should buy in the grocery store, it also distinguishes between the ingredient and a manufactured food. For instance, it's better to eat a pineapple rather than a soda with added fiber. (This is a thing. Please don't buy it no matter how pretty the label or sweet-sounding the name.) My intention is to make it easier for you to eat well for your gut and, by extension, your whole body.

If you are looking for a particular subject and I didn't address it, that is because I didn't feel I had enough evidence to write about it. All these topics are rapidly evolving, and it was my goal to present as accurately as I could what is known and what seems plausible based on the research.

ALL ABOUT THE

1

GUT

MICRO-

BIOTA

YOUR BODY IS HOME TO AN ESTIMATED 100 TRILLION MICROBES. These single-celled organisms make up communities known as microbiota that reside all over (and inside) your body. You have distinct microbiotas on your skin, nose, lungs, mouth, stomach, intestines, and genitals.

But the largest collection of microbes lives in what is commonly referred to as "the gut," (more specifically inside your large intestine), and so is known as the gut microbiota. The digestive system is a complex combination of mouth, esophagus, stomach, small intestine, liver, large intestine (which includes the caecum, appendix, colon, and rectum), and the anus. Each of these organs plays a part, as does another incredibly important "organ"—the gut microbiota.

Yes, you got that right, the gut microbiota functions like an organ. It's invisible to the naked eye, so until recently, it hasn't garnered much scientific attention or acclaim, but it's as essential to our health as the heart or brain.

Caring for Your Gut

A guide to caring for your gut microbiota
is really a guide to being well.

Ignoring what's happening in our guts is like
assuming we don't have thoughts because we can't
see our brains.

It's not just about how your stomach feels. In fact,
it's much more than that.

Food is the main lever we can pull to change our
gut microbiota because that is what the microbes
digest and thrive on.

The point isn't that diet affects your gut microbes,
but rather that this community, known as the gut
microbiota, modulates our body's health, and so
how we eat affects how we feel in every way.

Humans have co-evolved in a symbiotic relationship with our gut microbes—we give them a home, and they in turn contribute to our health through many known and as yet unknown processes. They do this by breaking down the parts of plants that are indigestible to humans and in turn creating chemicals that both act locally in the gut and travel throughout our bodies. We know that among the many jobs microbes do for us, they train our immune systems from the moment we are born, communicate with the brain and other organs, and even influence our circadian rhythms. When this community becomes imbalanced (through a variety of mechanisms), our bodies tip from healthy to unhealthy. This means it's important to feed our microbial friends the food they need to survive: vegetables and other whole plant foods. Without enough sources of these foods, the otherwise friendly microbes start attacking the protective mucus lining of our guts, which can lead to negative effects throughout the body like inflammation, joint pain, and itching. To add insult to injury, eating too many refined grains, too much added sugar, and ultraprocessed foods not only starves the microbes we need for health, it also encourages the growth of ones that have potentially harmful effects on the body.

The bottom line is, a healthy body is one that harbors an abundance of microbes from a wide variety of species. No two humans contain the exact same gut microbiota, but the output of those microbes can have a similar effect on our health.

The Age-Old Partnership Between Humans and Microbes

After the human genome was sequenced for the first time in 2000, a new picture started to emerge: Our genes don't determine as much of the fate of body and health as we previously believed, but microbes and their own genetic capabilities influence our gene expression and health. (In addition, environmental factors, and how those interact with our genes, play a role.)

This same breakthrough in science allowed for the genome of the microbiota to be decoded. While our human genome contains almost 21,000 individual genes, our gut microbiome contains over 300 million genes, according to recent estimates. These microbial genes combine with our own to comprise the body's total genetic capabilities. While reports on the number of microbe cells and genes vary, and it's likely this estimate will be revised again and again, the point remains the same: We are not just human but rather a superorganism.

Why would our bodies allow for this foreign invasion?

It turns out that this relationship has co-evolved through the entirety of human existence. Why should humans do all the work when we could have a hardworking factory housed in our guts to make life easier? This relationship between humans (the host) and our microbes is what's called a symbiotic relationship: We give the microbes a place to live, and in turn, they help us out. In the case of the gut microbiota, the microbes digest plant material human bodies can't, synthesize essential vitamins and nutrients, and produce chemical messengers that relay messages to our immune system, brain, and other

organs—functions that have far-reaching effects on our overall health. It's a mutually beneficial arrangement.

And while our human genome is inalterable, our microbial genome can change and does constantly.

Before I explain exactly how the microbiota does its job, communicates to the rest of the body, and determines our health, it's important to understand the bigger picture of how our digestion works. We often colloquially use the term "the gut" to refer to the microbiota or to our entire digestive system. However, the gut microbiota is one element of a greater digestive system.

GERMOPHOBIA: WHY MICROBES HAVE GOTTEN A BAD RAP

When bacteria were first discovered, it was in the context of disease-causing microbes like tuberculosis, cholera, and syphilis. The association between disease and these pathogenic bacteria led to the conclusion that all "germs" must inherently be bad. In fact, almost every microbe is harmless to humans, and even more than that, many species are essential to our health. Even though some microbes are pathogenic in a human body in certain contexts, there is actually no such thing as a good or a bad microbe. Bacteria like *E.coli* and *Streptococcus aureus* live harmlessly in many human bodies without causing disease. However, for the purposes of this book, I'll use the terms *good* or *beneficial* to speak about microbes that have a positive effect on our bodies and *bad* or *pathogenic* to speak about microbes that have a harmful effect.

How Digestion Works, from In to Out

While eating could be described as putting food in our mouths, tasting it, then swallowing—a rudimentary description of eating if there ever were one—it is so much more than that. As most people know, eating isn't so straightforward as simply ingesting fuel for health. We are not machines but complex human creatures. Desire, craving, our individual psychology and relationship to self, social connection, pleasure— all these intangible elements and more play into the question of what we put into our bodies.

The act of eating itself begins with visual or hormonal signals to the brain that get translated into a general sense of being hungry or a specific thought like "I want a bowl of pasta."

Mouth

Once the food is on the fork, the mouth comes into play. And play it can be! For most people, I would

A glossary of important terms

Microbe A single-celled organism. This overarching term includes bacteria, eukaryotes (which includes yeasts and other fungi, as well as protists), archaea, and viruses. For the sake of visualization, I think it's helpful to use the metaphor of a factory. The microbe is the factory worker in this scenario.

Gut microbiota The complex community of various microbe species that live in your gut, often referred to as the gut flora. Bacteria represent the largest proportion of microbes in the gut microbiota. In our factory metaphor, the gut microbiota is the entire cohort of workers—from the guy working the assembly line all the way up to the CEO.

Gut microbiome The collection of genetic material contained in those microbes. Just like humans have a human genome, microbes have a microbiome. The microbiome tells us about the collective capabilities of the factory workers. Those capabilities (determined by each microbe's genes) tell us about potential but not about the actual output.

Metabolites These are the chemical byproducts of cell metabolism. In this book, I use this term to refer exclusively to microbial metabolites. Metabolites are produced when a microbe encounters food or other substrates (a fancy word for things microbes can digest). What you eat determines which capability each microbe uses—basically, it's a matter of the input (food) and how it combines with the worker (the microbe). The resulting product is a metabolite. Each metabolite has a different role in the body—it might act locally in the gut, or signal a nerve to communicate to the brain, or even travel through the bloodstream to other organs.

Metabolome The entire collection of chemicals produced by microbes. This gives us an idea of what the functional profile of the microbiota is—essentially, what the microbes do rather than just knowing their names. Think of this as seeing the entire line of what a company makes at its factory. You're not just looking at one pair of shoes, but also the pants, shirts, jewelry, and so on.

Probiotics These are live microorganisms that have a positive effect on health when consumed in adequate amounts. They could be in a pill or powder, in fermented food, or even bacteria you ingest from exposure to dirt or pets. Think of these as guest microbes: while they don't necessarily stick around in the long term, they are believed to provide benefits including training immune responses and producing metabolites as they pass through the digestive tract.

Prebiotics Foods (and other substances) consumed by a host's microorganisms that have a health benefit on the host. Prebiotics include, but are not limited to, fermentable dietary fiber derived from whole plants, as well as HMOs, a type of prebiotic found in breast milk, and oligosaccharides like inulin, which are extracted from plants and added to processed food or sold as supplements. Plants that are not "readily fermentable," aka not easily turned into chemical byproducts, are not technically considered prebiotic. Back to the factory metaphor, these are important raw materials for the workers to produce their wares.

Microbiota accessible carbohydrates (MACs) This is a term coined by researchers Justin and Erica Sonnenburg to encompass all food sources that escape digestion by human enzymes and land in the gut, where they are gobbled up by microbes. MACs are food for microbes, but unlike prebiotics, they don't necessarily provide a health benefit to the host (although they can). Because each person has a unique collection of microbes, what counts as a MAC to one person might not to another. (Put very simply: if you don't have a microbe to break down spinach, then spinach does not count as a MAC for you.)

DIGESTIVE SYSTEM

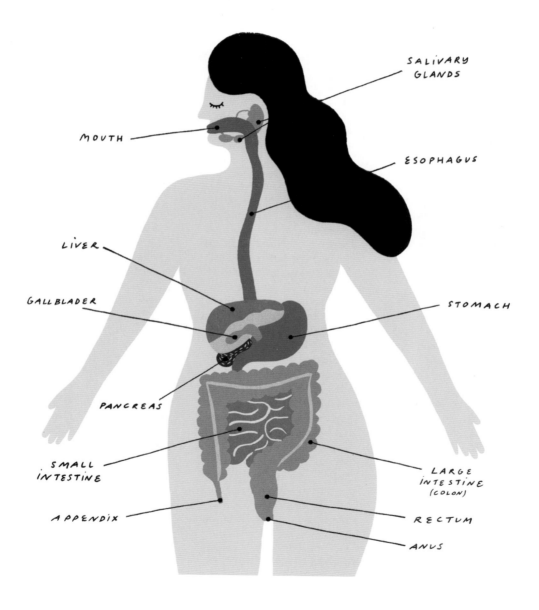

SALIVARY GLANDS

MOUTH

ESOPHAGUS

LIVER

GALLBLADER

STOMACH

PANCREAS

SMALL INTESTINE

LARGE INTESTINE (COLON)

APPENDIX

RECTUM

ANUS

bet that the sensorial element of eating—the taste, texture, and smell—is the best part.

From the second we take a bite of food, digestive enzymes are secreted in our saliva. These enzymes, along with the physical act of chewing, work to break down the food into smaller parts to make the job easier on the rest of the system. There's a reason for the advice to chew your food well—breaking the food into smaller parts enables the digestive enzymes in your saliva to then break it down even further. If food isn't properly chewed, it can cause bloating, gas, and cramping, and makes it more difficult for the small intestine and gut microbes to extract nutrients down the line. Chewing is also a moment to connect with the pleasure of eating—taking the proper time to pay attention to the meal, to taste it, and savor the food before swallowing.

You probably know the main elements of the mouth: teeth, tongue, gums, saliva. But did you know that the mouth also has its own rich community of microbes? Known as the *oral microbiota,* the bacteria in our mouths also play a role in digestion. As with gut microbiota, the foods you eat also affect the health of your oral microbiota. For example, eating sugar, highly processed foods, and refined grains can cause these bacteria to convert simple sugars into acid, contributing to bad breath, gingivitis, tooth decay, and even strep throat. On the other end of things, healthy bacteria can help fight tooth decay. To keep things in balance, don't eat a lot of added sugar, brush well (ideally with an electric toothbrush), use a tongue scraper, and floss daily.

When it comes to eating, chewing and swallowing are two of the three most important elements to pay attention to. Why? Because you can control these actions (after you swallow, your body takes over the rest via involuntary actions).

So, I try to chew well, to pay attention while I'm eating, and to swallow fully before taking another bite. I admit I do love to eat while watching TV, and sometimes I need to drink a smoothie while working or in the car—it's not a perfect system— but keeping this in mind most of the time helps my digestion. The third thing you can control, by the way, is which foods you put into your digestive tract, but we'll get to that later.

The Enteric Nervous System (ENS)

Along the entire digestive tract, starting at the esophagus and running all the way to the anus, is the enteric nervous system, a network of an estimated 100 million nerves that is often called the "second brain," a term coined by Dr. Michael Gershon to describe this system's complexity, which rivals the brain itself.

The ENS influences the functions of digestion including how the food moves through the tract, mucus secretion, blood flow, and the signaling of immune and endocrine cells. What's incredible is that the ENS is able to react to conditions in the gut and coordinate responses without the help of the central nervous system (the brain and spinal cord); however the two systems are in close communication through neurotransmitters, other chemical and hormonal signals, and the vagus nerve (a direct line of crosstalk between the gut and the brain, which is part of the parasympathetic nervous system).

Esophagus and Stomach

After swallowing, the food travels downward via the esophagus into the stomach. The stomach's clever shape—a bean-shaped lopsided pouch—allows liquids to slide through on the shorter side and food to sit on the larger side so that it can stick around to be broken down by mechanical churning as well as a combination of acid and enzymes. The acid also works to kill any potentially pathogenic microbes before the food travels into the small intestine.

Small Intestine and Friends (Liver, Gallbladder, and Pancreas)

After being thrashed about in the acidic environment of the stomach for about three hours, the food is released into the small intestine, which ranges in length but is on average about twenty-two to twenty-three feet long and an inch thick. While there are some microbes that live in the small intestine, it contains only about fifty million bacteria per teaspoon of contents—compared to trillions in the large intestine.

The small intestine further breaks the food down to extract the macronutrients—including proteins, fats, and simple carbohydrates—that are digestible to the human body, with the help of enzymes and bile from the liver, pancreas, and gallbladder. Then, villi, small finger-like projections that cover the wall of the small intestine, absorb those nutrients.

One particularly relevant element of the small intestine's job is to absorb glucose and fructose after they're broken down from simple carbohydrates (which happens in the stomach). Glucose is absorbed into the bloodstream, often referred to as *blood sugar*. This stimulates the pancreas to release insulin, which in turn signals uptake by the body's cells—either being stored as glycogen in muscle cells or lipids in fat cells. Fructose is absorbed by the liver, where it is either converted into glucose or into body fat. Too much of either of these sugars and the body's system can become imbalanced in the form of insulin resistance, diabetes, or other metabolic disturbances.

Large Intestine

After the food passes through the small intestine, what's left, the nondigestible elements of the food (mostly plant fiber) are delivered into the approximately five-foot-long large intestine, which comprises a small area called the caecum, the appendix, the colon, and the rectum. The large intestine is where the trillions-strong collection of microbes known as the gut microbiota get to work.

The caecum houses a large concentration of microbes that jump-start fiber fermentation. Dangling off the caecum is the appendix, which was long thought to be a useless vestige of evolution, no longer needed for modern purposes. This idea was popularized by Charles Darwin, and boy he couldn't have been more wrong. We now know that the appendix acts as a storehouse of microbes that the body can use to recover after an acute infection or a decimation of bacteria, for example after taking antibiotics. It's an incredible

Just to refresh before we get into the nitty gritty:

Microbes are single-celled organisms. This broad category includes bacteria, viruses, archaea, fungi, and protozoa. They live all over and inside our bodies, collecting in communities known as microbiota. The collective genes of those microbes are known as the microbiome. They produce chemicals called metabolites, which affect our health.

backup system, cleverly separated in case of emergency. Most of the time, that emergency supply sits unused, and the food passes through the caecum and into the main section of the colon, where the bulk of the microbial community lives—literally trillions of microbes, each with its own food preferences and its own resulting chemical byproducts.

The microbes work to break down the remains of the food not digested in the small intestine, mostly plant fiber that we humans are incapable of digesting ourselves. This is the slowest part of the digestion process because the microbes need time to do their job. Beneficial bacteria prefer plant fibers, with which they synthesize vitamins and produce essential chemicals for our immune system, brain function, and overall health. The chemical byproducts of each type of microbe inform how our body works on every level. Any food that the microbes don't or can't consume is sent along to the rectum to be disposed of in stool.

Rectum and Anus

It wouldn't be a fair tour of the digestive system to avoid talking about the rectum and anus, which might rival the words "gut" and "poop" for "top words I've said that make people squeamish." Personally, I appreciate this stage of my digestion because it's back on a level that I can see. Paying attention to the end stages of digestion is a good way to gauge whether things are going well for your gut and, by extension, your health. Stool (about 75 percent dead and living bacteria) accumulates in the rectum before passing through the anus and into the beyond.

The Bottom Line—Your Poop!

Skip this if you think reading about poop is just too gross. Talking about poop in a cookbook? It's insanity. But think of your poop as a free daily report on how your gut microbiota is doing.

You might think of feces as just waste, but it's a complex, ever-changing mixture of water, bacteria and other microbes, fiber that even those microbes weren't able to digest, and other substances like medications and chemicals. Going anywhere between one and three times a day is considered normal.

The gold standard for assessing the health of your poop is based on the Bristol Stool Form Scale, a tool commonly used by doctors and patients to describe its characteristics. You can find it online if you want more details.

The ideal is smooth, soft, easy to pass, and comes out in one long piece with no cracking. No splash? That means it's a perfect poo. Smaller, harder pieces indicate constipation, while a looser consistency indicates diarrhea. Constipation can be caused by too little plant fiber and fluids as well as by several diseases and medications. Anecdotally, I'd also add stress and travel to that list.

As for color, a range of dark to light in the scale of green to brown is healthy. Other colors like yellow, light brown, gray, black, or red are worth checking with your medical provider (unless you've recently eaten beets, which can tint your stool red).

Everything You Ever Wanted to Know about the Gut Microbiota

Now that there's context for the microbiota within the digestive system, we can get into the nitty gritty of how the microbes in your gut work.

What has become apparent in the last two decades is that our gut microbial community is the way station to health. Treat it right and our bodies thrive, treat it badly and our bodies decline.

You might be thinking, "That sounds like an extreme thing to say." I get it. Before I learned the hard way that decimating my community of microbes was the reason I went through years of chronic illness, I had a hard time believing it, too.

The Gut Environment

When we talk about the microbes in our gut, what we really mean is the community in the large intestine, also called the colon. They either attach to the epithelial lining on the walls of the gut, nestle into the mucous layer that protects that lining, or float independently in the lumen (the fancy name for the space between the walls).

Bacteria make up the largest proportion of this microbial community, but other microbes including viruses, fungi, protists, and archaea all coexist in this space. And it's not just microbes; several different species of bacteria can form communities known as biofilms, essentially tiny organisms that draw on the collective capabilities of the bacteria. There are also immune sensing cells, chemical byproducts of microbial metabolism, luminal fluid, and toxins that stay in the gut as long as the gut barrier is working well.

How You Get Your Gut Microbiota

You inherited your initial microbiota at birth. I won't go too much into it (although if you are pregnant, you might want to learn more and discuss with your obstetrician), but as a quick summary: An infant is exposed to bacterial cultures as they are born (and the microbes will differ for a vaginal birth versus a C-section). Feeding the baby in turn feeds their microbes. In particular, bacteria found in breast milk and indigestible complex carbohydrates called human milk oligosaccharides (or HMOs) help nurture an infant's microbiota. HMOs are now present in many baby formulas and probiotic supplements, although they are not the same as those found in breast milk.

As a child grows and transitions to solid foods, they gain exposure to a diversity of microbes, which trains the immune system to differentiate friend from foe, until at around 1,000 days (between 2½ to 3 years old), their microbiota is as diverse in species as an adult's.

Your Individual Gut Microbiota Is Like a Fingerprint

While most humans have similar types of microbes living in their gut, the exact breakdown of which and how many species, and hence, which chemical byproducts are produced, vary from person to person. Given the extraordinary number of microbes, it's no surprise that the complexity is likened to a fingerprint, since no two are exactly alike.

Your Gut Microbiota Is Relatively Stable Over Your Lifetime

Your gut microbiota can change very quickly over short periods of time, for instance, through an intense change in diet, but give up the dietary

changes and the community will likely revert to its original composition. That might seem stressful—the idea that you could try to change the community and it would snap back to its old-school state. However, rather than focusing on just the microbiota, I think it's more useful to think about the metabolome, which describes the functional output of the microbes. So it's not just about what microbes you house, but the chemical products they make, and then what those products are capable of doing. Those chemical outputs (metabolites) shift based on what you eat. Feed your microbes barley, they'll produce one chemical; feed them bell peppers, they'll produce a different one. This means that metabolite output shifts from meal to meal.

A Western diet (see page 41) and other environmental factors, such as taking antibiotics, can decrease its diversity, but it is possible that a long-term gut-friendly diet (like the one in this book) may restore some of the lost species, or at the very least, change the functional output, for instance, improving glucose tolerance or losing weight. As you'll see, this output can affect functions throughout the body.

How Microbes Influence Human Health

Starting from when we receive our first community of gut microbes at birth, through environmental influences like dirt, pets, and our family members, microbes train our immune cells to recognize them—essentially letting them know that they are not invaders but friends. Exposure to microbes also appears to regulate inflammatory

ONE SIZE DOES NOT FIT ALL

The unique makeup of each individual's microbiota means that it's impossible to prescribe a one-size-fits-all set of guidelines for how to eat for a "healthy" gut. In fact, it prevents the ability to say that there is one true "healthy" gut at all. What we know is that health is correlated with several factors, for instance the presence of microbes that ferment dietary fiber to produce short-chain fatty acids. Recent research has shown that the microbiota determines glucose response to foods to the point that for some participants, white bread might spike glucose *less* than whole-grain sourdough bread—basically, flipping the common health wisdom on its head. This study was conducted by scientists who advocate for personalized nutrition, which would use a combination of gut microbiota sequencing and blood tests to monitor glucose to tell you exactly which foods to eat or not. This is an exciting area of research, albeit one that requires a significant time and financial commitment. There is emerging evidence from these small studies that long-term diet can alter glucose response via the gut microbiota. The good news is that what you eat shapes the microbial metabolites produced at every single meal, and we know that beneficial microbes produce these by fermenting plant fiber!

responses, and the gut microbiota influences metabolism, glucose tolerance, and circadian rhythm.

Each microbe's own genetic code determines the job of that microbe. Some are experts at synthesizing vitamins, while others produce chemical messengers like serotonin (a chemical that regulates both bowel movements and psychological well-being) or simply help us extract calories from foods we can't digest ourselves. The gut microbes signal the immune cells in the gut and its mucus lining and communicate directly to the brain through numerous chemical and nerve pathways.

Metabolites

Each microbe has a set of genes that determine what kind of job they do (they can even transfer genes between one another). Which genes are switched on and how that microbe interacts with its environment will determine the chemical byproducts, called *metabolites,* produced by each microbe. The collection of all the metabolites produced by your microbes is called the *metabolome.* The metabolites—the chemical byproducts— are arguably more important than the types of microbes, since it's those chemical messengers that determine what occurs in our bodies.

Beneficial metabolites comprise a vast array of chemicals including neurotransmitters and short-chain fatty acids. These interface with the cells in your gut lining, enter the bloodstream, and can even speak to the brain via the gut-microbiota-brain axis (see page 46 for more on that). Additionally, metabolites include endocrine-signaling hormones, chemicals that signal immune cells and trigger nerve impulses, regulate inflammation, and influence the entire body via other methods still being discovered. The recipes in *Help Yourself* are about guiding your microbes to produce health-promoting metabolites, however, with too much red meat, ultraprocessed food, and added sugar, pathogenic microbes can thrive and produce inflammatory chemicals.

SHORT-CHAIN FATTY ACIDS (SCFAs)

When certain microbes in your gut eat dietary fiber, they can produce metabolites (chemical byproducts) called short-chain fatty acids (SCFAs). These incredibly important chemicals include butyrate, acetate, and propionate, and provide a variety of local and far-reaching services to promote good health.

SCFAs are the all-star players of metabolites. Their jobs include supporting the growth of other beneficial species inside our bodies, acting as an energy source for the cells of the intestinal lining (which strengthens the gut barrier) and regulating the release of anti-inflammatory immune cells. SCFAs do not just act locally but can transit to other organs. For instance, acetate increases a sense of satiety in the brain and butyrate signals the enteric nervous system to move things along through the digestive tract. While we don't yet know all the mechanisms through which SCFAs affect the whole body, scientists have recognized that they are beneficial to human health.

 Help Yourself *is your road-map to encouraging SCFA production through both abundance and diversity of plant foods. This is because the more fiber you eat, the more SCFAs your microbes can produce. And variety is key, too, since each plant source and microbe type combine to create different types of SCFAs.*

What Beneficial Microbes Like to Eat

Given the evolving nature of gut microbiota research, we are still learning exactly how microbes carry out their communication inside and beyond the gut. What we do know is that they can't promote health without the right food.

Your gut bacteria—the species that live there, the number, and the diversity—can shift according to diet and lifestyle. The makeup of our microbes reflects what we eat—the microbes (good or bad) that we feed thrive, the ones we starve either begin eating the lining of the large intestine or they die. This ability to shift is what's known as *microbiota plasticity*, and it enabled the microbiota of our ancestors to shift with the seasonal availability of hunter-gatherer diets. This was advantageous for a foraged diet because it allowed microbes to extract nutrients from what humans could find. However, it's not so great for our sugar- and animal fat–heavy modern diets. This Western diet starves beneficial microbes and allows pathogenic ones to proliferate in their place, setting off a chain of inflammation and chronic heightened immune response.

Each time the small intestine pushes the nondigestible remains of a meal into the large intestine, the microbes get to work. Each microbe has a specific kind of food it likes to eat. Beneficial microbes prefer fermentable plant fiber. You can find this in vegetables, whole grains, beans and legumes, nuts, and seeds. It might seem strange that large elements of these foods, long known to be beneficial for human health, would pass through the small intestine undigested. Humans haven't evolved to process this dietary fiber, but we actually have friends on board who do: our microbes. When the remains of, say, asparagus make it to the large intestine, asparagus-loving microbes will get to work. Depending on the substance they eat, the microbes produce metabolites including short-chain fatty acids and other chemicals like neurotransmitters.

What's the Deal with Fiber?

You may have heard things like "just eat fiber" or to eat "prebiotics" or "avoid all carbs," without an explanation of *why* this matters. Here's why: When you eat plants, you are eating food that your bacteria need to produce health-promoting metabolites like anti-inflammatory short-chain fatty acids and neurotransmitters like gamma aminobutyric acid (GABA), which can dampen anxiety.

Beneficial microbes—the ones you want to encourage—like to eat dietary fiber, which is a type of complex carbohydrate found in plants. "Carbs" have had a complicated reputation for decades, due to a fundamental misunderstanding of this broad group of organic compounds. What matters is the number of carbohydrate molecules that are linked together into a chain. A small number means they are quickly broken down and absorbed into the bloodstream; a complex number, as found in whole plant foods, allows them to escape digestion by human enzymes and make it to the microbes in your gut.

That's why I like the term *dietary fiber* better than *MACs* or the buzzword of *prebiotics*. For one, prebiotic fiber can be isolated outside of the food source and turned into a dietary supplement. Not only does this take away the quality control of choosing the plants you eat, it also ignores the fact that we really don't yet know exactly what every microbe on this earth loves and what chemical it

might produce. As for *MACs*, it insists that we look at food on a nutrient level rather than the whole food form. My overall advice? It's better to eat a variety of plants in their whole form to support a diversity of happy beneficial microbes.

Carbohydrates that human enzymes can digest. These are the simplest form of carbohydrates, and they're the kind that enter the bloodstream right after eating. These are what most people think of as "carbs" and come in the form of added sugar, refined grains, and hot, starchy foods like white potatoes.

This type of carbohydrate includes monosaccharides, which can be absorbed directly from the small intestine into the bloodstream (glucose) or by the liver (fructose); disaccharides like sucrose (aka table sugar) and lactose (the sugar found in milk), which during digestion are then broken down into glucose and fructose; and starches, which are polysaccharides, meaning they are made up of many monosaccharides linked together.

Honey and maple syrup (which are simple chains of carbohydrates including fructose and glucose), often considered to be healthier than white sugar, aren't any different when it comes to blood sugar. They each contain some minerals, and honey even has antimicrobial properties, but these refined sugar alternatives still quickly affect blood sugar and can be stored as fat.

 Cooking and completely cooling certain types of starch allows them to pass undigested through the small intestine. This type of starch is called resistant starch, *and it's processed by beneficial microbes in your gut. (See pages 120 and 310 for recipes.)*

Carbohydrates that neither you nor your gut microbes can digest. These nonfermentable fibers such as cellulose, one kind of fiber found in plants, pass through without being absorbed or used in the body. They are, however, great bulking agents for stool as they absorb water.

Carbohydrates that *can* be digested by your gut microbes, but not by you (aka MACs). These are complex carbohydrates mostly found in dietary fiber (aka from plants). Since these carbohydrates aren't absorbed via the small intestine, they do not affect your blood sugar right away, but instead slowly over time. When these microbiota-accessible carbohydrates arrive in the large intestine, they are fermented by your gut microbes, producing beneficial byproducts like the SCFAs mentioned on page 38. Without these foods, health-promoting bacteria starve, allowing harmful ones to gain a foothold. What counts as beneficial for your unique microbiota is determined by the species you harbor.

Prebiotic Fiber

A prebiotic is a substance that, when eaten by microbes, produces a positive health effect on the host's health (that's you). While a prebiotic can be many things like breast milk or even short-chain fatty acids, the majority of prebiotics are fermentable, soluble dietary fiber from plants. Soluble indicates that the fiber dissolves in water, and fermentable means that the microbes digest the substance. While certain foods are termed *prebiotics* (legumes, oats, green bananas, onions, and sunchokes, to name a few), it's more accurate to say that these plants contain prebiotic fiber. Despite the efforts of food corporations to market processed foods as containing added prebiotic

fiber, to reduce this category to an additive or a supplement is to miss the point. Fiber-rich plants contain "co-passengers" which might provide essential protection of fiber's health-promoting benefits. In short, fiber might benefit you significantly more when it's in the original form it grew in.

I prefer to consider dietary fiber, or even simpler, "whole plant foods," rather than focus on the label "prebiotic."

What Does a "Healthy Gut" Look Like?

In this book, I wanted nothing more than to be able to give a clear answer on what a healthy or unhealthy gut looks like. Turns out, it's not that simple. Recall that each human has a unique community of microbes, not unlike a fingerprint, so there's no one-size-fits-all definition. What we do know is that it's possible to look at someone who is healthy or unhealthy and make associations with certain features in the gut. For instance, diversity and bacterial gene richness appear to be an important indicator of health, while lower bacterial richness is associated with unhealthy levels of obesity, insulin resistance, and inflammatory disorders.

Beyond food, a person (of any age) is exposed to microbial diversity—which correlates positively with health—from parents, siblings, pets, and the natural environment. Food is the most effective way to address health because good microbes thrive off plant fiber, and the byproducts of their digestion benefit the entire body.

Can We Say What Constitutes an Unhealthy Gut?

An imbalance of good and bad microbes in the gut is known as *dysbiosis*. It's associated with human states that are considered to be "unhealthy." While beneficial bacteria can do things like produce anti-inflammatory chemicals like short-chain fatty acids, some pathogenic bacteria can make carcinogenic compounds.

After researching this topic for years, I have come to the conclusion that the tipping point between balance and dysbiosis is a result of myriad cumulative factors that are largely invisible until one day you feel the effects. Problematically, many of the contributing factors to a dysbiotic gut are normalized in our culture, which has given them a veneer of being either normal or right. Here is an overview of some of these:

- **Western diet:** A Western diet is characterized by not enough whole, plant-based foods, particularly vegetables, and too much of refined grains, added sugar, ultraprocessed food, and red meat. While this trend started in the Western hemisphere, hence the name, this type of diet has become increasingly common around the world. The media and the "wellness" industry would have you believe that it's simple enough to demonize one type of food or even an element within a food, but the problem is in the overall pattern—not one food, one meal, or even one day but rather a continual accumulation of not enough of the good and too much of the bad. Hand in hand with the Western diet are exposure to chemicals like endocrine disrupters in plastic packaging, pesticides used on conventionally grown produce, and antibiotics used on livestock, all of which may also contribute to dysbiosis.

- **Chronic stress:** Stress has a negative effect on our gut microbiota. It can cause the gut barrier to become leaky and potentially change the diversity and number of microbes. In our day-to-day lives, we experience an onslaught of stressors that constantly trigger the physiological fight-or-flight response, often without resolution. With chronic stress comes inflammation, and the immune system becomes less effective.

- **Excessive use of antibiotics:** There is no question that antibiotics have saved countless lives and made modern medicine safer. Antibiotics do their job by killing bacteria, which prevents contamination by pathogenic species during medical procedures or after an infection. However, antibiotics do not selectively kill only the exact bacterium causing the problem. Instead, they wipe out entire species indiscriminately, leaving the gut devoid of other important bacteria that we need. The absence of these good bacteria also makes room for unwelcome microbes to move in and colonize the gut. Sometimes taking an antibiotic is necessary, but they are also overprescribed— for example, for viral infections, which cannot be treated by antibiotics. If you must take antibiotics, it's important to feed what good bacteria remains (using the guidelines and recipes in this book) so they return to their job of crowding out pathogenic microbes before they gain a foothold.

- **Over-the-counter medications like NSAIDs, PPIs, and H2-receptor antagonists:** Here's the deal: Poor diet leads to inflammation and an imbalance of good and bad bacteria. This can result in taking OTC medications like ibuprofen to help manage pain or proton-pump inhibitors like omeprazole to quell heartburn. There's no question that there is an immediate benefit to these medications; however, what helps in the near term has a detrimental effect to the balance of good and bad microbes in the long run. I have come to see them as short-term gain for long-term pain. NSAIDs can cause the gut barrier to become permeable, and PPIs reduce the acid in the stomach, potentially allowing pathogenic bacteria to slip through.

I think of myself as a sensible person, so it seems silly in retrospect that I was paying for drugs I don't need now that I've shifted my diet and lifestyle. There was a long time when I was taking Prilosec, Zyrtec, a prescription anti-itching pill that was the equivalent of five Benadryl, and regularly popping Tums throughout the day. The cost was significant, adding up to around two hundred dollars a month. Since switching my diet? I take none. This is by no means a promise of the same results, but it worked for me, and I sure love having the extra money in my bank account.

- **Lack of exposure to certain microbes:** The "old friends" mechanism proposes that we evolved with nonharmful organisms like parasites, helminths, and viruses so that our immune system could learn to tolerate them. As modern life disrupts many of these traditional exposures, there is a question as to whether simply living in a nonagrarian society during the years that a child's gut is developing (from birth until about age 3) might lead to a state of dysbiosis. Humans have long been exposed to a diverse array of microbes through mechanisms that are now being disrupted in modern life. This includes the increase of C-sections (the vaginal birth canal is believe to be the first microbial exposure); a decrease in breast-feeding (a rich and varied source of bacteria); less common exposure to the microbial environment of dirt and nature, pets slobbering all over us, multiple siblings interacting, and parents sharing fluids (like sucking on a pacifier to clean it rather than throw it away). In other words, healthy immunoregulation may be a constellation of varied microbial exposure that encourages colonization in the gut microbiota and dampens inflammatory responses. Decreased exposure to these factors during microbiota development is associated with asthma, allergy, and inflammatory diseases.

Dysbiosis

Dysbiosis is a microbial imbalance associated with modern chronic illnesses. At its most basic, dysbiosis is just an imbalance between microbes, which tips the host's health toward illness.

Over the last 150 years, there has been an increase in noncommunicable diseases, what are called "modern chronic illnesses," that mirror the rise of a so-called Western diet and other lifestyle factors that also contribute to gut dysbiosis. These include inflammatory and autoimmune diseases, asthma and allergic diseases, type-1 diabetes, type-2 diabetes, insulin resistance, metabolic syndrome, Crohn's, ulcerative colitis, irritable bowel syndrome, colorectal cancer, gout, ADHD, Alzheimer's, Parkinson's, nonvascular dementia, multiple sclerosis, depression, and anxiety.

We can see a correlation between gut microbiota dysbiosis and these modern chronic illnesses (and potentially many more not listed

or yet to be discovered). But correlation alone doesn't indicate the cause—that is, dysbiosis might cause a disease, or the disease could be the cause of dysbiosis. However, analyzing the gut microbiota is emerging as a promising route for disease detection and diagnosis and potentially even treatment and prevention. For example, Parkinson's seems to start affecting the gut microbiota about ten years before neurological symptoms appear, which could make microbiota analysis potential tool for early diagnosis.

A decline in gut microbial diversity can predict how rapidly our health will decline. This is true of old age—the closer we get to death, the less variety we have in our gut microbiota. This parallel between old age and modern chronic illnesses highlights that dysbiosis is a precursor to death.

"Leaky Gut"

Leaky gut is the popular name for increased intestinal permeability or gut barrier dysfunction, when the normally tight junctions between the cells in your epithelial lining become more permeable than normal. This allows microbes and food particles that normally wouldn't get through to enter the bloodstream. Things like stress, extreme exercise, NSAIDs like Advil, an imbalance of gut microbes, and diet contribute to leaky gut.

When the normally beneficial bacteria that thrive on dietary fiber are starved of the food sources they need to survive, they start chomping at the carbohydrate-rich mucous layer lining the large intestine. Once the mucous layer is degraded, this exposes the one-cell-thick epithelial lining that is responsible for regulating the flow between the bloodstream and the contents of the gut. When this normally tight barrier is loosened, contents from the gut leak into the bloodstream. This can include food particles and chemicals that normally stay in the gut like inflammatory endotoxins.

While an abnormal intestinal barrier has been associated with a shockingly wide variety of gut-related and other diseases from irritable bowel disease to Parkinson's and rheumatoid arthritis, it is still unclear whether it contributes to development of these diseases or if healing the lining would improve symptoms.

Colorectal Cancer

Rates of colorectal cancer (CRC) are increasing in young people. Researchers now suspect that a Western diet specifically high in fat and meat shifts the gut microbiota in a way that may be a contributing factor. Recent studies have shown that there is a distinct microbial signature (basically, a recognizable fingerprint) associated with CRC, which will improve detection accuracy.

C. Diff Infection

Clostridium difficile, or *C. diff*, is infamous for causing horrific, relentless diarrhea, dehydration, abdominal pain, and rapid weight loss. The bacteria can live harmlessly in many people's guts, but after taking antibiotics depletes the microbiota, they can proliferate and wreak terrible havoc. The treatment has traditionally been more antibiotics, but the problem is that it causes a vicious cycle when it comes to the gut microbiota, and people who suffer from *C. diff* often experience repeat infections. An emerging alternative treatment, as unlikely as it may seem at first, is a fecal microbiota transplant, which is exactly what it sounds like. If you've suffered from *C. diff* infections, you may want to ask your health care provider about this.

Inflammatory Bowel Diseases (IBDs), Irritable Bowel Syndrome (IBS), and Celiac Disease

Inflammatory bowel diseases include Crohn's and ulcerative colitis (UC), which are characterized by inflammation of the gastrointestinal tract. Crohn's can affect any part of the digestive system, while UC is just in the large intestine. It is believed that IBD develops as a dysregulated response by the immune system to dysbiosis in the gut microbiota in genetically susceptible people. There is clear evidence of the relationship to the microbiota in the development. Irritable bowel syndrome (IBS) involves both the brain and the gut microbiota. Symptoms vary between people, some experiencing constipation, diarrhea, or both. It is estimated to affect between 10 to 25 percent of Americans, of which 90 percent experience depression or anxiety. Not only is that a staggering number of people just in the United States alone, it also underscores that IBS is a disorder of the gut-brain axis, which differentiates it from IBD. See "What About Gluten?" on page 57 for more about celiac disease.

I've grouped these together because, when it comes to diseases that specifically target the intestine, the recommendations for what to eat aren't straightforward. What works for someone who is healthy isn't necessarily the same as what works for someone with an inflamed intestine (as in the case of IBDs and celiac) or who is particularly sensitive to gas produced by microbial fermentation (as in IBS). Celiac sufferers often see a reduction of symptoms once they've eliminated gluten, but when the intestine is inflamed, a general high-fiber diet might cause irritation until the inflammation goes away.

SHOULD YOU TAKE A PROBIOTIC?

Research on probiotics is still developing. A probiotic is broadly defined as an organism that confers benefits on the health of its host—a definition that allows foods like kimchi, sauerkraut, and even breast milk to be deemed probiotic since they contain live organisms. But when people say, "take a probiotic," they're usually referring to over-the-counter pills. These capsules or tablets contain billions of bacteria. The strains included are believed to have beneficial effects on humans, but the sheer diversity of each human's individual gut microbiota means that proving the efficacy of these strains is not an exact science. One criticism I've heard of probiotics is that we don't naturally harbor these species in our guts— insinuating that these species don't stick around. It's possible that these guest stars could digest food and produce beneficial metabolites as they pass through the colon; for instance, a milk-eating bacteria might chow down on cheese and produce an anxiety-reducing neurotransmitter.

You may come across the term symbiotic on a label, which is the term for probiotics with prebiotic fiber added to the capsule. In this sense, the bacteria are provided with the food they like to eat rather than relying on the food that you are eating. But I'm skeptical about the source of this prebiotic fiber and prefer to get my fiber from food sources.

The term psychobiotic refers to probiotic bacteria that can produce neuroactive substances such as gamma-aminobutyric acid (GABA) and serotonin. These substances are believed to act on the gut-microbiota-brain axis to reduce anxiety and depression. I take probiotics for this reason: Having dealt with depression and anxiety my entire life, I am convinced enough by the research to take them with the intent of improving my mental health. I do notice less anxiety overall, but that is a murky, self-reported statistic. You will have to try for yourself, if you want.

Bottom line: You don't need to take a probiotic, but if you can afford it, it might be worth adding to your daily regimen. But it's more important to start eating vegetables and other plant foods every day. Probiotics have not been proven to be harmful, and some research indicates they might help digest food or even reduce depression or anxiety. They might work like extra troops on hand to help with the work your microbiota is already doing. However, because they don't stick around long enough to colonize the microbiota, this is an area of developing research.

The Gut-Microbiota-Brain Axis

Without even knowing the science of the links between the gut and the brain, it's likely you've internalized that a connection exists. It's baked into our language: When something feels off, we call it a gut instinct. When we feel bad about something, we say, "I'm sick to my stomach." When trying to make a tough decision, we "go with our gut." When we fall in love, we get butterflies in our bellies.

Gut feelings are more than just a metaphor—the gut is connected to the brain through several pathways, including a direct nerve connection, chemical messengers like short-chain fatty acids and neurotransmitters, and stimulation of the HPA-axis, a complex matrix of the hypothalamus, pituitary and adrenal glands, hormones, and other chemicals that controls stress response.

This is a bidirectional system of communication, meaning that the brain can influence the gut, and the gut can influence the brain. As awareness grows around the connection between gut microbes and mental health, diet is increasingly seen as an important aspect of maintaining good mental health, and nutritional psychiatry is an emerging area of focus.

While this is a complex system only beginning to be studied and understood by researchers, we know a fair amount about the circuits through which the brain and emotional states can affect the gut microbiota and associated physical states.

The Vagus Nerve

This bundle of nerves is the primary parasympathetic nerve in the body, and it directly links the gut microbiota and enteric nervous system to the brain. It is known to transmit information between the gut and the brain about activity in each location via neurotransmitters and short-chain fatty acids. The vagus nerve allows the brain to translate signals from the gut into mood-related cues like stress impulses or feelings like anxiety or depression. Hormones like ghrelin and leptin that relay a sense of fullness and satiety also use the vagal highway.

An estimated 10 percent of signaling runs from the brain to the gut through the vagus nerve, leaving the remaining 90 percent to go from brain to gut. When you think about the fact that diet is the largest lever we can pull in terms of modifying our gut microbes, it stands to reason that what we eat is a plausible route to improving mental health.

Neurotransmitters and Other Chemicals

The bacteria in your gut are capable of synthesizing and responding to neurotransmitters including dopamine, serotonin, gamma-aminobutyric acid (GABA), and brain-derived neurotrophic factor (BDNF), all of which affect mood. In addition to the vagus nerve, these chemicals enter the bloodstream and transit to other organs through which they influence body functions. The exact mechanisms still aren't entirely clear, but we know that they are produced in the gut and can pass the gut barrier in both directions. It seems that, when the body is experiencing stress, signals from these neurotransmitters play a role in activating the stress response via the hypothalamic-pituitary-adrenal (HPA) axis, causing a downstream cascade of chemicals that eventually spike cortisol, which dampens the immune system.

Flourish: Valuing Whole-Body Self-Care

Learning about the gut-microbiota-brain axis underscored for me how crucial it is to prioritize self-care and well-being. Being well is not as simple as just eating well. The way we live is equally important, and I believe that one enhances the other, just as one suffers when the other does. Factors such as stress, sleep, exposure to nature, and even having a sense of purpose affect the health of our bodies. To address just food without addressing the other areas of life is to expect to light an entire cave with just a flashlight. While not all these activities have been directly connected to the gut microbiota (yet), it is plausible that their effects on emotional and mental health can also benefit microbial health via the bidirectional nature of the gut-microbiota-brain axis.

Body care: Am I getting enough sleep, daily exercise, and stretching? Sleep disruption alters gut bacteria, and dysbiotic gut microbes alter circadian rhythm. Not getting enough sleep also reduces stress tolerance and increases systemic inflammation. Meditation and breathing exercises calm the vagus nerve, which not only connects the gut and the brain, but also relaxes the parasympathetic nervous system, which controls the fight-or-flight response.

Prioritizing downtime, disconnecting from technology, and welcoming quiet: It's easy to forget to prioritize health in an always-on culture. Escaping to nature not only reminds me that there's more than work, it also calms the nervous system. I try to prioritize time off screens and limit social media.

Managing my mental health: If the gut-microbiota-brain axis proves one thing, it's the value of taking care of mental health. I go to therapy regularly, practice advocating boundaries to reduce stress, and make time to connect with friends who I love and trust.

2 EAT GOOD TO FEEL GOOD

IF YOU STARTED THIS BOOK by reading Part I, then you'll know that eating for your gut microbiota is the same as eating for your entire body's health. There are lots of ways to improve your health, but experts agree that changing what you eat is the most effective.

In this section, I'll cover the guidelines for eating the *Help Yourself* way, give you my tried-and-tested strategies for eating with your microbes in mind, and rethink paradigms like the food pyramid. While I am reticent to use the word *rules,* I have come up with a manifesto of sorts—an approach to eating that not only keeps taste front and center, but also takes into account the gut, the planet, and a pattern of eating that promotes health.

My *Help Yourself* Maxims

1 **Focus on the abundance of what you can have instead of what you're cutting out.** When someone tells you not to think about pizza, what do you think about? Pizza, obviously! This is called *ironic process theory*—trying not to think about something only makes it more prominent in your mind. Understanding this is crucial to success when switching to a new way of eating. Instead of focusing on what *not* to eat, think about the foods you *can* eat. You can have all the avocado you want. And the most delicious pie I've ever developed (page 334). Obsessing over what you can't have just leads to a fixation with it and potentially to breaking down and bingeing. Which is why, when I crave cheese, I go ahead and eat a hunk of cheese.

2 **"Just eat the donut" only works if you have the will and the tools to get back on the wagon.** *Help Yourself* isn't about a total annihilation of pleasure, just a rethinking of how much, how often, and when you're going to indulge, and ideally doing so with intention.

If you want to eat a massive brownie sundae, do it, enjoy it, and don't feel guilty about it. Make a plan to eat vegetables and other plants at the next meal and for the days after that.

In the beginning of shifting how I ate, I was stricter, which not only set the ground rules but also shifted my microbes more effectively. Now, it's easy to eat with my microbes in mind at every meal. When I decide that I'm going to have cocktails and a cheeseburger, I'm conscious that the next meal will have to contain leafy green vegetables. The happy reality is that within the context of a genuinely plant-focused way of eating, one meal will not undo it all. But, if I don't have plans to cook healthful food or get back on track, this can lead to a detrimental downward spiral.

3 **This is about a dietary pattern, not green-lighting orthorexia.** Orthorexia is an eating disorder characterized by preoccupation with eating healthfully and distress as the result of breaking self-imposed dietary rules. If you find yourself obsessively thinking about healthy eating and weight loss, then it's gone too far.

4 **Nothing tastes as good as healthy feels.** I have Kate Moss to thank for the underlying sentiment here—that some things are more important than taste. Of course, she was promoting being skinny, while I'm all about *healthy*. I don't want joint pain, chronic itching, anxiety, weight gain, swollen fingers, racing heart, and incessant thirst more than I want to eat a grilled cheese and a milkshake at every meal. This trade-off is worth it for me.

5 **Not every meal has to be an "experience."** Shout-out to my brother-in-law Steve for coming up with this one. When he and my sister started shifting their diets to the *Help Yourself* way of eating, she often resisted his desires to cook a healthy dinner, wanting it to be "the most delicious meal ever." All too often that meant ordering pizza, ramen, or spaghetti and meatballs for dinner since that was what they thought of as delicious. As they worked to make these types of meals an occasional treat rather than the status quo, he told her, "Not every meal has to be an experience," and the mantra stuck. Sometimes roasted vegetables with beans and an avocado are what you have on hand for dinner, and no, it may not feel like a special-occasion indulgence. That's okay. You also might find (as I have) that healthful food only gets more delicious as you eat it more often.

6 **Treat your microbes like a pet.** Even though we are technically each a superorganism comprised of microbial cells and human cells, it can be hard to treat the gut microbiota with importance. Once I started seeing my microbes as friends I had to take care of, it was easier to keep them in mind. The idea that the good microbes would starve if I didn't feed them the right food (plant foods high in fiber) wasn't so different than making a beloved dog skip dinner.

Many people eat takeout or processed food for almost every meal, rarely exercise, and deprioritize sleep, and yet pamper their pets with the highest-quality chow, lavish them with affection, and pay for a regular dog walker. So if you can't be motivated to improve your own self-care, think of your microbes as a pet, and care for them accordingly.

7 **Reality-check nostalgia.** Ah, the glory days of shoving cookies into my mouth. I miss them sometimes, and I become convinced that I can go back to the days of sugar deluxe. The reality is, I didn't feel good, but a body state is much harder to recall than a visual like a stack of cookies.

When it comes to gut health, it's key to feed the good microbes and starve the bad ones—the ones we feed will proliferate, the ones we starve will die. And, since our microbes eat what we eat, this means an overall dietary pattern that preferences the things anti-inflammatory and other beneficial microbes like to eat.

There is no one-size-fits-all solution for improving your gut health, but the overall guidelines are these: Include high-quality, minimally processed whole foods, with a focus on a variety of plants (meaning vegetables, whole grains, nuts and seeds, beans and legumes, berries, and other fruits) at every meal. Integrate fermented foods daily, and limit or eliminate added sugar and ultraprocessed foods. If you do eat animal products, eat them only occasionally, and ensure that they are well-raised and ethically and sustainably sourced, which matters for the animals' well-being and the planet.

How to "Eat Good"

The thing with clichéd phrases is that they take on a tone and personality beyond the words themselves. Every time I hear someone say, "Eat well," I think, *Damn, that sounds like an obligation.* It's loaded with the feeling of "should," and that just makes me want to rebel. Eating "good" on the other hand, while not proper grammar, subverts my expectations and reminds me that good can mean a lot of things—good taste, good food, and good feelings. It just so happens that what is good for our gut microbiota is good for our bodies, too.

Eating good for your gut, and by extension your overall health, doesn't need to be limiting—in fact, it's about an abundance of delicious foods and navigating the greater food world with ease and pleasure.

When I was close to finishing the recipe development for this book, a family friend asked me what the biggest surprise had been. I thought a long time, wanting to pick one recipe as an example worthy of that prize. Was it the Seeded Chocolate-Tahini Bark (page 340)? Or the Roasted Pepper and Aioli Flatbread (page 201)? It was impossible to choose just one, which is what brought me to my answer: The surprise of the book was that plant-focused eating is a delicious, satisfying way to eat that happens to be good for you, too.

What This Food Isn't

It might seem weird to start the food section of a cookbook by talking about what the food isn't. But if I've learned one thing about writing a health-focused book, it's that there is rampant confusion about what health means, as well as a lot of dogma and judgment. What I can do for you is give you the evidence, talk about my personal choices, and then have you decide from there. However, there are three particular areas that differentiate *Help Yourself* from many of the books already out there.

THE RECIPES ARE NOT 100 PERCENT PLANT-BASED

I am conscious of the fact that the climate is affected by industrial meat, dairy, and poultry farming and our oceans are suffering because of overfishing. If veganism works for you, then I thank you, and so does the planet.

However, strict labels and boundaries incite resistance. I'd rather give myself room to wobble, to sway, to do well by my microbes some days and go all out on others. Labels like "vegan" or "vegetarian" are identity-based, whereas my preferred description, "plant-focused," allows for a wide variety while still remembering that whole plant foods are the goal, not deeply processed, reconstituted vegan foods that are just as detrimental to the gut as their non-vegan or -vegetarian equivalents. (You know what I mean if you've ever mindlessly eaten a carton of vegan ice cream.) I use "plant-based" rather than the term *vegan* because it's less rigid and might encourage people who are not motivated by the ethical reasons to be vegan.

While eating a lot of whole plant foods is good for your gut, it's not necessary to follow a strictly plant-based diet. My recipes are plant-*focused*, which is to say that most of the ingredients are whole plant foods; however, I do incorporate animal products. Personally, I'm much more likely to eat lots of vegetables with an occasional sprinkling of cheese or a tablespoon of fish sauce. If you are vegan, you can find a list of all seventy-two 100 percent plant-based recipes in the book on page 344. Where applicable, I've noted optional plant-based swaps on recipe pages.

THE FOOD ISN'T "CLEAN" OR "GUILT-FREE"

The intense competition for clicks in the 24/7 media landscape means that the words *clean* and *guilt-free* are casually associated with dietary advice with an alarming frequency. But these words imply that other foods are the opposite—"dirty" or a cause for feeling guilt. Not only is it problematic for our guts to not be exposed to dirt, but there's a lot of judgment baked into these word choices.

THIS IS NOT A WEIGHT-LOSS OR CALORIE-COUNTING BOOK

There is a good chance that if you adhere to the *Help Yourself* way of eating, you might lose weight. But weight loss is not the goal of this book. I am also completely against the use of calories as a measurement of food for many reasons (see sidebar). Our microbes determine the amount of energy we extract from food, and it varies based on the makeup of our microbiota. What this means is that one person might extract 100 calories from one food and another person might extract 104.

I knew that setting out to write a "health book" would be difficult; what I didn't expect was how little I knew when I started and how much my opinions would evolve throughout the process. First, while this book talks about "diet," meaning the food you eat, it's not about diet as in weight loss, or "being on a diet." This means that I don't consider this to be a diet book but rather a guide to the various ways healthful eating and well-being are aligned. Second, based on what the science shows, for most people, healthful eating can look like many different things provided a few underlying things are true (lots of vegetables and other plants, low sugar, etc.). It's more difficult to address nuance and gray areas than it is to say, "Don't eat this, do eat that." I resist black-and-white categorizations or marketable tactics like "under-500-calorie dinners." Sticking to those sorts of (frankly arbitrary) guidelines are at best a misguided marketing tactic and at worst detrimental to someone's comfort and excitement about improving their relationship to food.

If you internalize a way to eat that's good for the gut, you will establish a lifestyle that allows you the freedom to eat good and feel good, too.

What Does "Eating Healthfully" Even Mean?

Health is not a zero sum game but rather a long-term balancing act between several orders of importance.

First, there's the ingredient level—the quality of the food and the composition (whether it's processed or a whole food) count toward healthfulness.

Next, the individual meal, whether that's a sugary cookie or a plate filled with brown rice, beans, avocado, and roasted chicken with an herb vinaigrette. We can assess the healthfulness of each dish we eat.

Then there's the course of each day. This is something we know well, often saying, "This was a healthy day," or "I'll do better tomorrow."

Finally, on the largest scale, is the overall dietary pattern. A few days eating pasta and drinking red wine on vacation in Italy or one particularly indulgent day isn't going to disrupt your microbiota or health long-term. But an overall tendency to favor ultraprocessed foods and sugar rather than vegetables, whole grains, and other plant foods will have a deleterious effect on your health, especially if health-promoting species lose their foothold in your gut and die out.

The most important levels to think about are the ingredients and the overall dietary patterns. How you eat over time matters, and the building blocks of each meal (the ingredients) are essential, too.

WHY I DON'T COUNT CALORIES

For a long time, the conventional wisdom about calories (a measure of the energy stored in food) and weight loss was calories in versus calories out. In other words, to lose weight, burn more calories than you consume. But this leads to the erroneous belief that all calories are equal, whether they're from a Twinkie or a zucchini. In addition, believing in the logic of calories-in/calories-out ratio fails to take into account the differences in how the body processes the macronutrients of protein, fat, and carbohydrates as well as the way it uses these foods to burn as fuel, rebuild tissues and organs, or store as fat. Each person's unique community of microbes also determines the number of calories we extract from the food we eat. And switching to a high-calorie diet could preference microbes that extract more calories. What we eat affects which microbes we host, and those microbes determine how much energy (aka calories) we extract from food.

Other Diets that Address Gut Health

Over and over again in my research I came across the same dietary recommendation from the experts on gut microbiota and the connection to overall health: A general pattern that emphasizes vegetables and other plant foods, is low in added sugar, and minimizes processed foods is best

for the health of our microbial community and, by extension, our health. Whether that includes animal products or not is an individual decision, provided animal foods like red meat don't make up a large part of the diet. For this reason, I don't call this a "diet" book, nor do I categorize the *Help Yourself* way of eating as a specific diet. It's a way of eating sustainably that can fluctuate with your life as it changes.

A variety of dietary patterns and approaches have been shown to improve health outcomes, whether it's the DASH (Dietary Approaches to Stop Hypertension), Blue Zone, or Mediterranean diets. Many people have also found success with a vegan, vegetarian, paleo, or low FODMAP diet. Nutrition experts will often focus on the contradictions among the diets rather than look at the main similarity: By following one of these approaches, there is an increase in whole foods and a dramatic reduction in processed foods and added sugar.

Low FODMAP Diet

FODMAP is an acronym for fermentable oligo-, di-, monosaccharides and polyols, which are essentially a form of complex carbohydrate found in foods like onions, mushrooms, legumes, and pistachios. Low FODMAP is a dietary approach that eliminates foods containing these substrates in order to calm a sensitive gut or the symptoms of irritable bowel syndrome. Basically, the fermentation that happens by microbes in the gut (and produces beneficial byproducts) can be extremely painful for people who suffer from IBS. There have been numerous studies pointing to relief from IBS with a low-FODMAP diet. However, eliminating these foods cuts down on the very fiber that beneficial bacteria thrive on (the ones that, among other jobs, produce short-

chain fatty acids, those crucial chemicals we need to calm our inflammatory response and fortify the gut lining). Low-FODMAP also allows white sugar, which I do not recommend eating at all if you are in a health crisis. If your medical practitioner recommends a low-FODMAP diet, please consult them before starting on the *Help Yourself* regimen. But it's worth asking about when and how you can transition back to eating plant fiber.

Autoimmune Paleo Protocol Diet

The autoimmune protocol diet is a stricter version of the paleo diet (premised on eating only the foods our primitive ancestors would have eaten) that alleges entire categories are inflammatory for people with autoimmune disease and thus must be eliminated. This includes alcohol, gluten, eggs, nuts, seeds, sweeteners, nightshades (including potatoes, tomatoes, eggplant, and more), as well as grains like buckwheat, millet, oats, quinoa, and rice. This is a controversial diet; one small study seemed to improve IBD symptoms.

Paleo diets encourage eating a lot of meat, which isn't great for the balance of microbes in your gut. Beyond all that, according to a paper by Justin and Erica Sonnenburg, the preeminent researchers of hunter-gatherer microbiota, it's highly unlikely that there was even one single ancestral state at any point in evolution: As humans migrated across the planet, their diets changed and so did their microbes and genes.

This extremely restrictive diet does share two important tenets with the *Help Yourself* approach, which is to eliminate processed foods and reduce added sugar.

What About Gluten?

Gluten—a protein found in wheat—has a controversial reputation and is often misunderstood to be unhealthy. I want to clear some things up.

People who have celiac disease have an autoimmune reaction to the proteins in gluten. The disease manifests as a spectrum of symptoms that differ between children and adults. Children are likely to experience bloating, diarrhea, vomiting, weight loss, and fatigue among other things, while in adults, fatigue, bone or joint pain, canker sores, and more can signal celiac. You can review a complete list of symptoms at celiac.org or speak with your medical practitioner about testing. Cutting out gluten is essential for celiac sufferers.

Many people have non-celiac gluten sensitivity (NCGS), with similar symptoms to celiac but without the biomarkers for celiac. It could be caused by leaky gut walls, which allow gluten particles to enter the bloodstream through the intestinal lining, causing an immune reaction. It could be other mechanisms that aren't yet clear. Many people find that avoiding gluten helps improve gastrointestinal distress like bloating and diarrhea. That being said, "gluten-free" does not automatically mean healthy; in fact, it could be harmful if it means you stop eating whole grains.

Whether or not you eat gluten, it's important to remember that cutting out gluten is not an immediate guarantee of health—there is such a thing as unhealthful gluten-free food. Eliminating or drastically cutting down on *ultraprocessed foods* is important for your gut; cutting out gluten on the other hand, is only necessary if you have celiac or an allergy to gluten. It might not be the gluten that's irritating your gut but actually the lack of food for your beneficial microbes, basically if you're starving them of the whole plant foods they

need to survive (see more on page 64). If you do decide to go gluten-free, make sure to eat a lot of gluten-free grains and grainlike seeds like millet, quinoa, amaranth, and buckwheat.

I eat gluten-free because I have NCGS, but I want to stress that this decision is secondary to my commitment to eating whole-food ingredients with a focus on plants, with as little added sugar and ultraprocessed food as possible. This is why you won't find gluten-free flour or other similar substitutes used in the recipes in this book. These products are fine for special occasions, but they are mostly heavily processed and rely on additives like emulsifiers to imitate the signature chewiness that gluten adds to bread, cakes, pasta, and more. In their additive form, emulsifiers like maltodextrin, xanthan gum, and carrageenan have been linked to IBD and dysbiosis.

The bottom line is: If you are in good health and tolerate gluten well, there's no reason why gluten-containing whole grains can't be a part of your overall dietary pattern. Where I call for quinoa, brown rice, and so on in this book, you can substitute whole grains like barley, farro, spelt, and einkorn. Many gluten-sensitive people also find that they can tolerate naturally leavened sourdough, as the process of fermenting the dough reduces the gluten content.

The *Help Yourself* Eat Good Guidelines

If you grew up with the USDA food pyramid, it's likely that these guidelines and my food pyramid (page 60) will look a little different to you. Once you start eating with your microbes in mind, these are the things that are crucial. How you source ingredients matters, too, not just for your gut but for the health of the planet. These are by no means rules; rather, they are meant to encourage and educate you about the best-case scenario.

Choose Whole Foods
Buy minimally processed ingredients and avoid ultraprocessed foods.

Whole foods is a term that's been co-opted by mainstream brands, but its definition is an important one. The closer to its original state, the more likely a plant will escape digestion by human enzymes and make it all the way to the gut, where it will feed your beneficial microbes. The opposite of whole foods are ultraprocessed foods (see page 61), which are high in additives, stabilizers, and emulsifiers (all associated with dysbiosis). It's not so much that you can't eat a candy bar here and there, but if these synthetic, highly manufactured foods represent a majority of your energy intake, they not only introduce these harmful additives but also displace the whole foods that our microbes need to survive.

It's a **whole food *ingredient*** if it's recognizable in the form that you see it at the grocery store. Think: eggs, lemons, Swiss chard, a hunk of meat. These ingredients can also be minimally or beneficially processed; for instance, a sprouted grain is still a single ingredient but has undergone the sprouting process to increase the nutritional value.

It's a **whole food** if it's a minimally processed or beneficially processed food. This includes things like butter and cheese, fermented foods like kimchi, and meals prepared with multiple whole food ingredients.

Be skeptical of a packaged, processed food that promotes itself with a label like "Contains prebiotics." Processed food can harm the gut, so whether it markets itself as being good for you or not, the best thing is to skip it most of the time. To say just "fiber" is to lack context: Can it be extracted by a machine and added to processed food? Maybe, but that isn't going to benefit your gut in the same way that it would from a whole food source, since a food's complex nutritional matrix seems to promote fiber's health benefits.

Vegetables and other plants feed our beneficial microbes, which in turn produce chemicals that we need for good health. At the end of the day, eating more plants is the most important thing, whether they're high in prebiotic fiber or not.

2 Stay Plant-Focused

Eat a lot of vegetables and other plants like whole grains, nuts and seeds, beans and legumes, and fruit.

One of the common pieces of advice for healthy eating is to "eat the rainbow" or go for "lots of color." Within the context of whole foods, I like this as a useful shorthand for variety in your diet, and it tracks with research by the American Gut Project showing that eating more than thirty different types of plants in a week correlates with health.

This means you can't just pick one vegetable, one whole grain, one nut, and one bean and consider yourself set. It's important to vary the types of each plant category you eat, because that encourages a diversity of microbes to thrive in your gut. Diverse microbes produce diverse metabolites, which correlates with health.

3 Be Mindful When It Comes to Animal Products

If you eat them (dairy, eggs, meat, fish), source them from ethically minded producers and eat them occasionally.

Too much red meat and animal fat can tip the balance of microbes in your gut toward inflammation. Red meat specifically can result in harmful metabolites, while excessive consumption of all animal-derived foods in the absence of a variety of plants can starve beneficial microbes and promote precursors to cardiovascular-disease-promoting chemicals. Eat reasonable servings—just a couple times a week for fish, eggs, and dairy and once a week or less for red meat.

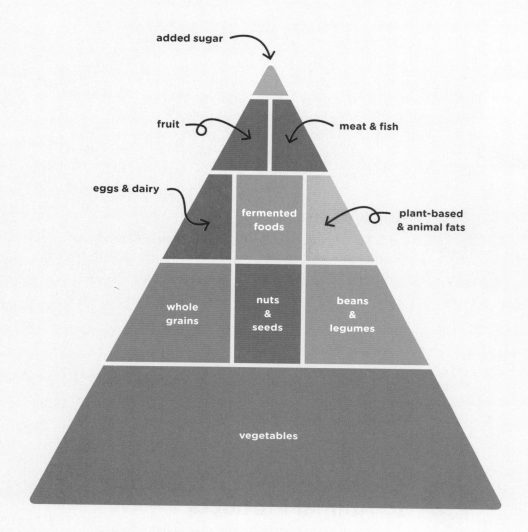

The following labels appear on the pyramid:

- added sugar
- fruit
- meat & fish
- eggs & dairy
- fermented foods
- plant-based & animal fats
- whole grains
- nuts & seeds
- beans & legumes
- vegetables

THE *HELP YOURSELF* FOOD PYRAMID

The USDA MyPlate diagram introduced in 2011 doesn't distinguish between things like whole and refined grains or fruit and juice, which have very different effects on your body, for instance whether they are likely to quickly enter your bloodstream (e.g., refined grains like white crackers), or make it all the way to the good bacteria in your gut (e.g., whole grains like farro or barley).

I actually think the format of the old-school food pyramid is an easier way to visualize how a balanced way of eating should function on a day-to-day basis, rather than the single-meal MyPlate diagram. Mine is updated with clear terms like *whole grains* and *fermented foods,* which align with gut-friendly eating. Additionally, the focus is on integrating vegetables into every meal, and several servings of other plant foods every day.

 For the purposes of this book and how I suggest you start thinking of food, I will use the terms *food* or *whole foods* to encompass whole food ingredients and whole foods that have been minimally or beneficially processed.

Integrate Live Fermented Foods Daily

Make kimchi, miso, tempeh, sauerkraut, and kefir (but not kombucha) everyday foods.

The process of fermentation essentially mimics what happens inside your gut. Microbes start feasting on the food, jump-starting the digestion process. So when you eat the food, you're also eating the microbes and potentially some beneficial byproducts of their digestion, too. In the case of kimchi, sauerkraut, and lacto-fermented vegetables like pickles, you're also getting dietary fiber. It's a symbiotic win-win!

Commonly available fermented foods include kimchi, sauerkraut, lacto-fermented pickles, kefir, yogurt, tempeh, gochujang, and kombucha. I include all of these except kombucha in my weekly rotation, since most commercial kombuchas are high in added sugar, which is inflammatory and spikes blood sugar. This means that kombucha falls under the special occasion category for me.

ULTRAPROCESSED FOOD, DEFINED

The Brazilian researcher Carlos Monteiro popularized the term *ultraprocessed food* to define the manufactured foods that are ubiquitous in modern diets.

"Ultraprocessed products are made from processed substances extracted or refined from whole foods—e.g., oils, hydrogenated oils and fats, flours and starches, variants of sugar, and cheap parts or remnants of animal foods—with little or no whole foods. Products include burgers, frozen pasta, pizza and pasta dishes, nuggets and sticks, crisps, biscuits, confectionery, cereal bars, carbonated and other sugared drinks, and various snack products."

With ultraprocessed food, it's about moderation. Having a little won't harm you, but these products are engineered in a way that overwhelms your body's satiety mechanisms due to the ubiquitous trifecta of high salt, fat, and sugar. And because ultraprocessed foods tend to be energy dense (read: high in calories), they displace other food sources, like vegetables and whole grains, which are essential to health.

NOTE I didn't include recipes for fermentation in this book for two reasons: First, just because you're looking to do better by your gut microbes doesn't mean you necessarily have a lot of time to experiment with fermentation. It's a fun and worthy project to pursue, but you can buy high-quality fermented foods across the country. Second, there are numerous guides to fermentation by true experts. Rather than crib from their work, I recommend you seek out *The Art of Fermentation* by Sandor Ellix Katz and *The Noma Guide to Fermentation* by René Redzepi and David Zilber. Many of the other gut-friendly cookbooks listed in the Resources section (page 356) also include fermentation recipes.

Shopping **TIP**

The process of heating or sterilizing food so that it is shelf stable kills beneficial microbes. Look for refrigerated fermented foods to ensure you get the probiotic benefits of the live microorganisms.

Eat Something at Every Meal that Feeds your Microbiota
Our microbes eat what we eat.

Humans have co-evolved with microbes in a mutually beneficial relationship. When we feed beneficial bacteria the foods they like, they thrive and so does our health. Beneficial bacteria thrive on dietary plant fiber (which includes microbiota-accessible carbohydrates [MACs] and prebiotics). The more variety of plants in your diet, the bigger the variety of beneficial microbes. A meal without plant fiber might feed you, but it leaves nothing for your friendly microbes.

 ## Reduce Added Sugar
Unless you've fed your microbiota adequately, don't eat any sugar at all, including sweeteners like honey and maple syrup.

When I say "added sugar," I am talking about any refined substance that's used to sweeten food. That means cane sugar, beet sugar, maple syrup, coconut sugar, honey, evaporated cane syrup, agave nectar, and more.

Simply put, if a sweet food is refined to where it can be scooped into a cup or poured into a batter and turned into a treat, then I consider it sugar. (I do not consider dried Medjool dates added sugar, as they contain fiber and minerals when eaten in their whole form. However, I do consider date sugar and date syrup to be "sugar.")

Sugar wreaks havoc on your gut microbes. It can cause bad bacteria to outnumber good bacteria, and sugar-loving yeasts can not only set up camp in your digestive tract, they send signals to your brain to feed them—aka eat more sugar! Eating sugar is also a major factor in the development of many chronic illnesses that are linked to the gut like type-2 diabetes, hormone imbalances, and metabolic issues. Excessive amounts can also contribute to inflammation.

I like a saying from the field of toxicology, "the dose makes the poison." While this is not true for every substance, I do think it's a useful way to think about sugar. A little sugar occasionally as part of a balanced overall diet is not a problem. It's when the doses outpace our body's ability to process it that problems arise. If you do eat added sugar—which I think is absolutely fine in moderation—make sure to eat it alongside fiber-rich plants so your beneficial microbes are well fed.

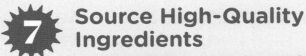

Source High-Quality Ingredients

For instance, local, organic, non-GMO, and antibiotic-free.

This is a controversial guideline since it requires the means and access to buy these frankly more expensive foods, but one I feel compelled to suggest if you have the financial resources and time to seek out high-quality ingredients. The best-case scenario is to buy with these qualifications, since pesticides on vegetables and even trace antibiotics in conventionally raised meat have a deleterious effect on gut microbes.

FIBER: LET'S TALK NUMBERS

As humans, we have gone from eating somewhere between 100 and 150 grams of fiber a day to the measly 10 to 15 grams of fiber that characterizes the Western diet. No wonder our gut microbes are struggling—we are literally starving them of 90 percent of the food they need to survive. Most experts recommend trying for between 30 and 40 grams of fiber per day. I don't count grams of fiber myself, and of course, it varies from day to day. I do try most of the time to eat foods and dishes that are mostly plants. The great thing is, you'll likely feel better and feel a difference in your body simply by eating more plants without needing to tally up the numbers from each meal you eat. (Though you can do that if you want; nutritional information for all the recipes starts on page 347.)

Our communities of microbes are different than those of our hunter-gatherer ancestors; consequently, we might lack the right microbes to digest a lot of fiber. If you are not used to eating a lot of vegetables and other plants, you might experience some bloating or gas as you increase your fiber intake. That's because those fiber-loving microbes are finally getting what they need to thrive—and that means they're going to produce chemical byproducts (read: gas). These symptoms should go down as you adjust to eating more plants. Drinking a lot of water also helps (see guideline 8 on the next page for more on that).

8

Drink a Lot of Water and Limit Alcohol

We know that lots of water is good for health. But for the microbes in your gut, why does it matter?

Well, water is absorbed by the fiber in plant foods, and if you increase fiber without increasing water, you're likely to get backed up. Not only is this uncomfortable, frequent bowel movements are essential to maintaining a healthy balance of good and bad microbes.

Excessive alcohol consumption can cause a spectrum of gut-related issues, including increased intestinal permeability (aka leaky gut), dysbiosis, and inflammation. Chronic alcohol use may disrupt circadian rhythm, which in turn can disrupt the gut microbiota. Alcohol also seems to encourage pathogenic bacteria, which produce endotoxins, a type of chemical that increases inflammation locally and—if it passes through the intestinal barrier—throughout the body. Of course, sugary cocktails are a double whammy of added sugar and alcohol.

And while this isn't entirely gut-specific, I want to make a note about alcohol use: Rather than advocate that people cut out alcohol entirely or limit to a single glass of wine a day, I say: start by paying attention to how you engage with alcohol. Are there times when you drink more than you wish you had? Do some drinks make you feel worse than others? How many drinks equal a "normal" night? Do you hate how often you're hungover, or wake up with a sense of guilt or shame about what happened the night before?

This is an incredibly personal area—like almost everything we put into our bodies—so rather than be proscriptive, I urge you to listen to how your body feels, and think about what role alcohol plays in that relationship.

The Strategy Stuff

Many books tell you what to eat to be more healthful but don't tell you how to make it happen in your real life. You know, the life that happens every day, not just the Instagram-filter version. These strategies have made the difference for me in shifting to a plant-focused way of eating.

Here are my tips and tools to set you up for success—in your kitchen, at the grocery store, and in your mindset. Doing a big overhaul at once isn't practical, cost-effective, or sustainable, so I recommend reading this section to get some inspiration and then picking out a few pieces at a time to apply to your life.

Organizing for Success: What to Keep Where

It matters where the healthful ingredients are kept (hint: in clear containers at eye level) and that jars of cookies aren't in the path of your most common activities. There's no reason you should have to resist a brownie every time you walk past the kitchen. It's just too dang taxing on your mind! Here are five organizational tips to make healthy eating easier:

1. Do a big cleanout: Get rid of foods that have a lot of added sugar or are ultraprocessed. If you want to keep these around, put them on a hard-to-reach shelf or in a low drawer in the fridge or freezer.

2. Rather than recycle (or, god forbid, throw out) glass jars from peanut butter or mustard, reuse them for salad dressings.

3. Use clear containers to store cooked grains, beans, vegetables, and other healthy prepped foods; store these at eye level in your refrigerator. I like glass ones best.

4. Prep greens and other vegetables when you get home from shopping. Wrap greens in clean dishtowels and store in the fridge in a salad spinner or in a container draped with a damp dishtowel.

5. Keep a permanent marker and masking tape on hand for labeling leftovers, prepped ingredients, and cooked grains, beans, legumes, and dressings.

Equipment for Healthier Cooking

I've noticed that friends who find cooking frustrating or a hassle often don't have the right tools. Rather than give a comprehensive overview of everything you need in a stocked kitchen, I want to highlight tools that make a big difference in healthier cooking.

- A HIGH-POWERED BLENDER: Smooth-textured soups, vegetable dips, and smoothies all rely on a strong motor to blitz ingredients to a silky puree.

- FOOD PROCESSOR: I keep an 8-cup and a mini food processor on my countertop at all times for things like crumble topping (page 338), pesto (page 132), and herb dip (page 197). I also love the slicing blade for quick prep.

- SALAD SPINNER: This might be the most important missing tool in many people's kitchens. Soggy lettuce is no good, and a salad spinner also doubles as a colander or storage container for prepped vegetables.

- DIGITAL SCALE: Healthful baking requires more exacting ratios of ingredients, because there's little to no added sugar to mask mistakes. This is why you'll notice weights on some recipes, which a digital scale allows you to measure exactly.

- **HIGH-QUALITY LEMON SQUEEZER:** I am a proselytizer for a heavy-duty lemon squeezer (my favorite brand is Chef'n). Citrus is expensive, and wasting any drop because the squeezer isn't up to the task is such a shame.

- **GARLIC PRESS:** Snobby cooks, look away. I love using a garlic press because it takes an entire step off my cutting board, and it saves me from getting those sticky garlic fingers.

- **CUTTING BOARDS IN MULTIPLE SIZES:** Yes, a beautiful, heavy-duty wooden butcher block set on a kitchen counter is the dream of beautiful kitchens. But for practical, everyday cooking, I also like to have several dishwasher-safe cutting boards in multiple sizes for a quick clean-up after I chop.

- **RIMMED BAKING SHEETS:** There is no such thing as too many rimmed baking sheets in my kitchen. I keep a stack of quarter-sheet (10 by 13-inch) and half-sheet (13 by 17-inch) pans at the ready for all sorts of tasks, from roasting vegetables to corralling prep ingredients. Look for heavy-duty sheets that won't warp in the oven.

- **OVEN THERMOMETER:** The right temperature is the key to crisp-edge vegetables, well-risen banana bread, and a fall-off-the-bone piece of meat. Over time, many ovens lose their ability to regulate temperature or they spike during cooking. Too low and you risk a rock-hard roasted vegetable; too high and you're looking at a charred lump of who-knows-what. Spend the five dollars on an oven thermometer so you know you're cooking at the right temperature,

TIP: GET A WHITEBOARD

If you're the type of person who always looks in the refrigerator, even a stocked one, and thinks, "There's nothing here," a magnetic whiteboard or even a piece of paper taped to the fridge can make healthy eating easier. Especially if cooking tends to fall on one person in the family, having a list of what's available to eat encourages everyone to take care of meals on their own.

I list what's ready to eat (full meals, leftovers, etc.) in one column and components that are available (prepped greens, salad dressing, frozen cooked grains, Trash or Treasure Broth, etc.) in a separate column.

and your food is likely to get significantly tastier.

- **KITCHEN SHEARS:** I still use the same pair of heavy-duty kitchen shears that I got in my culinary school toolkit. I use them for everything from snipping chives to carving a chicken (trust me, it's easier than using a knife) to releasing roasted shallots from their skins. Choose ones that are dishwasher safe and come apart so you can get all the gunk off.

Work Clean

If there's one thing I'm a fanatic about when it comes to cooking, it's keeping a clean and organized kitchen. It might seem funny to obsess over something that isn't food related, but I genuinely believe that these simple tools and tips can make the difference between regularly cooking and not, since a dirty kitchen makes cooking feel like a hassle. And when it comes to eating healthfully, cooking at home is crucial.

I never leave the kitchen without loading the dishwasher or handwashing my dishes. Then, I spray the counter and wipe it down, and put everything away in its right place. This makes it that much easier to walk into the kitchen next time to assemble a healthy meal from my fridge or to start cooking. Here are a few more useful things to help keep your kitchen clean:

- **A LARGE STACK OF REUSABLE DISHTOWELS**—not only do they help you cut down on paper towels (which will end up in a landfill), dishtowels are useful for pulling things in and out of the oven, drying dishes, drying vegetables and berries, and cleaning the countertop. I hang dirty towels on the oven bar and fold clean ones in a rectangle by the sink so I can tell them apart.

- **TWO SPONGES**—one for the countertops, one for dishes. Get two colors so you can tell them apart.

- **A SPONGE-HOLDER**—repeat after me: mildew is the enemy. When you let sponges sit in water or sogged up at the bottom of the sink, they grow smelly mildew. After dishwashing or counter-cleaning, rinse your sponge with clean water, then wring out and place in a dish that allows for air circulation.

- **A COUNTER SPRAY**—buy an ecofriendly one, or fill a spray bottle with equal parts distilled vinegar and water.

MY FAVORITE TREAT— DRIED MEDJOOL DATES

Dried Medjool dates are a wondrous fruit—they're incredibly sweet but not cloying, and they can stand in place of refined sugar in desserts and smoothies. Flavors range from butterscotch to caramel-esque to toffee-like. The point is, they are decadent!

High-quality ones are worth seeking either at your local health food store, farmers' market (if you live in California), or by ordering online. My favorite farm is Rancho Meladuco.

Look for plump, soft dates that aren't hard and shriveled. Store them in your fridge for up to six months.

Shopping

Shopping for groceries has never been more complicated. Is it best to get a CSA? Shop at the farmers' market? Is the grocery store fine? Or should I get things from a delivery service? What to buy where is often a factor of convenience and cost, and my goal is to get you to take quality into account, too.

To avoid food waste, the ideal scenario is to shop each day for what you plan to cook. We have the best intentions with a big shop, but often life gets in the way. That said, going to the store every day is just not realistic for most people. I keep a well-stocked pantry and freezer and try to make it to a farmers' market at least once a week.

My Gut-Friendly Staples

A stocked kitchen is the key to cooking healthfully off the cuff. Here are the ingredients I have on hand at all times:

PANTRY

- **WHOLE GRAINS AND GRAINLIKE SEEDS:** millet, buckwheat groats, amaranth, quinoa, barley, farro, oats (quick-cooking, rolled, and oat groats)

- **DRIED BEANS AND LEGUMES:** beans (adzuki, pinto, black beans are always on hand) dried chickpeas, lentils (green, Puy/French, and red)

- **NUTS AND NUT BUTTERS:** raw nuts (almonds, cashews, pistachios, pecans); no-sugar-added nut butters (peanut and almond)

- **SEEDS:** pumpkin, sesame, chia, hemp, flax and sunflower

- **BAKING INGREDIENTS:** coconut sugar, maple syrup, honey, baking soda, baking powder, kosher salt

- **SNACKS:** chips, crackers, brown rice cakes, unsulfured dried fruit (mulberries, prunes, apricots) (all without additives)

- **COOKING STAPLES:** oils, vinegars, flaky sea salt, kosher salt, pepper mill

- **SPICES:** particular favorites include cumin, coriander, turmeric, cinnamon, nutmeg, and smoked paprika

- **SEAWEEDS:** Kombu and wakame

- **AROMATICS:** onions, shallots, garlic

- **UNRIPE AVOCADOS**

FRIDGE

- **FERMENTED INGREDIENTS:** miso pastes, kimchi, sauerkraut, lacto-fermented pickles, kefir, Greek yogurt

- **LITTLE FLAVOR BOOSTERS:** capers, harissa paste, fancy green olives (Castelvetrano are my favorite), olive tapenade, Parmesan

- **CONDIMENTS:** tamari (gluten-free soy sauce), Dijon mustard, vegan mayonnaise, curry pastes

- **DRIED MEDJOOL DATES**

- **PERISHABLE STAPLES:** non-dairy milks, cultured butter and ghee, lemons, fresh ginger, herbs like parsley and cilantro, eggs, ripe avocados

- **SPROUTED CORN TORTILLAS**

FREEZER

- **SPECIALTY FLOURS AND STARCHES**

- **TRASH OR TREASURE BROTH** (page 129)

- **FROZEN VEGETABLES AND FRUIT** for smoothies

What's on My Shopping List

I supplement my staples with multiple trips to the store so that I am eating a rotating selection of fresh foods. This is when I stock up on pantry items that are running low, plus in-season vegetables, herbs, fruit, and more. I'll also pick up eggs and meat at the farmers' market or at my local butcher.

Navigating the Grocery Store with Health in Mind

You may have heard that the key to shopping healthfully is to stick to the perimeter of the store (where the fresh, unprocessed, whole foods usually are) and to steer clear of the aisles, where the processed foods lurk, waiting to tempt you. In theory, this should work, but marketers and supermarket chains are smart, and they stay on top of these types of consumer tactics—meaning you'll find processed foods in all areas of the store. So, what should you actually do? Make a plan, and a list, and stick to them. This is advice you've probably heard before, but it is worth repeating: Don't do your shopping on an empty stomach. I don't need a study to tell me that when I shop hungry, I buy more than I plan to and am more likely to succumb to junk-food temptation.

MY SHOPPING LIST STRATEGY

The key to my incredibly efficient shopping is my organized grocery lists and my standardized plan of attack. I categorize my shopping list by area of the store—bulk items, then shelf staples, refrigerated items, and finally produce. That way, I can find what I need as I work through the store.

ONCE I'M AT THE STORE

List and pen in hand, I start with the bulk bins (filling up compostable bags that I order online and reuse).

Most health food stores now have bulk bin sections, which is a great way to find inexpensive organic ingredients. Bulk bins are also great for reducing waste, as you can bring a bag or a reusable jar. I've heard a lot of fear and hesitation from friends who are intimidated by the bulk bin aisle, but it's worth getting over. Beyond the environmental benefits (less packaging), the format corrals so many ingredients in one spot: It's a convenient, one-stop shop for everything from beans and legumes to nuts and seeds. I also get all my grains and even some flours from the bulk bins.

Next, I stock up on the canned goods and other shelf staples I can't get from the bulk bins, like coconut milk and specialty baking ingredients. Then I hit the refrigerated staples like sprouted corn tortillas, kefir, kimchi, and sauerkraut. If I didn't get eggs at the farmers' market that week, I'll add those, too. Finally, I swing through the produce section for anything I can't get at my farmers' market.

IF YOU CAN, MAKE TIME FOR YOUR FARMERS' MARKET OR A CSA SHARE

Much has been written about the reduced carbon footprint of buying local, and there's also the lovely goal of supporting local businesses. From a nutrition perspective, fresh food begins losing nutrients from the moment it's picked until you eat it. For this reason, shopping at your local farmers' market or buying a CSA share is the way to go for the best in-season produce. And, from the perspective of your gut, foods that are locally and organically grown are likely to still have some good dirt on them—aka microbes that can help your gut!

The Wellness Industrial Complex

"Wellness" has become big business for food
manufacturers, websites, and brands who survive by stoking consumers'
fear about doing the wrong thing for their health.

Instagram and Internet "Healthy"

Nowhere is the wish to have our cake and eat it, too, more evident than in the "healthy" blog and internet food arena. As likes have come to determine popularity, so-called healthy bloggers and Instagrammers have popularized a certain look for food that simultaneously reads as healthy and decadent. Take a scroll through social media and you'll find towers of pancakes dripping in almond butter sauce and maple syrup, and pictures of skinny bodies in spandex between ones of matcha frozen yogurt. Taking these photographs at their word either results in a feeling of personal failure (it's not) or success in the eyes of social media, adding more noise to this problematic sphere.

Somewhere deep down, I think most people know that these accounts are an exercise in contradiction, that sharing is curated to sell something, even if that something is "just" likes and followers.

Wellness Websites

I am skeptical of any article that promotes gut health with magic bullet–style headlines. The ones that say things like, "Adding this one ingredient to your smoothie can majorly boost gut health" or "Pop a probiotic to prevent stress"—these are causal claims that obscure the nuance inherent in the variation between each person's microbiota.

The wellness media industry has something to gain by keeping us afraid of food and of making the "wrong choice." When we are scared and insecure we are more likely to incessantly search for answers, to read articles with clickbait titles that rely on scare tactics.

Many foods are vilified by media doctors based on spurious claims, especially in relation to gut health. One oft-maligned nutrient is called lectin, which is a protein famously found in legumes, but actually also found in most foods. Lectins have not been shown to be dangerous in the amounts we consume them in. In fact, one notable study found that legume consumption was inversely associated with non-cardiovascular mortality and a reduced risk of a type of heart disease caused by narrowed arteries. And to bring it all back to our microbes: Lentils and other legumes are a great source of resistant starch, a particular type of fiber that beneficial bacteria thrive on.

The same goes for nightshades, which is a catch-all term for edible members of the *Solanaceae* plant family such as potatoes, eggplant, peppers, and tomatoes. Nightshades are routinely called pro-inflammatory despite any scientific evidence to substantiate the connection. Eliminating an entire family of plants will only reduce the variety in your diet and thus the variety of gut microbes you house.

These examples highlight the way wellness media often ignores the greater good of foods and overly stresses the negative aspect of one element in isolation, doing so with exaggerated certainty.

You are welcome to come to your own conclusions, but my takeaway has been to be deeply skeptical of any dietary advice that advocates cutting out entire categories of vegetables and other plant-based whole foods.

8 Ways to Be a Critical Thinker

in the Face of Wellness Media, Big Food, and "Because I Told You So" People

1. Question anyone who makes a health claim based on an isolated nutrient or component of a food without contextualizing within the food or dietary pattern.

2. When only one study done on mice is cited, don't immediately assume it translates to humans.

3. Pay attention to misattribution of causation instead of correlation.

4. Beware health claims that don't explain why or give evidence.

5. Who's paying? Big Food and Big Pharma are also big funders of research, which can bias outcomes.

6. Learn how to spot intellectual loopholes—the "have your cake and eat it, too" type of advice.

7. Consider the source: Does the purveyor of this information have something to gain?

8. Question black-and-white statements like "antibiotics are bad."

EAT GOOD TO FEEL GOOD

Ideas and Strategies for Forming and Sticking to New Habits

I am by no means a habit expert, but I am interested in habit formation and like to treat myself like a guinea pig. These strategies and ideas were ones that worked for me over time as I shifted how I ate, and help me stay on track with my goals to eat with my microbiota in mind.

Tracking

One of the hardest things about shifting how you eat is quantifying baby steps in the face of a bigger, longer-term picture. It's hard to see change on a day-to-day basis, and it can feel frustrating to commit to healthier eating to feel better twenty, thirty, or fifty years down the line. Small daily wins in the form of tracking, using the tools below, are an essential strategy for me. It's a tiny reward that gives me a sense of the good work I'm doing for my long-term health.

People also tend to overestimate how healthfully they eat; tracking can be a reality check when assessing where you're at in terms of fitting in vegetables or reducing added sugar and processed food.

Scorecards

To motivate myself to incorporate more plants into my diet—essentially eating from the perspective of my microbiota—I created a scorecard system (see page 342). The idea is that you start with easy, achievable goals, and level up as you get accustomed to *Help Yourself* eating. I love the satisfaction of checking off the boxes as I move through my day and have found this to be an incredibly effective tool. You'll notice that each recipe includes check marks for using the scorecard.

Sticker Journal

I'm not sure if anything makes me sound more like a kid than when I mention my sticker journal. But, if I were to share one thing that made the difference in adjusting my eating habits, it was this—rewarding myself with stickers I collected in a small notebook. (I used one with a week on each page, but you could create your own out of a blank notebook.)

I came up with the idea as a way to motivate myself to shift what I ate as well as my lifestyle habits. I made a key on a notecard with a sticker to represent each goal. For instance, I'd get a different sticker for each day that I didn't drink alcohol, didn't eat sugar, and didn't eat processed food. I also included work and life things like "reached out to a friend" and "spent an hour on a freelance project." These were bigger-picture goals than on the scorecard, which tracks servings of microbe-friendly foods throughout the day.

Originally, my idea was that after I earned a certain number of stickers, I'd treat myself to something I wanted like a new dress or a massage. But it turned out that simply seeing the stickers pile up in my journal made me feel a boost of accomplishment and helped establish new habits.

What to Track

I'm not a fan of keeping a detailed food journal—it's just too much work—but if you want to do that or your medical practitioner has requested you keep one, go for it. Since the body is a complex, interconnected system, it's worth tracking other elements, even in just a word or two. Ideas include exercise, what you drink, how you are feeling emotionally, and something you're grateful for. You can also add this to the bottom of your scorecard or to your sticker journal.

Listening to Your Body

It's important to listen to your body, because how you feel physically is an indicator of how things are going in your gut, and how your gut microbiota is doing affects the entire body. Gurgling, growls, and bloating can all be normal outcomes of adjusting to a plant-focused diet and finally feeding beneficial bacteria what they want. But they can also be symptoms of SIBO (small intestine bacterial overgrowth) or a food intolerance. They should abate as your microbiota shifts; if they don't, speak to your medical practitioner.

Building Healthy Habits

I have a secret. My favorite section of the bookstore isn't the cookbook section, it's the self-improvement area. Give me a book about habits, psychology, and self-help and I will devour it, highlighter in hand and notebook at the ready. Next, I set to putting the ideas into practice in my own life. (Yes, it's exhausting to live with me.) I've put experts' theoretical advice to the test and come up with five real-life strategies for creating new habits, breaking old ones that no longer serve you, and taking some of the mental work off eating healthfully.

AUTOMATICITY AND BABY STEPS

The goal with a habit is that it eventually becomes a behavior you don't have to think about. This is called *automaticity*. It relies on the repetition of the task, not on the time spent. Rather than choose a huge habit like "I'm going to eat healthfully," it's useful to break it down into small, manageable tasks that can be repeated daily. Baby steps! This might be as simple as eating fermented food every single day until you no longer notice you heap sauerkraut on a grain bowl. Or, it could be deciding that you'll cook dinner every night of the week until it doesn't feel so arduous. I used to loathe cleaning the kitchen until I made a practice of clearing dishes and wiping down the counter after every time I cooked. Now it's automatic, and I don't have to think about it.

HABIT LOOPS

Habit loops are a concept popularized by Charles Duhigg in his book *The Power of Habit* and expanded on by James Clear in *Atomic Habits*. Instead of relying on willpower or feeling decision fatigue, a habit loop can be harnessed to shift behaviors toward things you want to do rather than things you're accustomed to. Clear breaks the loop into four stages: cue, craving, response, reward. Once you get the reward, it's associated with the cue, which starts the cycle again. Here's how I've built off both their ideas to form healthy eating habits:

It starts with a cue (for instance, hunger). That leads to a craving, like "I want something delicious!" In the past, my response would be to go for what was easy—pasta, bread, cured meats, all of it together! But that is where *Help Yourself* recipes come in—offering an easy alternative response. By having a fridge stocked with ready-to-eat foods from the Prep City section (page 92) or a preassembled grain bowl that you made before you got hungry, you can intervene in the old habit loop by easily choosing something else (the response). This is the reward—hearty, healthful food that satiates. Eventually, the habit loop reinforces your association with this food and feeling good.

PAIRING

I learned about the strategy of pairing from one of my habit gurus, Gretchen Rubin. The concept is simple: Pair a task you don't want to do with one you want to do. I use this all the time, especially with cooking. Healthy eating requires cooking at home, and it can be time-consuming. I listen to a podcast while I do dishes, call a friend while I prep, or blast my favorite music as I stand over the stove. You can use this in any area of your life—saving a favorite TV show for the elliptical machine or buying a special tea for when you fill out insurance paperwork. It's a simple trick, but it makes many tasks less annoying.

MAKING FRIENDS WITH FUTURE YOU

Research shows that we view our future selves as entirely distinct from who we are at this moment, which can lead to all sorts of undermining behavior like neglecting to save money, procrastinating on a deadline, or assuming healthy eating can start somewhere down the line. The more similarly we view our future self to our present self—when we think of them vividly and as a continuum of who we are now—the easier it makes sacrifices, like healthful eating, in the present. Given this information, I do something that might sound hokey, but works: I take time to talk to Future Lindsay. I think of her older, with a family and a shelf of published books, and I imagine her without joint pain or itching or depression—all things that my actions now can help prevent. This makes it easier to practice self-care and do the work to maintain long-term health.

SHORT- AND LONG-TERM REWARDS

Apparently, rewards can undermine habit creation. The thinking goes that reward-based change makes the habit extrinsically motivated, so when the reward disappears, the habit theoretically does, too. But this is one situation where I have found the research to not hold up in my real life.

For me, rewarding myself in the short- and long-term has made sticking to difficult new habits palatable. Then, once the habits are ingrained, they are just that: habitual. I no longer need a reward for going a day without sugar, but when I started easing away from my daily cookie or ice cream sundae, it felt good to do something to recognize that achievement. I've used rewards like putting a dollar in a jar for each day I successfully completed a habit and choosing something I could buy when it hit a certain goal. This reward strategy makes use of short term (a dollar each day) and long term (a milestone to achieve).

My feeling is that it's fine to reward with food or alcohol occasionally, but only if it's not tying one bad habit to a good one. It does no good to crush the expert level of my scorecard (page 342) and then drink a whole bottle of wine to celebrate. However, after a day of finally getting around to my taxes, it feels good to know that there's a delicious glass of red wine (or two, let's be honest) waiting for me at the end. Context matters.

Identity and Mindset

How you think about your identity and the mind-set you maintain are two crucial elements to success when adapting to a healthy lifestyle.

When I first started to realize that changing how I ate was going to be essential to feeling better, I resisted, since winning people over with food was a major part of my identity and why I got into the food industry in the first place. I was a socially anxious kid who developed a strategy of approaching new people with a tub full of home-baked brownies. Post-college, this evolved into elaborate dinner parties. Who would I be if I weren't hosting my friends for decadent meals? In the decade I spent as a recipe developer and food writer, I built much of my career on developing over-the-top desserts and even mastering the perfect chocolate chip cookie.

There was also the matter of the identities I strongly *didn't* identify with. I resented friends who put their health first, and I considered thin people who watched what they ate to be the opposite of me. I looked at healthy food as negative by association—the women who were lean and beautiful ate this food, and I felt jealous of them, therefore I hated the food they ate.

Choosing to change the way I ate required me to completely give up long-entrenched identities and redevelop my relationship to healthy food from square one. It didn't happen overnight, and without therapy to help me value myself over what others thought, as well as determination to stop feeling so bad all the time, I couldn't have done it. I had to mourn the loss of what once was—my cookie-loving self—to start putting my health first.

In the end, I had to choose a new identity that trumped my old one: Now, I value feeling good in my body and mind above all else. If that doesn't jive with regularly binge drinking and mindlessly shoving chips in my face, so be it.

How do you feel when you think about changing how you eat in order to feel better? Do you feel stressed? Annoyed? Angry? Confused? Doubtful?

I cycled through all these feelings and more as I adapted to my microbe-friendly way of eating. Until I felt genuinely better, was able to start cutting out medications (and saving money), and started seeing the difference in my body, I fought back at my new reality. This was a direct result of rethinking my identity.

One thing that helped was reminding myself of another aspect of my identity—that I like to learn, grow, and challenge myself. This is called having a growth mindset, and while it's often invoked in academic or business settings, I find it highly applicable to implementing lifestyle changes.

Overcoming Common Excuses

Change is hard. Even once I understood that changing how I ate would likely improve how I felt, I resisted. After all the research I'd done, I was so stressed as I finished the manuscript for this book that I ate pizza four days out of seven. It happens. Here are some of the excuses I've used while shifting how I ate and a couple I've come across during the process of writing this book. (One person in particular was adamant that this simply didn't apply to her. I've got news: Everyone on this planet has a gut microbiota. This most definitely does apply to you!)

Long story short: Change is hard, but feeling good in your body and prioritizing health can be the difference between living and thriving. Start by paying attention to your excuses, and challenge them.

"I DON'T HAVE ENOUGH TIME."

If you're already in the habit of cooking dinner every night or even prepping meals for the week, then all you have to do is swap in these recipes for your usual ones. But many people don't have time because it's not baked into their schedule. Some ways I've addressed this in my own life are by cutting down on TV or setting up my iPad while I chop vegetables. I cook and do dishes while on the phone with my close friends and family, and I keep my freezer stocked with ready-to-eat meals. When I really feel pressed for time, I make a vegetable-packed smoothie for dinner. It takes five minutes, and I can soak the blender in the sink overnight. Sure, in the short term, time can feel precious, especially when there is a world of immediate gratification at our fingertips via social media and streaming services. However, putting in the work to benefit your long-term health is well worth it.

"I DON'T LIKE THOSE FOODS."

Are you sure? Or are they just unfamiliar? What if you commit to trying one new ingredient a week? There is evidence that our microbes influence what foods we crave, so the more you eat new plant-based foods, the more you will crave them.

"I FEEL FINE."

You may have become accustomed to things like allergies, joint pain, and heartburn. Because these symptoms have become normalized, you might think you feel fine. Pause, listen to your body, and reflect—have you been complaining about recurring health issues? It's worth taking these symptoms seriously and considering how a gut-friendly way of eating might help.

"IT'S TOO EXPENSIVE."

A head of cabbage and a bag of dried beans are not expensive. Whole food ingredients do not have to break the bank, and there's even a chance that by changing how you eat, you won't need expensive medications like proton pump inhibitors.

"THEY DIDN'T HAVE ANYTHING AT THE RESTAURANT."

Most restaurants have vegetable side dishes—order two or three and you've got a meal. If they have beans and brown rice, great. Ask for a side of avocado and voilà! A burrito bowl. Vegetable soups work, too. The point is, this kind of excuse is about projection rather than reality. And if you are finding that you eat often at restaurants that truly don't serve vegetables, change the places you frequent.

"I DON'T WANT TO CHANGE THE WAY I EAT."

I feel you. I didn't want to either, but no challenge has ever been more worthwhile than improving how I felt in my body.

Fuzzy Boundaries

Most healthy cookbooks require you to live in a contracted state of restriction, insisting that pairing a slice of bacon with vegetables negates any good. That is an exhausting way to live, and it's not as delicious. The thing is, a rigid mindset won't do you any good, nor is it realistic, whether you came to this book to feel better, to stay healthy, or because you're "gut-curious."

When you expect perfection (an impossible goal), there's inevitable failure. When you expect good enough (a realistic goal), there's room to wobble and still consider your efforts a success.

It can be tempting to feel that boundaries or extremes will help you control habits, but in my experience, they just lead to a binge or breakdown. Life isn't neat and it resists being squeezed. Much better to go for an overall trend. If you want a rule, I like James Clear's suggestion from *Atomic Habits*, which is to feel fine about skipping one day of a habit but never two in a row. As he writes, "Too often, we fall into an all-or-nothing cycle with our habits. The problem is not slipping up; the problem is thinking that if you can't do something perfectly, then you shouldn't do it at all."

Pistachio Butter
Thumbprints
with Raspberry-
Chia Filling
332

3 THE RECIPES

MAKING A GREAT RECIPE is about more than just throwing together tasty ingredients and hoping it will work. Before I started eating with my microbes in mind, a few goals drove my creations: they had to be streamlined, not use too many pots and pans, and call for everyday ingredients. Once I shifted to plant-focused eating, I raised the bar even higher. Getting from vegetables to dinner without relying on shortcut flavor ingredients like a blanket of cheese or a hunk of butter meant learning how to be clever and resourceful. While most recipes use standard grocery store items, I have introduced some ingredients that might be new to you (see page 87). I understand that you are trusting me with your time and grocery budget, so please know that if I call for something unique, it's because I think you'll like having it as part of your gut-friendly repertoire.

With all this said, I've created four promises to you for these recipes. Beyond those, you'll find an introduction to the "slugs" (icons) that run on many of the recipe pages, and some guidelines for entertaining the *Help Yourself* way.

The Four *Help Yourself* Recipe Promises

1 **These recipes aren't pretending to be something else.**

I'd rather eat a plate of salmon with vegetables and quinoa than mac and cheese made with almond milk, nutritional yeast, and chickpea noodles. Not only will it taste bad, many allegedly "healthy" substitutes are rife with stabilizers and emulsifiers, which can be harmful to the gut. I'd rather you eat a delicious plate of four-cheese macaroni topped with buttery bread crumbs and then see how you feel afterward. You might feel fine, and that's great. But if you don't, then you know something about where your body is right now. No matter what, real food is the goal.

2 **The food looks appetizing.**

When it's cooked well and thoughtfully put together (with variety in mind), plant-focused food is colorful and looks beautiful.

3 **The food tastes great.**

As a professional recipe developer and author, I have a track record of creating delicious recipes for over a decade. I know what goes together and the best cooking methods for drawing out their incredible flavors.

4 **These recipes work in your real life.**

Help Yourself is about what I call "actual cooking." The recipes don't use too many pots and pans, the ingredient lists are short, and there aren't a lot of steps or prep. With recipes that are easy and doable, you're much more likely to have success.

TIME: THE SECRET INGREDIENT

I've discovered that time is its own ingredient in healthy cooking. Letting the chickpea flatbread batter (page 123) sit for eight hours is the key to its dense, satisfying texture, and sprouting beans and grains takes a couple days of rinsing and straining. Soups, too, when they're focused on plants and don't use shortcut flavor ingredients like cream, require a little more time on the stove. I can promise you that I never include a step where there shouldn't be one, but if you're used to my recipes in my previous book, *Healthyish*, don't be surprised if these take a little longer.

Delicata Rings with Kefir-Ranch Dip 309

About the "Slugs"

When I was working at *Real Simple* developing recipes, we used the word *slug* to delineate different types of service for each recipe. I like the simple categorization, and the name has stuck, along with the service-based approach to how I develop recipes. While each recipe in *Help Yourself* is delicious, has smart steps, and is as streamlined as possible, I wanted to call out four levels of extra service throughout the book. You can also find a list of recipes in each category on page 344.

Quick and Easy

I am a fundamentally lazy cook—my love of cooking never outweighs my desire to get to delicious faster—and I know you don't have all day to put together a complicated dinner. This means that I generally develop with time in mind. As a rule, I don't include times on my recipes because what takes one cook five minutes might take another fifteen. Rather than promise a total time, I marked the quickest and easiest recipes in the book, which you can flip to when time is tight.

100% Plant-Based

While I strive to eat vegetables and other plants at every meal (what I call plant-focused), recipes with this icon are made *entirely* of plants. If you are a strict vegan or are just trying to eat more plant-based meals, you can look for these recipes throughout the book.

One Pot/One Pan

I have made friends with washing dishes since the invention of the podcast and wireless headphones, but that doesn't mean that I'm down to scrub up for hours every night, and I'm guessing you feel the same. The recipes marked with this symbol use just one pot or pan.

"Good for a Sensitive Gut"— What to Eat When Your Gut Is in Crisis

If you have IBD, IBS, leaky gut, or severe dysbiosis, many foods won't sit well with you until the gut lining has been repaired and you have enough beneficial microbes to digest plant foods. Because the spectrum of dysbiosis is so wide and the causes are varied, no two inflamed or irritated guts will act the same. In these cases, you may need to follow a more restricted diet for a short period of time while your gut heals, after which you can reintroduce some foods. The key, however, is to *continue to feed the beneficial microbes* while calming down the painful symptoms like cramping or diarrhea.

A common approach is to eliminate some foods—often dramatically so, as in the autoimmune protocol or low-FODMAP diets (see page 56 for more on these diets). But these diets, in addition to being more restrictive than *Help Yourself,* also exclude many sources of food for the good microbes. When I was suffering from an imbalanced gut, I was not comfortable cutting down on vegetables, whole grains, and beans, since I knew that my beneficial microbes needed fiber to thrive. Instead, I focused on heavily cooked and pureed vegetables and legumes while completely avoiding added sugar. Heavily cooking plant foods jump-starts the digestion process, which can make those foods more tolerable for people with sensitive gut.

This is the most extreme version of the *Help Yourself* way of eating. It is meant to be a temporary solution as a first step on the road to feeling better. I've marked these throughout the book with a "Good for a Sensitive Gut" symbol.

Potentially-New-to-You Ingredients

ARROWROOT, POTATO, AND TAPIOCA STARCH

Gluten-free baking requires something to thicken and bind in place of the gluten naturally present in wheat (which adds structure and texture). These starches are great binders that don't have a strong taste, and they're gut-friendly, too.

CHICKPEA/GARBANZO BEAN FLOUR

Chickpeas are high in resistant starch (which beneficial microbes love), and they have a mellow flavor that doesn't compete with other ingredients. Because it absorbs so much water, chickpea flour makes a great binder or thickener in place of wheat flour.

SUNCHOKES

Also known as Jerusalem artichokes, sunchokes are a nutty-flavored tuber that looks like ginger. They're incredibly high in fiber, which is great for your microbes. If your gut is in distress, skip sunchokes, as they cause a lot of fermentation (aka gas).

BUCKWHEAT GROATS

Buckwheat is a gluten-free seed that looks and performs like a grain. A "groat" is the name for its most intact version. The little pyramid-shaped seeds can be found with the other grains at your grocery store.

AMARANTH

These tiny seeds have a fantastic, nutty flavor and are high in protein and calcium. I like adding them to porridges because they contribute a sticky

WHAT ABOUT COOKING OILS?

You'll notice in my recipes that I generally call for you to use your "preferred cooking oil." This is because, while there is a set smoke point for each kind of fat at which the heat denatures the oil and releases potentially carcinogenic compounds, I think obsessing over types of cooking oil is simply missing the point. Instead, my focus is on eating vegetables and a variety of plants and reducing added sugar. I use an organic olive oil for most cooking and a cold-pressed, fancier one for finishing. Many gut health books recommend cooking with lard or another rendered animal fat—but since the research points to excessive animal fat as having a negative effect on the balance of good and bad microbes, I don't use it to excess (though I certainly love a duck fat–roasted potato here and there).

It is better, from the perspective of your gut, to use whatever oil you like if it's going to get you to eat more vegetables. You can take the smoke point into account when choosing your preferred oil. But in all the studies, books, and expert interviews I conducted, not one mention was made of smoke points in home cooking with oils. Eating home-cooked food using oil to roast, sauté, or dress food is not the same as consuming the highly refined oils that are in ultraprocessed food. To overly focus on oil type is to lose sight of the bigger picture, and creates a barrier to cooking and eating healthfully.

consistency that is particularly comforting. When I cook amaranth on its own, I follow the package instructions for the absorption method (unlike the other big-batch grains on page 124, which I boil). It makes for a delicious sick-day treat with cultured butter and chopped dates folded in.

MILLET
Like quinoa and amaranth, millet is a seed that cooks up like a grain. It's mushier (in a good way) than quinoa, which makes it feel more comforting and less like "health food."

CULINARY-GRADE MATCHA POWDER
Matcha, a powdered green tea, has been used for centuries in China and Japan and has recently become more popular in the West as an alternative to coffee. Matcha is high in antioxidants and has a grassy flavor with nutty undertones. The powdered form makes it easy to add to smoothies and baking recipes, but combining it with too much sugar undermines its healthful benefits.

PSYLLIUM SEED HUSKS
Psyllium seed husks are high in dietary fiber so they've long been used to relieve constipation. I like them for their ability to bind recipes that don't contain gluten, like the Magic Seed-and-Nut Bread on page 177. Because they're often sold as a health supplement, you might find them in the vitamin aisle. I'll also add a tablespoon or two to smoothies to boost the fiber content or stir some into whole-grain pancake batter.

HARISSA PASTE
A traditional North African condiment, harissa is a paste made from dried chiles, garlic, and spices like coriander and cumin. The exact ingredients and proportions vary by brand—it's worth trying a few different ones to find your favorite. Harissa adds a lot of heat and deep flavor even in a small dose, so start with just a little and adjust from there.

GOCHUJANG
Gochujang is a Korean fermented hot pepper paste. You can find shelf-stable versions at most grocery stores, but the process it undergoes kills the beneficial bacteria from the fermentation process. Instead, seek out a tub of refrigerated paste at a Korean grocery store or at a specialty food shop.

KOMBU
Kombu is a type of seaweed traditionally used in dashi, a Japanese broth. You'll find it in wide planks—one sheet adds minerals to broth or beans. The enzymes in seaweed also start breaking down the beans during cooking, making them easier to digest. I mail-order all my seaweed from Salt Point Seaweed, a sustainable-harvesting company out of California.

Cooking for a Crowd

Hosting dinner parties is my absolute favorite way to socialize, and I didn't want to give that up just because I changed how I ate. I worried about imposing on friends—I didn't want anyone to leave feeling grossed out or hungry—but I also wanted to stay aligned with my values and what I needed to be healthy.

The key to this was in making sure the food looked abundant—if it looked beautiful, people were likely to dig in. Brightly colored dips like the ones you'll find starting on page 204 and sumptuous desserts that look decadent (like the Sweet Potato, Squash, and Carrot Pie on page 334) did the convincing for me. In fact, I rarely mentioned that these were recipes light on added sugar and heavy on vegetables. When someone asked, I shared that, yes, this was 100 percent plant based or, no, there is no added sugar. Better to convince through deliciousness than make someone feel like they're not getting it right in their own life.

The template for setting up a gut-friendly dinner party is the same as for any great spread:

- Something that people can dig into right away—a dip (page 204) or a dish of fancy olives and spears of cucumber sprinkled with flaky sea salt

- An appetizer to start the meal, like Chickpea Hush Puppies with Herb Dip (page 197)

- A hearty main dish like Oven-Poached Salmon (page 263) or Slow-Roasted Chicken with Extra-Crispy Skin (page 276)

- A side dish or two—usually one with grains and one with vegetables (some of my recipes for mains also include side dishes that pair well, but you can play around)

- A gorgeous dessert, like Pistachio Butter Thumbprints with Raspberry-Chia Filling (page 332)

- A dish of flaky sea salt and freshly ground black pepper

I also like to set out one, two, or three of the dishes from the Three Magical Transformations chapter (page 98).

Here are a couple sample menus to get you started:

Hearty Wintry Feast
(see photo on page 6)

- Olives and cukes (see page 194)

- Special Occasion Short Ribs with Olive Oil–Kefir Mashed Potatoes (page 274)

- Garlicky Sautéed Chard (page 113)

- Sweet Potato, Squash, and Carrot Pie (page 334)

Summer Vegetarian Spread
(see photo on next page)

- Whipped Cauliflower and Harissa Dip with Herb Oil and Sesame Seeds (page 212)

- Roasted Eggplant and Chickpeas with Herbed Oat Pilaf (page 253)

- Marinated Cucumber-Tomato Salad (page 303)

- Roasted Pineapple Parfaits, assembled family-style (page 331)

Roasted
Pineapple
Parfaits
331

Whipped
Cauliflower
and Harissa Dip
212

Roasted Eggplant and Chickpeas with Herbed Oat Pilaf 253

Marinated Cucumber-Tomato Salad 303

PREP CITY

These are the kind of recipes that I tucked away in the back of my first cookbook, *Healthyish*. My thinking was, things like boiled grains and salad dressings are the supporting cast for the flashier stars of the show—the dinners, complete grain bowls, hearty salads, etc. In making the shift to a plant-focused lifestyle, however, I have found that these small recipes are the building blocks of most of my meals. When I have a recipe or two from each section in my fridge, I am so much more likely to choose in favor of my gut microbes.

So here, I give the simplest recipes top billing, and I recommend making these part of your weekly rotation as I do.

Slow-Roasted
Shallots
109

If You Want to Meal Prep

If you're in the habit of cooking regularly, then I think preparing components ahead of time is a great way to ensure you always have healthful foods on hand. I love throwing together a bowl of lentils, brown rice, and roasted vegetables with a pile of sauerkraut and a grating of cheddar. The ease of those meals is worth taking a couple of hours out of my week to facilitate. That being said, I found that when I was adjusting to eating more healthfully, even when I had prepped food ready to go in the fridge, I often wanted something other than what was right in front of me. This meant that those best intentions led to food waste. Until I knew I'd follow through with all the plant-focused food in the fridge, I pushed pause on meal prep.

This book works equally well whether you like to plan out prepped food or choose what to cook for dinner day-of. Let your (realistic) schedule, rather than your wishful thinking, be your guide.

Little Pockets of Time, Big Results

Rather than put the burden of massive meal prep on a weekend day, I find it much easier to fit small amounts of prep, cleaning, and strategy into my day-to-day life. My friend and mentor Sarah Copeland recommends a similar approach in her cookbook *Every Day Is Saturday*. It's a great strategy if you're a kitchen putterer or can delegate tasks to people who want to help out.

If you do want to meal prep in one big session, I also have suggestions (on the next page) for getting everything done in a couple of hours. With the right game plan, it's totally doable.

When you have 2 minutes (a great moment for quick cleaning to-dos—they add up):

- Load the dishwasher.

- Wipe down the counter.

- Take out the trash.

- Start soaking a cup or two of grains or beans.

- Assess what's in the fridge—should it go into the bag for Trash or Treasure Broth (page 129)? Compost?

- Put some cans of coconut milk in the fridge for Coconut Whipped Cream (page 326).

When you have 20 minutes:

- Whisk up a dressing (see pages 130–137).

- Pickle some shallots (see page 101).

- Prep hearty greens (see page 141)—use anything from kale to chard to collards to turnip greens.

- Wash and spin dry some fresh herbs, then wrap them in a clean dish towel.

- Use a mandoline to thinly slice fennel or cabbage—toss with a little kosher salt and store for hearty salads.

- Make your grocery list.

- Freeze coconut ice cubes for Sesame Matcha Shakes (page 183).

- Freeze sliced bananas for "nice" cream (see page 327).

- Make the spicy paste for Turmeric-Coconut-Ginger Lattes (page 318).

When you have 1 hour:

- Choose a few tasks from the previous lists and jam them all out at once.

- Pick a whole grain to cook (see page 124) and roast, steam, or sauté some vegetables.

- Cook just one of the dishes marked Quick and Easy (see page 344 for a list)—which will leave you time to do all the dishes, rather than letting a cleaning hangover await you.

Big-Batch Prep

If you do want to set aside a couple of hours to get a bunch of cooking done, here's my suggested game plan for prepping meal components for the week.

I choose one or two vegetables, a grain, a bean or legume, and a dressing, and then pick up some extras like Persian cucumbers and feta to add to meals throughout the week. Since I always have citrus, avocado, and flavor boosters like capers and cornichons on hand, I can add those easily. When I know I'll be making time to get a big prep job done, I'll start sprouting my grains three days before.

Here are some suggested combinations for big-batch prep.

- Melted Onions (page 119) + Garlicky Sautéed Chard (page 113) + Slow-Roasted Chicken (page 276) + Cheater's Romesco (page 133)

- Lemony Roasted Broccoli Rabe (page 110) + quinoa (see page 124) + Pickled Shallots (page 101) + Marinated Cucumber-Tomato Salad (page 303) + White Tahini Sauce (page 134)

- Roasted Mushrooms (page 107) + steamed hearty greens (see page 141) + Cauliflower "Bread Crumbs" (page 102) + Chickpea Flatbread (page 123) + Parsley, Kale, and Pumpkin Seed Pesto (page 132)

- Perfectly Steamed Broccoli (page 116) + Roasted Romanesco (page 108) + brown rice (see page 124) + pinto beans (see page 124) + Spicy Miso Mayo (page 136)

- Blanched Haricots Verts or Green Beans (page 114) + steamed fingerling potatoes (see page 120) + Oven-Poached Salmon (page 263) + millet (see page 124) + Faux Caesar (page 135)

Five Ways to Make Off-the-Cuff Meals

When I have pre-prepped and cooked components ready-to-go in my fridge, it makes healthy eating so much easier, especially when I'm busy. Here are my flexible formulas for making meals on the fly from things I have in the fridge.

1. SKILLET EGGS

Heat some oil or butter in a nonstick skillet (you could also cook some bacon and use the bacon fat for cooking—crumble the bacon over the eggs at the end). Add some cooked vegetables and/or grains and cook until heated through. Crack eggs into the skillet, cover, and cook until the egg yolks are set, about 3 minutes. Season with salt and pepper. Top with herbs or avocado, or just eat plain.

THE RECIPES

2. HEARTY SALAD

Choose one or two greens—I like a bitter one like radicchio or endive and something hearty like escarole, kale, or chard. Add a cooked grain and/or bean or legume, one or two cooked veg, and something pickled. Drizzle with your favorite dressing to your liking.

3. SOUP

Heat a little butter or oil in a pot and sauté some garlic or an onion. Add some spices if you want, along with some salt and pepper. Pour in a quart of broth and bring to a boil. Add cooked grains, beans, or lentils and a cooked veg or two. Simmer until hot, adding more broth to adjust consistency. Season to taste and top with some flavorful extras like fresh herbs, chopped avocado, and/or pickled shallots.

4. A JUMBLE-Y SAUTÉ

Heat some oil or butter in a nonstick skillet. Add some cooked vegetables and/or grains and cook until hot. Add a little broth or water—just enough to add sauciness—and cover, then steam everything through until hot. You can either leave a little liquid or let it all cook off. Season to taste and top with extras like cheese, pickles, kimchi, or avocado, or just eat as is. It's meant to be easy.

5. GRAIN BOWL

Combine a cooked grain, bean, or legume, vegetable(s), dressing, and any extras you want (see opposite).

Roasted Romanesco
108

Nine Ways to Dress Up Your Meal

1. Drizzle with cold-pressed extra-virgin olive oil or another flavorful oil like pumpkin seed or walnut oil.

2. Sprinkle with flaky sea salt and a few grinds of black pepper.

3. Add citrus: Fold in chopped lemon (see page 296) or add a squeeze of lemon at the end.

4. Shake some seeds all over (bonus: it's even prettier this way).

5. Shower with chopped fresh herbs.

6. Add ¼ cup chopped nuts (raw or just-toasted).

7. Finish with half an avocado.

8. Use a vegetable peeler to shave some hard cheese (like aged cheddar or Parmesan) directly onto the dish.

9. Add ¼ cup fermented food like kimchi, sauerkraut, or lacto-fermented pickles.

~~~~

Three Magical Transformations

There are only three recipes in this short chapter, which at first glance might seem like they don't have much to do with each other. But there are a few common threads:

- Each is a humble ingredient transformed through cooking.
- They're meant to be kept in your fridge and casually added to a variety of meals.
- They add big flavor to simple dishes.

I give specific serving ideas for each recipe, but my suggestion is to make one, two, or all three of these for dinner parties. I set them out at the end of the serving line or disperse dishes of each along a table set family-style.

Cauliflower "Bread Crumbs" 102

Crispy Roasted Chickpeas 100

Pickled Shallots 101

Crispy Roasted Chickpeas

Truth be told, there's a limit to how crispy a chickpea can get in the oven—when you have crispy chickpeas at a restaurant, they're almost certainly deep-fried. Either way, they're a great (albeit messy) snack, but I love them best as an addition to salads and grain bowls—used where I would croutons—which is why they're in my weekly meal-prep rotation. I like this savory spice combo, but you can adjust to your liking.

Scorecard

✔

Beans and Legumes

Makes

3

cups
(½ cup per serving)

3 cups cooked chickpeas (see page 124), or 2 (15.5-ounce) cans, drained and rinsed

¼ cup preferred cooking oil

1 teaspoon smoked paprika

1 teaspoon ground cumin

1 teaspoon onion powder

¾ teaspoon kosher salt, plus more if you want

½ teaspoon freshly ground black pepper, plus more if you want

A couple of meal ideas for the chickpeas:

Mashed avocado + steamed broccoli (see page 116) + sauerkraut + shaved parm

Chopped grilled romaine + capers + poached shrimp (see page 268) + Faux Caesar (page 135)

Preheat your oven to 400°F with a rack in the center position.

Spread the chickpeas in an even layer on a rimmed baking sheet. Bake until the chickpeas are very dry, about 10 minutes.

In a small bowl, whisk together the oil, paprika, cumin, onion powder, salt, and pepper. Toss the hot chickpeas with the spice-oil mixture on the baking sheet. Return the baking sheet to the oven and bake, stirring once to bring the chickpeas from the outside of the pan into the center and vice versa, until the chickpeas are crispy, 25 to 30 minutes more.

Taste and adjust the seasoning with salt and pepper if you like. Serve warm, or let cool completely before storing.

To Store

Refrigerate in an airtight container for up to 5 days. To crisp the chickpeas back up, spread them over a rimmed baking sheet and reheat in a 400°F oven for 8 to 10 minutes.

Pickled Shallots

Without fail, whenever I set out a big spread for a dinner party, someone asks for my pickled shallot recipe before the end of the night. I'm always surprised to find it's a favorite, especially when they're competing with more elaborate dishes. After some reflection, I think I know why: Most store-bought pickles are just too intense on the vinegar. These are sour just enough to add acidity without overpowering a dish. Also, most pickling recipes call for sugar to mellow the acid, but there's no need here. These shallots are brighter and more flavorful without it.

Makes
2½
cups
(¼ cup per serving)

1 pound shallots (about 5 medium), very thinly sliced from stem to tip

2 teaspoons kosher salt

1 teaspoon whole black peppercorns

1 teaspoon mustard seeds (optional)

1 bay leaf (optional)

1 cup red wine vinegar

1 cup water

Place the shallots in a deep (not wide) bowl. Add the salt, peppercorns, mustard seeds (if using), and bay leaf (if using).

Combine the vinegar and water in a small pot. Bring to a boil over high heat. Pour the vinegar mixture over the shallots and stir well. The liquid should cover the shallots. Let cool to room temperature, about 1 hour 30 minutes.

Use tongs to transfer the shallots to a jar. Top off with the pickling liquid, then seal tightly.

To Store
Refrigerate for up to a month, adding water as needed to keep the shallots submerged.

These pair especially well with:

Southwestern Chicken Burgers with Sweet Potato Fries (page 280)

Crispy Chicken Thighs with Kale and Black-Eyed Peas (page 279)

Lentil and Chard Cakes (page 240)

Brothy Tomatoes, Spinach, and Chickpeas with Herbs (page 228)

Egg, Bacon, and Kale Breakfast Tacos (page 142)

Roasted Pepper and Aioli Flatbread (page 201)

THE RECIPES

Cauliflower "Bread Crumbs"

One day after roasting cauliflower, I was picking up all the little extra-crispy pieces that are too small to count as a floret but make it onto the tray anyway. I realized they're totally delicious and look like a bread crumb, but with the bonus of caramelized umami flavor that comes from roasting. They have the magical effect of transforming food that feels "too healthy" into something comforting and satisfying. I sprinkle them on just about everything—whether it's a grain bowl, steamed broccolini, or on top of eggs. And to really gild the lily, I suggest serving them with Special Occasion Short Ribs (page 274) or Long-Braised Lamb (page 285). Here's my method for getting that effect on purpose by sawing off the scrubby tops of the florets.

Makes
2
cups
(2 tables-
poons per
serving)

2½ pounds cauliflower (2 medium-small heads or 1 large)

½ cup preferred cooking oil

2 teaspoons kosher salt

1 teaspoon freshly ground black pepper

Preheat your oven to 400°F with racks positioned in the top and bottom thirds.

Pull off any green leaves from the cauliflower head(s). Set the cauliflower on a rimmed baking sheet and use a serrated knife to shave the florets into very small pieces. (The rimmed baking sheet helps keep rogue cauliflower crumbs from flying all over your counter.) Continue until all you have left are the stems. (Save the stems to roast separately; see page 108.)

Toss the shredded cauliflower with the oil, salt, and pepper. Transfer half the cauliflower to a second rimmed baking sheet and spread in a single layer. Roast, tossing the cauliflower once and switching the baking sheets from top to bottom and vice versa, until golden brown and crispy, 35 to 40 minutes.

Drain on a paper towel–lined plate. Use immediately for maximum bread-crumbiness. To store, cool completely and refrigerate in an airtight container for up to 4 days. To re-crisp the bread crumbs, reheat in a nonstick pan or on a rimmed baking sheet in a 400°F oven for a few minutes.

Note

Store-bought cauliflower rice doesn't work as well, but will do in a pinch. Use 6 cups/1½ pounds prepared cauliflower rice.

~~~

Basic Vegetable Recipes

It might feel silly to follow instructions for something as simple as roasted broccoli rabe with a little lemon, some oil, salt, and pepper. However, properly cooking vegetables is the difference between feeling excited about plant-focused eating and feeling like it's a chore. If you're not comfortable cooking vegetables without a recipe, following these recipes to the letter will teach you the basics, until cooking off the cuff becomes more natural.

Vegetables make your gut microbes happy, and what makes your gut microbes happy makes your body feel good. So use this section as bible, as inspiration, or whatever gets you to as many servings of veg a day as possible.

You'll notice that I've called for you to use your "preferred cooking oil" throughout—see page 87 for an explanation on why that is. Whatever oil you have on hand is fine.

Smoky Roasted Fennel

Sweet and crispy roasted fennel pairs perfectly with the mellow intensity of smoked paprika, and I double down on the vegetal flavor with crushed fennel seeds. Save any nice stems for a Ginger, Lemongrass, and Fennel Infusion (page 317).

3   fennel bulbs (1½ to 1¾ pounds total), ends trimmed, halved lengthwise and sliced ½ inch thick

½   teaspoon smoked paprika

½   teaspoon fennel seeds, crushed in a mortar and pestle or ground in a spice grinder

2   tablespoons preferred cooking oil

½   teaspoon kosher salt

½   teaspoon freshly ground black pepper

Preheat your oven to 425°F. Toss the fennel, paprika, fennel seeds, oil, salt, and pepper on a rimmed baking sheet. Roast, tossing once, until tender, 30 to 35 minutes.

To Store

Refrigerate in an airtight container for up to 4 days.

Scorecard

✔

Other Veg

Serves

4

as a side

HOW TO PREP RAW FENNEL FOR SALADS

When I was healing from extreme gut issues, I cut out most raw vegetables, as they irritated my digestion too much. But I did love the fresh crunch of an occasional shaved fennel salad. I use a mandoline to shave the bulb into thin strips and then rub the fennel with salt and olive oil. After marinating for 30 minutes, the fennel is not only tasty, it's softer and easier to digest, too.

Serving ideas:

Baked white fish

Lamb meatballs (see page 221; skip the soup and just sear the meatballs until cooked through) + Greek yogurt + roasted red peppers

Cannellini beans (see page 124) + avocado + olive oil–packed tuna

Roasted White Turnips

I don't turn the turnips while roasting, which allows the side sitting on the sheet pan to get deeply caramelized. Save their edible stems, wash and dry with a salad spinner, and steam or sauté them (see page 113 for a how-to).

1 pound small white turnips (1 regular bunch with about 8 turnips), halved

2 tablespoons preferred cooking oil

½ teaspoon kosher salt

⅛ teaspoon freshly ground black pepper

Preheat your oven to 425°F. Toss the turnips, oil, salt, and pepper on a rimmed baking sheet. Roast until tender, 24 to 28 minutes.

To Store

Refrigerate in an airtight container for up to 4 days.

Pair with:

Long-Braised Lamb (page 285)

Brown rice (see page 124) + Spicy Miso Mayo (page 136) + crispy tofu (see page 246)

Scorecard

✔

Other Veg

Serves

4

as a side

THE RECIPES

Roasted Celery Root

Roasting celery root pulls out its underlying sweetness to balance any bitterness.

1 celery root (about 2 pounds), top and bottom trimmed, peeled with a serrated knife and cut into 1-inch pieces

10 to 12 sprigs thyme

Pinch of ground nutmeg

2 tablespoons preferred oil

½ teaspoon kosher salt

½ teaspoon freshly ground black pepper

Preheat your oven to 425°F. Toss the celery root, thyme, nutmeg, oil, salt, and pepper on a rimmed baking sheet. Roast, tossing once, until golden brown and tender, 35 to 40 minutes. Discard the thyme.

To Store

Refrigerate in an airtight container for up to 4 days.

Great with:

Grilled steak + cultured sour cream + parsley

Pork chop + Dijonnaise (see page 280) + tarragon

Scorecard

✔

Other Veg

Serves

4

as a side

CLOCKWISE FROM TOP LEFT

Smoky Roasted Fennel *104*

Roasted White Turnips *105*

Roasted Mushrooms
opposite

Roasted Celery Root *105*

Roasted Mushrooms

I am a big fan of the trumpet mushroom—they stand in for bacon in a wedge salad (see page 202) and can be used in place of scallops (see page 250). In fact, I can down this whole batch of roasted mushrooms in one go. Trumpets satisfy in a fork-and-knife type of way, and unlike portobellos, trumpets don't weep an off-putting dark liquid. You can use this method for any type of mushroom, but keep an eye on the oven since the timing will vary depending on the size of the mushroom.

1½ pounds trumpet mushrooms, cut into 1½-inch-thick rounds, or oyster, or cremini, or button mushrooms, halved (or quartered if large)

2 tablespoons preferred cooking oil

¾ teaspoon kosher salt

¼ teaspoon freshly ground black pepper

Preheat your oven to 425°F. Toss the mushrooms, oil, salt, and pepper on a rimmed baking sheet. Roast, tossing once, until golden brown and tender, 28 to 32 minutes.

To Store

Refrigerate in an airtight container for up to 4 days.

Scorecard

✔

Other Veg

Serves

4

as a side

THE RECIPES

Great with:

Whole-grain or gluten-free pasta + brown butter + fresh herbs + lemon zest

Crispy Roasted Chickpeas (page 100) + White Tahini Sauce (page 134) + Marinated Cucumber-Tomato Salad (page 303) + quinoa

Roasted Romanesco

Romanesco is a stunning cone-shaped vegetable about the size of a cauliflower head. It comes in green, orange, and purple and is covered in little cones that look like fractals. Looks play a big part in our food choices—beautiful food is more appealing, which counts for a lot when you're adjusting to a plant-focused way of eating.

2   medium heads romanesco (2 pounds total), halved through the stem and cut into ¾-inch-thick wedges

3   tablespoons preferred cooking oil

1   teaspoon kosher salt

¼   teaspoon freshly ground black pepper

Preheat your oven to 425°F. Toss the romanesco, oil, salt, and pepper on a rimmed baking sheet. Roast, tossing once, until tender, 30 to 35 minutes.

To Store

Refrigerate in an airtight container for up to 4 days.

Scorecard

✔

Other Veg

Serves

4 to 6

as a side

Eat alongside:

Slow-Roasted Chicken (page 276)

Millet (see page 124) + White Tahini Sauce (page 134) + avocado

Chopped and tossed with capers, chopped lemon (see page 296), toasted almonds, and tons of Parm

Slow-Roasted Shallots

Shallots are a great source of prebiotic fiber, and they're beautiful, too. Even though they're just a humble allium, the gorgeous purple and magenta hues always draw *oohs* and *ahhs* from guests, which is why this is one of my go-to dinner party sides.

2 pounds shallots (about 15 medium), scrubbed, peels left intact unless they're extremely dirty, ends trimmed to just above the scraggly root parts (halved, if large)

¼ cup preferred cooking oil

¼ teaspoon kosher salt

¼ teaspoon freshly ground black pepper

Serving ideas:

Slice and fold into scrambled eggs for breakfast tacos

Slow-Roasted Chicken (page 276) + Dijon vinaigrette (see page 130) + chives

Roasted butternut squash + goat cheese + brown rice (see page 124)

Preheat your oven to 400°F. Line a 9 by 13-inch baking dish with aluminum foil.

Place the shallots, oil, salt, and pepper in the prepared baking dish and toss to coat. Roast, tossing once, until you can easily pierce one of the larger shallots with a fork, 45 to 55 minutes.

Let cool slightly, then use kitchen shears to snip off the end of each shallot. Squeeze them out of their skins into a serving dish.

To Store

Refrigerate in an airtight container for up to 4 days.

Scorecard

✔

Other Veg

Serves

6

as a side

THE RECIPES

Lemony Roasted Broccoli Rabe

There's a case of mistaken identities happening to two green vegetables. Broccoli rabe, also known as rapini, is related to turnips, while the similar-sounding Broccolini is a hybrid of broccoli and gai lan, a type of Chinese broccoli. I've also seen Broccolini called broccolette at supermarkets. They're both delicious—rabe is tougher and more bitter, while Broccolini is more tender and milder. I find the cooking time of the two to be fairly similar (as long as you halve any extra-thick Broccolini stalks lengthwise).

2   **bunches broccoli rabe or Broccolini (1½ pounds total), any thick stems halved lengthwise**

1   **lemon, very thinly sliced crosswise, seeds poked out of the slices**

3   **tablespoons preferred cooking oil**

1   **teaspoon kosher salt**

¼   **teaspoon freshly ground black pepper**

Pairing Tip

Broccoli rabe is best with rich foods, as its bitterness balances fat and salt well. Broccolini, on the other hand, is better with spicy flavors.

Preheat your oven to 425°F with racks positioned in the top and bottom thirds.

In a large bowl, toss the broccoli rabe, lemon slices, oil, salt, and pepper. Rub the oil well over the heads and leaves of the broccoli rabe. Divide between two rimmed baking sheets.

Roast, tossing once and swapping the baking sheets from top to bottom and vice versa, until the broccoli rabe is tender and the leaves are crispy, 14 to 18 minutes. Discard the lemon slices if not serving immediately.

To Store

Refrigerate in an airtight container for up to 4 days. I like to chop the broccoli rabe or Broccolini into bite-size pieces before storing. It saves the step of pulling out a cutting board every time I want to throw together a quick meal.

Scorecard

✓

LGVs

Serves

4 to 6

as a side

Garlicky Sautéed Chard

You know that scene in *Annie Hall* where Alvy Singer is telling Annie that he doesn't just love her, he loafs her, he luffs her, etc.? That's how I feel about garlicky sautéed greens. My favorite is chard (Swiss or rainbow) for its tender stems, but you can use this method for any and all hearty, leafy greens. Kale, collards, turnip greens, spinach, you name it—they all work (with or without the garlic). Cooking times will vary based on the green, so keep an eye on the pan.

2 large bunches Swiss chard or other greens

2 tablespoons olive oil

5 garlic cloves, chopped

½ teaspoon crushed red pepper

1 teaspoon kosher salt

¼ teaspoon freshly ground black pepper

2 tablespoons fresh lemon juice

I particularly love serving this with:

Roasted Eggplant and Chickpeas with Herbed Oat Pilaf (page 253)

Pinto beans (see page 124) + millet (see page 124) + avocado + drizzle of olive oil

Scrambled eggs + toasted Chickpea Flatbread (page 123)

Pull the chard leaves from the stems and slice the leaves into 1-inch-wide strips. Wash and dry thoroughly in a salad spinner. Wash the stems well and slice them ½ inch thick. You should have about 12 cups packed leaves and 2 cups stems.

In a large nonstick skillet, heat the oil over medium-high heat. Add the garlic and crushed red pepper and cook until fragrant, 30 seconds to 1 minute. Add the chard stems, salt, and black pepper. Cook, stirring frequently, until the stems are just barely tender, 5 to 7 minutes. Add the chard leaves and cook, tossing with tongs, until the leaves are tender but still have a bite to them, 2 to 3 minutes. Stir in the lemon juice and serve.

To Store

Refrigerate in an airtight container for up to 4 days.

Scorecard

✓

LGVs

Serves

4 to 6

as a side

THE RECIPES

Blanched Haricots Verts or Green Beans

Haricots verts beat grocery store green beans on all accounts: they're thinner and crisper, which makes for a snappier texture when cooked. During summer, I make sure to load up on in-season green beans and yellow wax beans instead.

1   pound haricots verts, green beans, or yellow wax beans, stem ends trimmed

2   teaspoons kosher salt

Plays well with:

Le Petit Aioli (page 198)

A quick Niçoise: Nine-Minute Eggs (page 141) + olive oil–packed tuna + steamed potatoes (see page 120) + Dijon vinaigrette (see page 130)

White Tahini Sauce (page 134) + toasted sliced almonds + Aleppo pepper flakes

Fill a large bowl with ice and water. Set a strainer in the sink.

Bring a large pot of water to a rolling boil. Add the haricots verts and salt. Cook until just barely tender, 2 minutes (if using green beans or wax beans, cook for 3 to 4 minutes).

Drain the beans in the strainer, then plunge the whole strainer into the ice water and leave for 30 seconds. Pull out and shake dry.

To Store

Refrigerate in an airtight container for up to 4 days.

Scorecard

✓✓
Other Veg

Serves
4
as a side

Extra-Crispy
Roasted
Asparagus
117

Blanched
Green Beans
114

Perfectly
Steamed
Broccoli
116

Perfectly Steamed Broccoli

How many kids have turned their noses up at mushy steamed broccoli? I confess to being one those kids well into adulthood, until I learned that the key to delicious broccoli is timing. Not too long—just 6 to 8 minutes—and then a shock in ice-cold water at the end, if you're prepping ahead, are the keys to crisp-crowned florets.

1 large head broccoli (about 1½ pounds), cut into florets

See page 297 for a tip on using tough broccoli stems.

To Store

Refrigerate in an airtight container for up to 4 days.

Fill a pot with 1 inch of water and put a steamer insert inside. Cover and bring the water to a simmer. Add the broccoli, re-cover, and steam until tender but with a little bite, 6 to 8 minutes.

If you're making the broccoli to prep ahead, fill a large bowl with ice and water. Shock the broccoli in the ice water for 30 seconds, then drain well.

Scorecard

✓ LGVs

Serves

4

as a side

Grilled Romaine

I like romaine as much cooked as raw, and grilling adds a deliciously smoky char to the leaves. This method works well with radicchio, too.

For a *Help Yourself* take on a Caesar salad, I top the wedges with Cauliflower "Bread Crumbs" (page 102), Faux Caesar dressing (page 135), and some shrimp, chicken, or Roasted Mushrooms (page 107).

3 tablespoons preferred cooking oil, plus more for the grill grates

3 romaine hearts, halved through the core, halves kept intact

½ teaspoon kosher salt

½ teaspoon freshly ground black pepper

Heat a gas grill to high, cover, and leave to preheat for 10 minutes. Clean and oil the grate.

Set the romaine halves on a rimmed baking sheet. Brush them all over with the oil and sprinkle on both sides with the salt and pepper.

Place the romaine cut-side down on the grill and cover. Grill for 3 to 4 minutes, until dark golden brown and crispy on the bottom, then flip and grill for 1 to 2 minutes more, until golden brown and slightly wilted. Serve right away.

Scorecard

✓ LGVs

Serves

4 to 6

as a side

Extra-Crispy Roasted Asparagus

I could easily house a pound of roasted asparagus on my own, which is why this serves two to four, unlike most of my other roasted vegetable recipes. These roast a bit longer and have more oil than many recipes, but I find it's the difference between a limp spear and a crispy delight.

1   bunch asparagus (about 1 pound), tough ends trimmed by about 1 inch

2   tablespoons preferred cooking oil

¾   teaspoon kosher salt

¼   teaspoon freshly ground black pepper

Preheat your oven to 425°F. Toss the asparagus, oil, salt, and pepper on a rimmed baking sheet, making sure to rub the oil into the tips of the spears. Roast, tossing once, until tender, 12 to 16 minutes.

To Store

Refrigerate in an airtight container for up to 4 days. I like to chop the asparagus into bite-size pieces before storing. It saves the step of pulling out a cutting board every time I want to throw together a quick meal.

Scorecard

✔
Other Veg

Serves

2 to 4

as a side

THE RECIPES

Serving ideas:

Oven-Poached Salmon (page 263) + dressing of kefir, fresh dill, and lemon juice

Olive oil–packed tuna + brown rice (see page 124) + capers

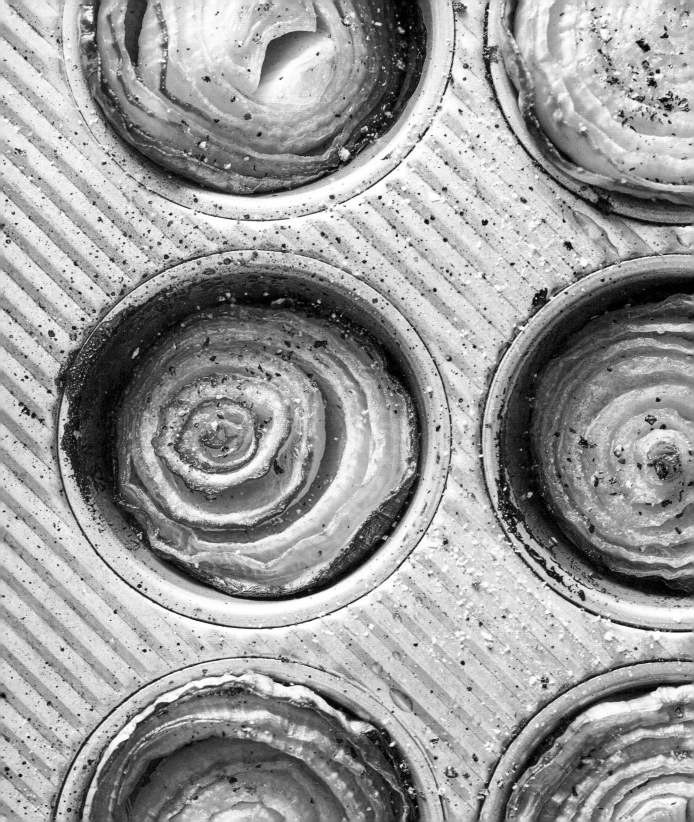

Melted Onions

I love how onions become meltingly tender and sweet after a long roast in the oven, but it's not such an elegant look to plop roasted onions on a platter. Here the petals stay together in a pretty rosette, thanks to a muffin pan. If you don't have one, use a small rimmed baking sheet or an ovenproof dish and pack the onions tightly together.

Scorecard

✔

Other Veg

6   medium onions (each 3 inches in diameter/2½ pounds total), halved crosswise through the center (not the root and stem), ends trimmed by ¼ inch

½   teaspoon kosher salt

3   teaspoons freshly ground freshly ground black pepper

2   tablespoons ghee or unsalted butter, melted, or your preferred cooking oil

Serves

4 to 6

as a side

If the stem is the North Pole, you're cutting through the onion's equator.

Preheat your oven to 425°F with a rack in the top position.

Place the onion halves cut-side up in the cups of a 12-cup muffin tin. Sprinkle the onions with the salt and pepper.

Roast for 20 minutes, until the onions have softened slightly and sunk into the cups. Brush with the ghee and return to the oven. Bake until extremely soft and golden brown, about 40 minutes more.

To Store

Refrigerate in an airtight container for up to 4 days.

Great with:

Buckwheat groats (see page 124) + soft goat cheese + arugula

Slow-Roasted Chicken (page 276) + Cheater's Romesco (page 133) + parsley

Resistant Starch Potatoes

Normally, the simple starches from foods like potatoes and grains get absorbed by the small intestine, spiking blood sugar. Cooking and cooling starch-rich whole plant foods, like these potatoes, allows the starches to travel undigested all the way to the large intestine, where your beneficial microbes are ready for a feast. The key is to cook them, then let them cool fully, and eat them either at room temperature or cold. Don't reheat the potatoes, or the starch stops being resistant.

Beans, lentils, and grains also become "resistant" when they're cold (see page 124 for cooking instructions).

Choose one

1 **pound Yukon Gold potatoes (3 medium)**

1 **pound fingerling potatoes (18 small to medium)**

1 **pound new potatoes (20 small to medium)**

Fill a large pot with 1 inch of water and put a steamer insert inside. Bring the water to a simmer, add the potatoes, cover, and steam until you can insert a fork into a potato with just a little resistance, 35 to 40 minutes for Yukon Golds, 15 to 18 minutes for fingerlings, and 25 to 30 minutes for new potatoes. Let cool to room temperature before serving.

To Store

Refrigerate in an airtight container for up to 3 days. To maintain their resistant starch qualities, serve cold or bring them to room temperature before serving, but do not reheat them.

Scorecard

✔
Other Veg

Serves

4

as a side

TiP

I recommend using a scale to weigh out the chickpea flour to make sure you get the texture of the batter just right.

Chickpea Flatbread

You may have heard of socca or farinata, the old-school chickpea flatbread popular in Southern France and Italy. Unlike that traditional recipe, my version isn't fermented, just soaked, and it's sturdy enough to stand up to hearty toppings. The result is wonderfully breadlike, except it's full of beneficial plant fiber that your microbes love.

2½ cups chickpea (garbanzo bean) flour (10.5 ounces/300g)

2 teaspoons kosher salt

1 teaspoon freshly ground black pepper

3½ cups water

¼ cup plus 2 tablespoons olive oil, plus more for the pan

Make the flatbread batter In a medium bowl, whisk together the chickpea flour, salt, and pepper. While whisking, pour in the water in a steady stream and whisk until incorporated. Whisk in ¼ cup of the oil.

Cover and let stand at room temperature for 8 to 10 hours, or refrigerate for at least 18 hours and up to 24 hours.

Bake the flatbread When ready to bake the flatbread, preheat your oven to 425°F with a rack in the top position.

Brush a 9 by 13-inch baking pan with oil. Pour the batter into the prepared pan. Bake on the top rack for 25 to 35 minutes, until the flatbread is firm. There should be no soft bits and no indent when you press the bread with your finger. (The baking time will vary based on how long you rested the batter. The longer it rested, the quicker the bread will bake.)

Remove the flatbread from the oven and switch the oven to broil on high.

Brush with the remaining 2 tablespoons oil and return the flatbread to the oven. Broil until the top is golden brown and begins to bubble, 2 to 5 minutes. (A gas broiler will brown the flatbread much faster than an electric one, so keep an eye on it.)

Run a flexible spatula around the edges of the flatbread and flip it from the pan onto a wire rack, then flip it again, this time right-side up onto a cutting board.

Serve hot, or cut into squares and refrigerate in an airtight container for up to 4 days. Reheat in a toaster oven or microwave until hot.

The chickpea flatbread is a delicious canvas limited only by your imagination. Here are a couple ideas for toppings:

Soft goat cheese + chopped broccoli rabe + crushed red pepper + squeeze of lemon juice

Parsley, Kale, and Pumpkin Seed Pesto (page 132) + Oven-Poached Salmon (page 263) + chopped avocado + 1 tablespoon Seed Shaker (page 180)

Scorecard

✓
Beans and Legumes

Serves

4

as a meal, 8 as an appetizer

THE RECIPES

How to Cook Grains, Grainlike Seeds, Beans, and Legumes—
Including a Guide to Sprouting

You might wonder what the big fuss is about soaking and sprouting grains. It turns out that grains, seeds, and beans contain an antinutrient called phytic acid, which is an evolutionary adaptation to protect the seed from being eaten. Smart in terms of evolution, not so great for our guts.

The way to remove the phytic acid is to soak or sprout the grain before cooking or consuming it. Sprouting causes the seed, bean, or grain to germinate, which is why you see a little tail. Not only does sprouting make the grains more nutritious, it's a fun science project, and only requires a couple of minutes at each step.

Whichever method you choose, it does require planning ahead. If you forget or don't have the time, and it's the difference between you cooking millet or not, then by all means, just rinse it and get to cooking. I don't think phytic acid is make-or-break in terms of gut health. Rather, cutting down on sugar, processed foods, and red meat and focusing on increasing vegetables and other plant-based foods in your diet is way more important than obsessing over the perfect way to cook your beans or grains.

Scorecard
½ cup cooked
= either

✔

Whole Grains
or

✔

Beans and
Legumes

You'll need:

A fine-mesh strainer for rinsing

A bowl for soaking

A large glass jar

Something to cover the jar that also lets air and water through—either a lid with a fine-mesh screen, or cheesecloth and a rubber band

Something to set the jar in at an inverted, slightly diagonal angle. This could be in a dish rack or in a tall bowl (I splurged on a sprouting rack and I love it).

A rimmed baking sheet to set multiple jars on at once (this is not required, but I find it makes it easier to move the jars from their sprouting location to the sink and back).

1. Rinse the ingredient in a fine-mesh strainer until the water runs clear, then transfer to a large bowl. Fill the bowl with water to within 1 inch of the top. Cover with a clean dish towel.

2. Set aside to soak at cool room temperature for the recommended time (see the chart on page 126). Refrigerate if it's hot in your kitchen.

If you are just soaking, not sprouting:
1. Rinse the ingredient in a fine-mesh strainer until the water runs clear

2. Follow the cooking instructions and recommended times in the chart on page 127.

CONTINUES

If you are sprouting:

1. If you have a mesh lid for your jar like I do, transfer the soaked ingredient to the jar, put the mesh lid on, and rinse the ingredient directly in the jar. (It's way easier this way.) If you are using cheesecloth, rinse the ingredient in a fine-mesh strainer until the water runs clear, then transfer it to the jar, cover the top with cheesecloth, and secure it with a rubber band.

2. Tilt on an angle, lid-side down, and rest in a dish rack or sprouting rack.

3. Rinse the ingredient twice a day until it has sprouted a tail and the tail is as long as the grain, seed, bean, or legume—I find between 2 and 3 days is normal, but this will vary based on the age of the ingredient and the temperature of the water and your kitchen.

4. Cook according to the instructions below.

SOAKING TIMES FOR GRAINS, GRAINLIKE SEEDS, BEANS, AND LEGUMES

Grain, grainlike seed, bean, or legume	(If sprouting) Soak before sprouting	(If soaking but not sprouting) Soak before cooking
Brown rice	10 to 12 hours	10 to 12 hours
Oat groats	6 hours	8 to 10 hours
Lentils	8 to 10 hours	8 to 10 hours
Dried beans and chickpeas	12 hours	8 to 12 hours
Quinoa	4 to 6 hours	8 to 12 hours
Buckwheat	n/a	2 to 4 hours
Millet	8 hours	12 hours

HOW TO COOK DRIED GRAINS, GRAINLIKE SEEDS, BEANS, AND LEGUMES

Fill a large (at least 8-quart) pot with water. Cover and bring the water to a rolling boil. Add the ingredient and 1 teaspoon kosher salt (omit the salt if cooking beans); if cooking beans, I also like to add 1 (6-inch) piece kombu. Return to a boil, then reduce the heat to maintain a simmer and cook according to the cooking times in the chart below until tender but with some bite remaining. (The cooking time for beans will vary widely depending on the brand, how old the beans are, and how long you've soaked them.) Season the beans with 1 teaspoon kosher salt when they are nearly finished cooking. Drain and serve hot. Or, for meal prep, spread on a rimmed baking sheet and let cool, then transfer to an airtight container and refrigerate for up to 4 days or freeze for up to 2 months.

APPROXIMATE COOKING TIMES FOR GRAINS, GRAINLIKE SEEDS, BEANS, AND LEGUMES

Grain, grainlike seed, bean, or legume (1 cup)	Yield (from 1 cup uncooked)	Cooking time (if sprouted)	Cooking time (if soaked)	Cooking time (if rinsed only)
Short- or long-grain brown rice	2½ cups	24 minutes	24 minutes	28 minutes
Oat groats	3 cups	40 minutes	45 minutes	50 minutes
Green, Puy, or black lentils	3½ cups	8 minutes	10 minutes	25 minutes
Dried beans and chickpeas	3 cups	1 hour 30 minutes	1 hour 30 minutes	n/a
Quinoa	2½ cups	12 to 14 minutes	14 to 16 minutes	14 to 18 minutes
Buckwheat	2¼ cups	n/a	4 to 6 minutes	10 to 12 minutes
Millet	3¼ cups	20 to 22 minutes	25 minutes	25 minutes

A FEW MISCELLANEOUS NOTES

OAT GROATS Groats are the most intact version of an oat—the inedible outer hull is removed, but the germ, bran, and endosperm are left intact. They have a texture similar to barley, and none of the slimy texture I've come to associate with steel-cut oats.

LENTILS I have seen recipes that call for eating sprouted lentils raw, but I don't recommend that. Not only can sprouted raw lentils be hard on your digestion, but boiling kills off any potential pathogenic bacteria.

BUCKWHEAT Despite its name, buckwheat is in fact not wheat, but a gluten-free seed. I do not recommend sprouting buckwheat, as it basically turns to mush before you even start to see a tail.

MILLET Millet bursts from a round seed into a split, irregular shape. When it's fully cooked, the little dot in the center should no longer be distinct.

Trash or Treasure Broth

Growing up, I loved a radio show called *Trash or Treasure*. The concept was simple: One person would call in with their "trash"—say, used tires—and then someone else would call in to claim the item, because to them, it was "treasure." Anything that reduces waste is good by me, particularly in the kitchen, and the trash-or-treasure concept is perfect when it comes to making broth. Of course, you can buy vegetables at the store to simmer into broth, but it's cheaper and more environmentally friendly to use the scraps from your vegetables and bones from your meat.

Here's how I do it: As I cook, I set a bowl on the counter for scraps that will go into my broth. I add these to a gallon-size zip-top bag that I store in my freezer. And if there are herbs or vegetables in the crisper drawer that are past their prime, into the bag they go. When the bag is full, I make a batch of broth. I do the same with bones from meat; after roasting a chicken (see page 276) or braising short ribs (see page 274), I remove the meat and add the bones to the bag.

For a plant-based version, omit the bones and double the vegetable scraps.

Makes

4

quarts

THE RECIPES

1 pound bones from chicken, beef, pork, lamb, or a mix

1 pound vegetable scraps (see sidebar)

4 quarts water

2 teaspoons whole black peppercorns

1 bay leaf

 For a seasoned broth, add 1 tablespoon kosher salt.

Combine all the ingredients in your largest pot. Bring to a boil over high heat, then reduce the heat to maintain a gentle simmer. Cook for about 30 minutes, then remove from the heat. Let cool completely, then strain the broth, discarding the solids, and divide it among airtight containers.

To Store
Refrigerate for up to 4 days or freeze for up to 3 months.

YES vegetables (pull off any stickers, but include peels)	NO vegetables
Onions	Tomatoes
Leeks	Asparagus
Garlic	Eggplant
Carrots	Broccoli
Celery	Bell peppers
Mushrooms	
Fennel	
Parsley	
Scallions	

~~~

Dressings & Sauces

Some recipes don't need to be followed to the letter, leaving room for improvisation. But when it comes to dressings and sauces like the ones in this chapter, it's all about the precise ratios to get the ideal balance of tang, richness, and a hit of intense flavor.

These dressings are at home drizzled over a bowl of grains or greens, or added to leftovers to punch them up. They can improve the simplest of meals, draw disparate elements together under a blanket of flavor, or play the role of a dip for almost any raw or cooked vegetable.

I'm always thinking of new ways to reframe the classic bottle of wine or box of chocolates to bring as a gift to a party—and let me tell you, a jar or two of one of these dressings, plus a tag with serving suggestions, is always greeted with excitement.

In addition, I also want to share my perfect Dijon vinaigrette—cribbed from my first cookbook, *Healthyish*: Whisk together $\frac{1}{3}$ cup Dijon mustard, $\frac{1}{3}$ cup apple cider vinegar, 1 teaspoon kosher salt, and $\frac{1}{2}$ teaspoon freshly ground black pepper. Slowly drizzle in $\frac{1}{2}$ cup olive oil, whisking as you go.

White Tahini
Sauce
134

Cheater's
Romesco
133

Spicy Miso
Mayo
136

Faux
Caesar
135

Parsley, Kale,
and Pumpkin
Seed Pesto 132

Kimchi
Dressing
137

Parsley, Kale, and Pumpkin Seed Pesto

Blanching the kale removes its bitterness and leafiness, resulting in a smoother, tastier pesto. It also sets the color into a beautiful vibrant green that doesn't oxidize the way regular pesto does. To make this using frozen kale, use 10 ounces (4 cups).

1 large bunch lacinato or curly kale, stems and leaves coarsely sliced (4 cups packed)

1 cup packed fresh parsley leaves and stems (just squeeze them into the cup, don't chop them)

1 cup raw hulled pumpkin seeds

¾ cup plus 1 tablespoon olive oil

4 garlic cloves, smashed and coarsely chopped

2 tablespoons lemon juice

1½ teaspoons kosher salt, plus more as needed

½ teaspoon freshly ground black pepper, plus more as needed

Ideas for the pesto:

Spread over Chickpea Flatbread (page 123).

Dollop on roasted vegetable and whole-grain bowls.

Slather on a cauliflower pizza crust and top with roasted squash and red onions.

Spread on corn tortillas and top with scrambled eggs.

Fill a large bowl with ice and water. Bring a large pot of water to a boil, add the kale, and cook for about 1 minute, until just barely tender and still bright green. Use tongs to pull the kale out of the water and plunge it into the ice water. Transfer the kale to a salad spinner to get as much water out of it as you can. Repeat with the parsley, cooking it for only about 30 seconds.

In a medium skillet, toast the pumpkin seeds over medium heat until golden brown and fragrant, 3 to 5 minutes. Transfer to a plate to cool. In the same skillet, heat 1 tablespoon of the oil over medium heat. Add the garlic and cook until fragrant, about 30 seconds. Let cool.

In a food processor or blender, combine 1½ packed cups of the kale, the parsley, pumpkin seeds, remaining ¾ cup oil, the garlic and any oil in the pan, the lemon juice, salt, and pepper. Process until smooth, 1 to 2 minutes. Taste and adjust the seasoning.

To Store

Refrigerate in an airtight container for up to 10 days.

Scorecard

✓ A double serving counts as LGVs

✓ Nuts and Seeds

Makes

2

cups (¼ cup per serving)

Cheater's Romesco

Romesco is a classic Spanish sauce made with blended almonds. My thought: Why use almonds when almond butter is already at the perfect consistency? It's a creamy, tangy delight, perfect with just about anything it touches. This is my favorite dressing, so a batch doesn't stay around long.

1   cup packed drained store-bought roasted red peppers

¼   cup natural almond butter

2   tablespoons olive oil

1   tablespoon sherry vinegar

1   tablespoon tomato paste

2   garlic cloves, smashed

1   teaspoon kosher salt

¼   teaspoon freshly ground black pepper

In a blender or mini food processor, combine all the ingredients. Blend on high until smooth.

To Store

Refrigerate in an airtight container for up to 5 days.

Makes

1½

cups (¼ cup per serving)

Here are my favorite ideas for this dressing:

Nine-Minute Eggs with Steamed Greens (page 141)—swap it in for the kimchi dressing

Millet and Black Bean Cakes (page 239)

Crispy Tofu Steaks with Broccoli Rabe and Romesco (page 246)

Slow-Roasted Chicken with Extra-Crispy Skin (page 276)

Roasted trumpet mushrooms (see page 107) + brown rice (see page 124) + Roasted Romanesco (page 108)

THE RECIPES

White Tahini Sauce

This simple sauce was inspired by the classic white sauce that comes with falafel.

½ cup tahini

⅓ cup water

¼ cup lemon juice

2 tablespoons olive oil

1¼ to 1½ teaspoons kosher salt

½ to ¾ teaspoon Aleppo pepper flakes or crushed red pepper

In a small bowl, whisk together the tahini, water, lemon juice, 1¼ teaspoons of the salt, and ½ teaspoon of the Aleppo pepper. Taste and add more salt and Aleppo pepper depending on your taste preference.

To Store
Refrigerate in an airtight container for up to 5 days.

Scorecard
✔
Nuts and Seeds

Makes about
1
cup
(2 tablespoons per serving)

My favorite ways to use it:

Nine-Minute Eggs (page 141) + quinoa + Crispy Roasted Chickpeas (page 100) + Marinated Cucumber-Tomato Salad (page 303)

In place of the aioli in Le Petit Aioli (page 198)

As a dipping sauce for lamb meatballs (see page 221; skip the soup and just sear the meatballs until cooked through) + Garlicky Sautéed Chard (page 113)

Faux Caesar

This shortcut Caesar dressing takes a fraction of the time of the traditional recipe, and it lasts longer in the fridge, since it's egg- and dairy-free. If you don't like the taste of raw garlic, skip it. This still tastes shockingly Caesar-esque without it.

Adjust the fish sauce to taste if you are worried about sodium, or omit it to make the dressing plant-based (you'll need to season to taste).

¾ cup vegan mayo

2 tablespoons fish sauce

2 tablespoons lemon juice

1 tablespoon Dijon mustard

1 small garlic clove, grated (optional)

¼ teaspoon freshly ground black pepper

In a small bowl, whisk together all the ingredients.

To Store

Refrigerate in an airtight container for up to 1 week.

Makes

1

cup
(2 tablespoons per serving)

WHY I USE VEGAN MAYO

Vegan mayo is less processed than the regular kind, plus frankly, I feel weird about buying a product made with shelf-stabilized eggs (as regular mayo is). My favorite—Sir Kensington's Fabanaise—is made of just the water left over from cooking chickpeas, with no stabilizers at all. Find it or other plant-based mayonnaises in the refrigerated section of the grocery store.

Gets along nicely with:

Grilled Romaine (page 116) + Cauliflower "Bread Crumbs" (page 102)

Steamed potatoes (see page 120) + Oven-Poached Salmon (page 263) + chopped parsley

THE RECIPES

Spicy Miso Mayo

This dressing is not shy: it announces itself with every bite, so pair it with mellow flavors like steamed vegetables and plain grains. I keep a store-bought fermented hot sauce in my fridge at all times, but if you can't find one, a regular hot sauce (ideally without added sugar) will work, too.

¼ cup white miso paste

3 tablespoons no-sugar-added hot sauce

½ cup vegan mayo

1 tablespoon rice vinegar

In a small bowl, whisk together the miso and hot sauce until you have a smooth paste. (This ensures a smooth, not chunky, dressing.) Add the mayo and vinegar and whisk to combine.

To Store

Refrigerate in an airtight container for up to 10 days.

Try it with:

Steamed broccoli (see page 116) + brown rice (see page 124)

Nine-Minute Eggs (page 141) + sesame seeds + flaky sea salt

Scorecard

✔
Fermented
Food

Makes

1

cup
(2 table-
spoons per
serving)

Kimchi Dressing

Even if I know that the beneficial microbes in my kimchi or sauerkraut are great for me, adding one or the other on top of my meals can start to feel repetitive. That's why I came up with this rich and creamy dressing, which packs a cup of kimchi into each batch.

1 cup packed kimchi

¾ cup vegan mayo

½ cup water

1 tablespoon fish sauce

Pinch of kosher salt, or more as needed

In a blender or food processor, combine the kimchi, mayo, water, and fish sauce. Start blending slow to incorporate the ingredients evenly, then blend until you have a smooth dressing. Taste and season with the salt—I like a little more than just a pinch, but preferences differ.

To Store

Refrigerate in an airtight container for up to 1 week.

Perfect with:

Poached shrimp (see page 268) + shredded napa cabbage + avocado

Adzuki beans (see page 124) + steamed carrots (see page 335) + pea shoots

Scorecard

✓
Fermented Food

Makes
2¼
cups
(2 table-spoons per serving)

THE RECIPES

BREAKFAST

There's some debate over whether breakfast is the most important meal of the day in terms of your health, but for me, there's no question that it keeps me on track with plant-focused eating. From the perspective of your microbes, this matters, too. A meal that's high in plant fiber keeps you full longer, because the fiber can't be easily digested and absorbed by the human digestive enzymes in the stomach and small intestine. A slice of white toast with jam might seem like it's filling, but it's actually starving your gut microbiota of the indigestible plant fiber it needs to thrive.

But whether I'm thinking of my microbes or not, breakfast sets the tone for the day. A satisfying and delicious meal keeps me from snacking or obsessing over when my next meal will be. This section features realistic recipes that taste great and factor in whole, plant-based ingredients like vegetables, whole grains, and fresh, in-season fruit, without sacrificing the other things that matter in your life like time, accessibility of ingredients, and cost.

There are a variety of types of meals, divided into ideas for eggs, sweet breakfasts that taste indulgent and help you get more fiber into your day, quick smoothies for taking your greens and other veg on the go, and three simple whole-grain porridges.

Nine-Minute
Eggs with
Steamed Greens
and Kimchi
Dressing
141

~~~

Easy Eggs

Eggs are delicious and complement vegetal flavors, making them a great partner for plant-focused eating. And while these recipes are filed under "breakfast," I eat them at any time of day.

Please buy the best eggs you can afford—it's not just important for the planet and the welfare of the animals, but it also matters to your body. Happy chickens lay eggs that are higher in nutrients, and they taste better, too. It's worth seeking them out from a local farmer through your farmers' market or CSA. If you're shopping at the grocery store, choose eggs from pasture-raised hens, fed organic, non-GMO feed. The "Certified Humane" label is a good one to look for, too.

Nine-Minute Eggs
with Steamed Greens and Kimchi Dressing

Think of this recipe as a template for a balanced breakfast. Pair nine-minute eggs with whatever vegetables you have on hand—whether it's the hearty leafy greens in the recipe or Perfectly Steamed Broccoli (page 116) or Roasted Romanesco (page 108)—plus your favorite dressing.

4   large eggs

4   cups packed hearty green leaves, such as rainbow or Swiss chard, kale, or collard leaves (from 1 large bunch)

½   cup Kimchi Dressing (page 137), at room temperature

2   teaspoons sesame seeds

Kosher salt and freshly ground black pepper

Boil the eggs Fill a medium bowl with ice and water. Bring a small pot of water to a boil. Using a long-handled spoon, gently lower the eggs into the boiling water. (Roughly dropping them in can crack the shell on the bottom of the pot.) Reduce the heat to maintain a gentle simmer and set a timer for 9 minutes.

When the timer goes off, use a slotted spoon to carefully transfer the cooked eggs to the ice water and set aside until cool enough to handle (alternatively, run them under cold water until cool). Tap each egg gently on the counter and roll to crack the shell all over. Peel the shell off and then halve the eggs lengthwise.

Steam the greens Meanwhile, fill a large pot with 1 inch of water and put a steamer insert inside. Cover, bring the water to a simmer, add the greens, re-cover, and steam until tender but with a little bite, about 6 minutes.

Serve Use tongs to remove the greens from the strainer, shaking them gently to let any extra water drip off. Put them in a shallow bowl, then top with most of the dressing. Top with the eggs, remaining dressing, sesame seeds, and a pinch each of salt and pepper. Eat right away.

To Make Ahead
Store the peeled cooked eggs and the vegetables in separate airtight containers in the refrigerator. Assemble and let come to room temperature before eating.

Scorecard

✔
LGVs

✔
Fermented Food

Serves
2

THE RECIPES

Egg, Bacon, and Kale Breakfast Tacos

The point of this recipe is to show that with just a little bacon—only one slice per serving—you can still enjoy satisfying and delicious breakfast tacos without going too hard on the processed meats (which are a just-once-a-week situation if you're going for optimal gut health). You do this by cooking the kale in the bacon drippings and then folding the crumbled bacon into the scrambled eggs so there's salty, smoky flavor in each bite.

Scorecard

✓
LGVs

Serves

2

2   slices no-sugar-added bacon

3   garlic cloves, minced

1   large bunch curly kale, stems finely sliced and leaves chopped (4 cups packed)

½   teaspoon kosher salt

¼   teaspoon freshly ground black pepper, plus more as needed

1   cup water

4   sprouted or regular corn tortillas (see shopping tip), toasted over a gas flame or microwaved until hot

1   tablespoon unsalted butter, ghee, or preferred cooking oil

4   large eggs, beaten

Hot sauce, ideally fermented, for serving

Cook the bacon Lay the strips of bacon in a large nonstick skillet. Cook over medium-high heat, turning occasionally, until crisp, 4 to 5 minutes. Transfer the bacon to a plate, leaving the drippings in the pan. Let the bacon cool and then crumble it into small pieces. (You can do this while the kale cooks.)

Sauté the kale Return the pan to medium-high heat. Add the garlic to the bacon drippings and cook until fragrant, 30 seconds to 1 minute. Add the kale leaves and stems, ¼ teaspoon of the salt, and the pepper. Use tongs to toss the kale so it is evenly coated in the drippings, then pour in the water. Cook, tossing occasionally, until the kale is tender and the water has evaporated, 8 to 10 minutes.

Divide the tortillas between two plates and top evenly with the kale; set aside.

Last but not least, scramble the eggs In the same skillet, heat the butter over medium-high heat. Pour in the eggs, then season with the remaining ¼ teaspoon salt and a few grinds of pepper. Cook, stirring continuously with a flexible spatula, until the curds are just set. This happens quickly, so don't walk away from the stove. Fold in the crumbled bacon.

Divide the eggs among the tacos. Dot with hot sauce and eat right away.

Any LGV would taste great in these tacos—try spinach, Swiss chard, or collard greens. These will release more water than kale, though, and take less time to cook, so omit the water from the recipe and adjust the cooking time accordingly.

Shopping TIP

When I can find them, I buy sprouted corn tortillas for these and other taco recipes. However, you can use regular corn tortillas if you prefer. Just make sure to choose an additive-free brand that uses organic, non-GMO corn. Despite what many people would like you to believe, GMOs aren't inherently bad for your gut. However, GMO corn is engineered to tolerate herbicides like Roundup, and it's the herbicide residue that appears to cause health issues; some research conducted on animals indicates that glyphosate (the main ingredient in Roundup) is harmful to the gut microbiota.

Refried Beans and Fried Eggs
with Avocado, Spinach, and Pico de Gallo

Real life means that I don't always have time to DIY refried beans myself, and it's better, in my opinion, to sub in a can of refried beans paired with avocado and spinach than it is to say "screw it" and just eat a sugary energy bar. That's what my fuzzy boundaries approach is about—not choosing to give up entirely because something can't be "perfect."

When it comes to picking the can for this recipe, I choose a low-sodium kind that has no additives. The ingredients? Beans, water, onions, oil, salt, garlic, and spices. All things I can stand behind. It's a shortcut staple I always have in my pantry for quick, healthful meals. Like I said, there's no doubt that homemade is the ideal, so substitute 1½ cups of your favorite refried bean recipe, if you'd like.

- 2 tablespoons preferred cooking oil
- 1 bunch fresh spinach (8 ounces)
- ¼ teaspoon kosher salt, plus more as needed
- ¼ teaspoon freshly ground black pepper, plus more as needed
- 4 large eggs
- 1 (15-ounce) can low-sodium vegetarian refried beans, microwaved in a bowl until hot
- ½ cup fresh pico de gallo or tomatillo salsa
- 1 ripe avocado, sliced
- Fresh cilantro leaves
- Flaky sea salt (optional)

Sauté the spinach In a medium nonstick skillet, heat 1 tablespoon of the oil over medium-high heat. Add the spinach, salt, and pepper. Cook, stirring continuously, until wilted, 2 to 3 minutes. Transfer to a plate and cover to keep warm.

Fry the eggs Wipe out the skillet and heat the remaining 1 tablespoon oil over high heat. Add the eggs and cook until the edges are crispy and the yolks and whites are set, 2 to 3 minutes. (I like to tilt the pan and use a spoon to baste the whites with the hot oil to help them cook quickly.) Season the eggs with a pinch each of salt and pepper.

Assemble the bowls Divide the refried beans between two plates and use an offset spatula or the back of a spoon to spread into a pretty schmear. Add the spinach and fried eggs. Top with the pico de gallo and avocado. Drizzle with any leftover oil from the skillet, then sprinkle with the cilantro and some flaky sea salt, if you want. Serve immediately.

Scorecard

✓ Beans

✓ LGVs

THE RECIPES

Serves
2

~~~

Breakfasts on the Sweet Side

Ever since I started freelancing four years ago, I've started my day in an identical way—breakfast and coffee, writing and reading. My morning routine is sacred to me, since it is the only time I guard as my own before the workday begins.

The formula stays the same: I alternate between sips and bites, write for an hour or so, then do my morning reading. Once this is complete, I can start the rest of my workday.

As for the food? In the past, I regularly paired a sugary treat with a bottomless pot of black coffee to slice through the sweetness. Whether it was a pancake doused with syrup or a *pain au chocolat*, these breakfasts had one thing in common: I was starting my day with the absolute worst foods for my gut. Refined grains and a lot of added sugar—even in the form of more "natural" options like honey and maple syrup—are a recipe for spiked blood sugar and no plant-fiber left over for the good microbes in your gut. The result? Inflammation.

When I started to change the way I ate, I worried that I would have to give up this sacred combination for the sake of my health. Rather than be a martyr to my microbes, I set about making recipes that fully satisfied both my taste buds and my friendly bugs.

Whether it's a waffle or a bowl of granola, these breakfasts are as comfortable with my mug of bitter coffee as any chocolate chip scone, but they feed my beneficial bacteria, too.

Coconut,
Pumpkin Seed,
and Buckwheat
Granola
156

Salty-Sweet Kefir and Olive Oil Fruit Bowl

A salty-sweet yogurt bowl might seem unusual, but it's now the only way to go for me. Kefir offers a hearty dose of beneficial microbes as well as calcium, and fresh, in-season fruit is a great source of fiber. The sea salt is optional if you're watching your sodium, but if you're not, I insist you finish the bowl with a few flakes.

1   cup plain kefir

1   cup local, in-season fruit, like berries, stone fruit, or grapefruit

¼   cup almonds, toasted and chopped

1   tablespoon olive oil

1   tablespoon hemp seeds

    Flaky sea salt (optional)

Pour the kefir into a shallow bowl and top with the fruit and almonds. Drizzle the oil all over and sprinkle with the hemp seeds and some flaky sea salt (if you want).

Get-Ahead TIP

This sits well overnight if made with berries, but cut stone fruits, apple, or grapefruit will curdle the kefir, so add those just before serving.

Scorecard

✔✔
Nuts and Seeds

✔
Fermented Food

✔
Fruit

Serves
1

Turmeric-
Coconut-Ginger
Latte
318

Make-Ahead

TiP Arrange room-
temperature waffles
in a single layer on
a baking sheet and
freeze. Transfer
the frozen waffles to an airtight
container or zip-top freezer
bag. Freeze for up to 2 months.
Reheat at 350°F until warm,
6 to 8 minutes.

Almond, Date, and Chia Waffles

My goal when developing this recipe was to make a genuinely healthful waffle that wasn't loaded with butter and sugar. It took six tries, but the result is a richly flavored waffle, dense with seeds for protein and fiber but crisp enough to satisfy a brunch craving. Since the batter doesn't have added sugar, make sure to chop the dates well so there's a nip of sweetness in every bite.

Scorecard

✔✔
Nuts and
Seeds

Makes about

6

waffles

For the waffles

- 3 cups unsweetened almond milk
- ½ cup chia seeds
- ¼ cup hemp seeds
- 3 large eggs, separated
- ½ cup unsalted butter or ghee, melted
- 12 large, soft Medjool dates, pitted, mashed, and finely chopped (1 cup)
- 1 tablespoon pure vanilla extract
- 1½ cups (6.5 ounces) scooped-and-leveled natural almond flour
- ¾ cup (3.5 ounces) scooped-and-leveled brown rice flour
- 3 tablespoons arrowroot starch or potato starch
- 1 tablespoon baking powder
- 1½ teaspoons kosher salt
- ½ teaspoon ground cardamom
- ½ teaspoon ground nutmeg
- ½ teaspoon cream of tartar
- Preferred cooking oil, for the waffle iron

For the raspberry flax smash

- 6 ounces fresh raspberries (1½ cups)
- 2 tablespoons flaxseeds
- Pure maple syrup, for serving (optional)

Make the batter Preheat your waffle maker to its highest setting. In a large bowl, whisk together the almond milk, chia seeds, and hemp seeds. Let sit for 10 minutes. Whisk in the egg yolks, butter, dates, and vanilla until completely incorporated.

In a small bowl, whisk together the almond flour, brown rice flour, arrowroot starch, baking powder, salt, cardamom, and nutmeg. Fold the flour mixture into the almond milk mixture. Set aside.

Place the egg whites in a clean bowl. Using an electric mixer or a handheld whisk, beat the egg whites until they start to foam up. Sprinkle the cream of tartar over the egg whites and beat until soft peaks form. Fold one-quarter of the egg whites into the batter until combined, then fold in the remaining egg whites.

Cook the waffles Brush the waffle iron with oil. Cook the batter according to your waffle maker's instructions. Transfer the waffle to a plate and repeat with the remaining batter.

Make the raspberry flax smash In a small bowl, mash the raspberries well. Stir in the flaxseeds.

Serve the waffles hot, dolloped with the raspberry flax smash. Drizzle with a little maple syrup, if you want.

THE RECIPES

Salted Smashed Sweet Potatoes
with Miso-Date Butterscotchy Sauce

When I'm craving a rich, hearty breakfast that still feels like a treat, I make this delicious loaded sweet potato situation. It's topped with Miso-Date Butterscotchy Sauce (page 325), which adds salty-sweet decadence as well as a dose of probiotics, thanks to the fermented miso paste. Make sure to eat the skin of the sweet potato—it's a great source of indigestible plant fiber, aka exactly what your good microbes want to eat!

Scorecard

✔
Other Veg

✔
Nuts and Seeds

✔
Fermented Food

Serves
1

- 1 **skinny medium sweet potato (about 9 ounces)**
- ¼ **cup Miso-Date Butterscotchy Sauce (page 325)**
- ¼ **cup large unsweetened coconut flakes, toasted**
- 2 **tablespoons chopped pistachios**
- 1 **tablespoon torn small fresh mint leaves**
- **Flaky sea salt (optional)**

Tip To toast coconut flakes, spread them over a rimmed baking sheet and bake at 350°F for about 3 minutes, stirring once, until golden brown and fragrant. Watch carefully—they can burn quickly.

Fill a large pot with 1 inch of water and put a steamer insert inside. Cover and bring the water to a simmer. Add the sweet potato, re-cover, and steam until you can stick a fork very easily into the center, 20 to 30 minutes, depending on the size of the sweet potato.

Cut the sweet potato in half from tip to tip. Place the halves cut-side up on a plate and smash the flesh with a fork, then spoon the butterscotch sauce over the top. Sprinkle with the coconut flakes, pistachios, mint, and some flaky sea salt (if you want).

Big Batch

This breakfast is so filling and delicious, I'll often eat it for several days in a row. I steam 3 or 4 sweet potatoes at once and reheat them one at a time. Add more water to the pot and steam for an additional 5 to 10 minutes.

Get Loaded

I originally developed this recipe with a combination of tahini, butter, maple syrup, sesame seeds, and flaky sea salt. Then, as we were shooting photos for this book, another cookbook came out with almost the exact same combination! Great minds think alike, but it inspired me to change up my recipe to use my supremely delicious and addictive Miso-Date Butterscotchy Sauce. However, if you want to make my original version, here are the ingredients, plus a couple other delicious combinations to try with steamed sweet potatoes.

1 tablespoon unsalted butter + 1 tablespoon tahini + 1 tablespoon sesame seeds + 1 teaspoon pure maple syrup + sprinkle of flaky sea salt

—

½ chopped avocado + ½ cup cooked or canned black beans + handful of fresh cilantro leaves + dollop of cultured sour cream + hot sauce + sprinkle of flaky sea salt

—

½ cup plain kefir + 2 chopped pitted Medjool dates + 2 tablespoons Seed Shaker (page 180) + dusting of ground cinnamon

Caramelized Baked Apples
with Yogurt and Granola

Raw apples give me and many others a terrible stomachache, while cooked apples are no problem. Not to mention that they taste sweet like dessert, without requiring a lot of sugar. Add a sprinkling of granola and a dollop of yogurt and the result is reminiscent of an apple cobbler.

4 medium baking apples, such as Jonagold, Honeycrisp, or Braeburn (1½ pounds total), halved and cored

1 tablespoon unsalted butter, ghee, or coconut oil, melted

1 tablespoon coconut sugar

½ teaspoon pure vanilla extract

¼ teaspoon ground nutmeg

¼ teaspoon ground cinnamon

¼ teaspoon kosher salt

2 cups plain yogurt or kefir, (or coconut yogurt for a plant-based option), for serving

2 cups Coconut, Pumpkin Seed, and Buckwheat Granola (page 156), or your favorite store-bought

Preheat your oven to 350°F. Place the apples cut-side down in a 9-inch round cake pan or similar-size ovenproof dish. Pour 1 cup water over the apples and cover the pan tightly with aluminum foil. Bake for 35 to 40 minutes, until the apples are soft and you can stick a fork very easily into the center of one. Remove the apples from the oven and switch the oven to broil. Remove the foil and use tongs to turn the apples cut-side up.

In a small bowl, stir together the butter, coconut sugar, vanilla, nutmeg, cinnamon, and salt. Divide the mixture among the apples and use a pastry brush to spread it evenly over the cut side of the apples.

Broil until the apples are caramelized, 2 to 5 minutes, depending on the kind of broiler you have. If it's gas, keep an eye on them the whole time!

For each serving, place ½ cup yogurt in a bowl and top with 2 apple halves and ½ cup of the granola. If there are any juices in the pan, I like to drizzle them over the apples.

To Store

Refrigerate the baked apples (without the toppings) in an airtight container for up to 5 days. Microwave or bake at 350°F to reheat, then top as directed.

Scorecard

✔
Nuts and Seeds

✔
Whole Grains

✔
Fermented Food

✔
Fruit

Serves

4

THE RECIPES

Coconut, Pumpkin Seed, and Buckwheat Granola

Most granola is the poster child for a sugary treat masquerading as a health food. In fact, many brands have as much sugar in a single serving as a scoop of ice cream (!!!).

For *Help Yourself*, I had a dream of creating a granola with as little added sugar as possible, but the reality is that a granola with no sugar at all is just muesli, which—while delicious in its own right—doesn't satisfy with granola's signature crispy snap. After making many, many batches, I've found that ¾ cup is as low as I can go with maple syrup before losing the classic crunch, which translates to about 2 teaspoons maple syrup, or 5 grams added sugar, per serving.

A roster of high-fiber plant-food superstars balances out the sugar, including oats (a source of essential prebiotic fiber), buckwheat, pumpkin seeds, and sunflower seeds, as well as coconut flakes. Your gut will thank you.

Scorecard

✔
Whole Grains

✔✔
Nuts and Seeds

Makes about

14

cups
(½ cup per serving)

- 4 cups old-fashioned rolled oats
- 2½ cups buckwheat groats (1 pound)
- 2 cups raw hulled pumpkin seeds
- 1 cup raw hulled sunflower seeds
- 1 cup unsweetened large coconut flakes
- 1 cup unsweetened finely shredded coconut
- 2 teaspoons ground cinnamon
- 2 teaspoons kosher salt
- 1 cup coconut oil, melted
- ¾ cup pure maple syrup
- 2 teaspoons pure vanilla extract

Optional toppings

- Unsweetened nondairy milk, kefir, or yogurt
- Fresh fruit
- 1 tablespoon Seed Shaker (page 180), for an extra boost of seeds

Preheat your oven to 375°F with racks spaced evenly in the top, bottom, and center positions. (You can cook this in batches if you only have two oven racks.)

In a large bowl, stir together all the ingredients until evenly combined. Divide the mixture among three rimmed baking sheets and smooth into an even layer.

Bake, stirring halfway through and rotating the baking sheets front to back and shifting the slots, for 22 to 26 minutes, until the granola is golden brown and fragrant. Remove from the oven and let cool completely.

Serve with your favorite toppings.

To Store

Store in an airtight container at room temperature for up to 2 weeks or in the freezer for up to 3 months.

Jicama, Avocado, and Grapefruit Breakfast Salad

One of the best ways to get enough fiber into your day is to start with breakfast, and in the case of this simple salad, there are 16 grams of fiber in each bowl. I know I'm asking you to rethink what breakfast is (salad for breakfast?!), but the combination of creamy avocado, crunchy jicama, and tart grapefruit is a winner, and—most important—it'll tide you over until lunch.

1   small grapefruit

1   cup sliced jicama (cut into matchsticks)

½   ripe avocado, sliced or chopped

1   tablespoon olive oil

1   tablespoon fresh mint leaves, preferably the smallest you can find in the bunch, or torn if large

⅛   teaspoon flaky sea salt, or to taste

    Freshly ground black pepper

Slice the grapefruit Using a sharp knife, cut a small slice from the bottom of the grapefruit so it will sit flat on your cutting board. Working for the top down, cut the peel off the grapefruit, making sure there's not a lot of white pith left on the outside. Cut the grapefruit in half, then slice it into ½-inch-thick half-moons. Pull out and discard any seeds.

Assemble the salad In a small bowl, gently toss the grapefruit, jicama, avocado, and oil until evenly coated. Pile into a serving bowl and sprinkle the mint, flaky sea salt, and a few grinds of pepper over the top.

Scorecard

✔✔
Other Veg

✔
Fruit

Serves

1

THE RECIPES

~~~

Porridges

I always thought of porridge as something a strict British nanny had to force down the gullet of her charges. But in recent years, there's been a resurgence of whole-grain porridges in restaurants, magazines, and cookbooks—seemingly reinventing the gruel of yore. For me, the appeal lies in the remix of a whole grain in both texture and format, which is one of the keys to plant-focused eating on a regular basis—it can't be grain bowls and salads all the time. Any of the three recipes in this section offers a deeply comforting, delicious meal to enjoy on a chilly morning. The best part is, you're starting the day with a serving of whole grains, which means your microbes will thank you.

Each of these recipes makes a big batch perfect for large groups, getting ahead on breakfast for the week, or stocking the freezer. I freeze in individual portions, then defrost a serving overnight in the refrigerator, heat it in the microwave or on the stovetop, and top it with whatever I have on hand.

Creamy Coconut and Millet Porridge 162

Peanut Butter and Amaranth Porridge with Saucy Strawberries 163

Creamy Coconut and Millet Porridge

Honestly, the bland looks of this porridge belie its delicious flavor. As my friend and fellow cookbook writer Casey Elsass wrote me after testing it, "What is this miracle?! So delicious!"

Soak the millet before you go to bed so it's ready to cook in the morning.

For the porridge

- 6 cups water
- 2 (13.5-ounce) cans light unsweetened coconut milk
- 2 cups millet, soaked overnight and rinsed or sprouted (see page 124)
- ¼ cup pure maple syrup
- 2 teaspoons ground turmeric
- ½ teaspoon ground ginger
- ¼ teaspoon ground cardamom
- ½ teaspoon kosher salt
- 1 teaspoon pure vanilla extract

To serve (per bowl)

- ¾ to 1 cup fresh figs, mashed mixed berries, or other in-season fruit
- 2 tablespoons hemp seeds or Seed Shaker (page 180)

  Fresh mint leaves

  Toasted coconut flakes (see Tip, page 187)

In a medium pot, whisk together the water, coconut milk, millet, maple syrup, turmeric, ginger, cardamom, and salt. Cover and bring to a boil over high heat, then reduce the heat to maintain a gentle simmer. Cook, covered, stirring occasionally, until the millet is almost completely broken down and the porridge has a thick but still pourable consistency, about 30 minutes. Remove from the heat and stir in the vanilla.

Ladle a generous cup of hot porridge into each serving bowl. Top with whatever fruit you are using, sprinkle with the seeds, and top with the mint and coconut flakes.

To Store

Refrigerate the porridge in an airtight container for up to 4 days or freeze for up to 2 months.

Scorecard

✓
Whole Grains

✓
Nuts and Seeds

✓
Fruit

Serves
8

Peanut Butter and Amaranth Porridge **with Saucy Strawberries**

Many plant-based porridge recipes call for cooking grains in almond milk or another dairy substitute. Often, though, cooking in store-bought nondairy milks results in an unappetizing gray slush. Here I cook the grains in water with a scoop of peanut butter, which has the effect of infusing the water just like a regular nut milk would, and adds more body.

Scorecard

✓
Nuts and Seeds

✓
Whole Grains

✓
Fruit

THE RECIPES

Serves
4 to 6

For the saucy strawberries

- 1 pound strawberries, stemmed and sliced
- 1 teaspoon pure maple syrup (optional)
  Splash of pure vanilla extract
  Pinch of kosher salt

For the porridge

- 8 cups water
- 1 cup amaranth, rinsed
- ½ cup quinoa, soaked, sprouted, or rinsed (see page 124)
- ½ cup natural peanut butter
- 2 tablespoons pure maple syrup
- ½ teaspoon kosher salt
- 1 teaspoon pure vanilla extract

To serve

  Splash of unsweetened nondairy milk, canned coconut milk, or kefir
- 2 tablespoons Seed Shaker (page 180) or your favorite seed
  A spoonful of peanut butter (optional)

Make the strawberries In a small bowl, mash half the strawberries, the maple syrup (if you want), vanilla, and salt. Stir in the remaining strawberries.

Make the porridge Bring the water to a boil in a large pot. Add the amaranth, quinoa, peanut butter, maple syrup, and salt. Cover and return to a boil over high heat, then reduce the heat to maintain a gentle simmer. Cook, covered, stirring occasionally, until the amaranth and quinoa are almost completely broken down and the porridge is smooth but still thin, about 30 minutes. Remove the lid and simmer for 10 to 15 minutes more, until the porridge reaches the consistency of a thin pudding.

Finish and serve the porridge Remove the porridge from the heat and stir in the vanilla. Ladle the porridge into serving bowls. Top with a scoop of the saucy strawberries and their juices. Add a splash of something creamy and sprinkle with the seeds. For extra decadence, I like dolloping on a spoonful of peanut butter.

To Store

Refrigerate the porridge and the strawberries in separate airtight containers; the porridge will keep for up to 4 days. The strawberries will keep for about a day. The porridge can also be frozen for up to 2 months.

Broccoli and Quinoa Congee

One of my favorite spots in LA, Destroyer, used to make a delicious broccoli congee. I was inspired to create a microbe-friendly version, since theirs was made with white rice and—by the taste of it—probably a pound of butter. I wanted to mimic that satisfying taste, but with a blend of brown rice and quinoa.

2 heads broccoli (1½ pounds total—get ones without long stems)

¼ cup unsalted butter or ghee, melted, or your preferred cooking oil

1 teaspoon crushed caraway seeds

2½ teaspoons kosher salt, plus more as needed

¼ teaspoon freshly ground black pepper

¾ cup short-grain brown rice, sprouted, soaked, or rinsed (see page 124)

¾ cup quinoa, sprouted, soaked, or rinsed (see page 124)

8 cups Trash or Treasure Broth (page 129) or high-quality store-bought broth

8 cups water

2 medium onions, sliced ½ inch thick from root to stem

Use a knife to cut the small, scrubby green tops off the broccoli (to make 1 cup). Set those aside and chop the rest of the broccoli into small florets.

In a large pot, heat 2 tablespoons of the butter over medium-high heat. Add the broccoli florets, caraway seeds, 2 teaspoons of the salt, and the pepper. Cook, stirring, until slightly tender, 3 to 5 minutes, then add the brown rice and quinoa. Cook, stirring continuously, until the grains are fragrant and toasty, 3 to 5 minutes.

Add the broth and water. Cover and bring to a boil over high heat, then remove the lid and reduce the heat so the liquid is simmering generously but not aggressively. Cook, stirring and scraping the bottom of the pot occasionally, until the rice and quinoa are broken down and completely soft, 45 to 50 minutes.

Meanwhile, preheat your broiler to high with a rack set 4 to 5 inches from the heat source. Toss the onions, remaining 2 tablespoons butter, and ½ teaspoon salt on a rimmed baking sheet. Broil, tossing once, until crispy and dark brown, 6 to 8 minutes. (Keep an eye on them, since broiler heat varies drastically.) Remove from the oven and set aside until ready to serve.

Using an immersion blender, blend the congee directly in the pot to create a smooth, porridgelike consistency. (You can also use a regular blender, in batches.)

Serve the congee in bowls, topped with the onions, reserved scrubby broccoli tops, and any extras you like (see headnote).

To Store

Refrigerate the congee, onions, and scrubby broccoli tops in separate airtight containers for up to 4 days. The congee will also freeze well for up to 2 months.

Scorecard

✔ LGVs

✔ Other Veg

✔ Whole Grains

Serves
6 to 8

Plant-based option
Use oil and all water or
plant-based Trash or
Treasure Broth (page 129).

TIP

I like to add extras like
kimchi, a Nine-Minute Egg
(page 141), avocado, or
Crispy Roasted Chickpeas
(page 100). For a crowd, I'll
make a platter of toppings
and let everyone top their
own bowl.

~

Smoothies

From the perspective of your gut microbes, smoothies are a mixed bag. This is because the process of blending the ingredients into such small pieces jump-starts the digestive process, meaning that more of the food is accessible to your human digestive enzymes and less is left over by the time the food reaches your gut microbiota. However, I'm all about being practical and not obsessing over perfect, so I'm a fan of plant-focused smoothies on occasional mornings when time matters most. Also, they taste great.

I developed each these recipes to pack in whole plant foods that beneficial gut bacteria thrive on, with only dates or fruit for sweetness. This is best-case scenario for a smoothie, as far as your gut is concerned.

The recipes all make two servings—split them between yourself and another lucky recipient, or save half for the next day. I've found that these all refrigerate quite well in an airtight container overnight—just stir well before drinking the next day.

WHAT'S THE DEAL WITH JUICE?

The process of juicing removes all the plant fiber, leaving only the simple chains of carbohydrate molecules (sugars) behind. So, it not only spikes your blood sugar, by the time that plant-derived drink gets to your gut microbes, there's nearly nothing left. In fact, you'd be better off eating what's leftover in the juicer, since that is the very stuff the friendly creatures in your gut thrive on.

Blueberry,
Chia, and Beet
Smoothie
171

Immune-
Boosting Super
Smoothie
172

Spiced
Pumpkin Shake
169

Turmeric
Pineapple
Smoothie
170

Mango, Mint,
and Kale
Smoothie
168

Spinach
and Squash
Smoothie
173

Mango, Mint, and Kale Smoothie

Fresh mint adds a refreshing twist to this green smoothie. I pour extra coconut milk from the can into a glass jar and refrigerate it to use for smoothies throughout the week.

1 cup packed frozen kale, spinach, or a mix

1 cup frozen mango chunks

2 tablespoons packed fresh mint leaves

2 tablespoons hemp seeds

1 large, soft Medjool date, pitted

1½ cups unsweetened nondairy milk

½ cup unsweetened canned coconut milk

Combine all the ingredients in your blender, adding the nondairy milk and coconut milk last. Blend until smooth, and drink right away!

For easy measuring, buy frozen kale, spinach, or other greens that come in a bag, not in a box.

Scorecard

✓
LGVs

✓✓
Nuts and Seeds

✓
Fruit

Serves
2

Spiced Pumpkin Shake

Pumpkin is high in fiber and, importantly, high in flavor. I particularly like it in smoothies because it reads as sweet without any added sugar.

I also like to make this recipe with leftover steamed sweet potato or carrot, if I have it on hand, instead of the pumpkin. Feel like trying that version instead? Use the instructions for steaming in the Sweet Potato, Squash, and Carrot Pie recipe on page 334; canned sweet potato will work, too.

1½	cups canned pure pumpkin puree
2	small or 1 large frozen banana
2	large, soft Medjool dates, pitted
½	teaspoon pumpkin pie spice, or ¼ teaspoon ground cinnamon
½	teaspoon pure vanilla extract
1½	cups unsweetened nondairy milk
1	cup unsweetened plain kefir

Combine all the ingredients in your blender, adding the nondairy milk and kefir last. Blend until smooth, and drink right away!

Plant-based option

Replace the kefir with your favorite nondairy milk. I like a blend of oat and coconut milks.

Scorecard

✓
Other Veg

✓
Fermented Food

✓
Fruit

Serves

2

THE RECIPES

Turmeric Pineapple Smoothie

Curcumin, a compound found in turmeric, is famous for its anti-inflammatory properties, but what many recipes don't mention is that eating it in combination with black pepper is helpful in making those benefits accessible to your body. I include just ¼ teaspoon of pepper here, which balances the sweetness of the pineapple without being too spicy.

Letting the oats soak for a bit before continuing with the smoothie allows them to thicken up for body, as well as making them easier to digest.

1½ cups unsweetened nondairy milk

¼ cup quick-cooking oats (or rolled oats, if that's what you have on hand)

1 cup frozen pineapple chunks

1 small banana

2 tablespoons flaxseeds

2 teaspoons ground turmeric

¼ teaspoon freshly ground black pepper

Combine the nondairy milk and oats in your blender. Blend until smooth, then let sit for at least 10 minutes to soften while you get the rest of the ingredients ready.

Blend on high until no large pieces of oat remain, then add the pineapple, banana, flaxseeds, turmeric, and pepper. Blend until smooth, and drink right away!

Scorecard

✔
Whole Grains

✔✔
Nuts and Seeds

Serves

2

Blueberry, Chia, and Beet Smoothie

Beets have anti-inflammatory benefits and are great for relieving constipation (sorry, I said it). And with their naturally sweet taste, they are a perfect match for blueberries and spicy ginger. If you have fresh, in-season blueberries on hand, use those; otherwise, frozen ones are your best bet, since they're picked at the peak of freshness.

It was tempting to call for beet juice in this smoothie, rather than steamed beets, because it's easier and, frankly, less work. But since juicing removes the beets' beneficial fiber and leaves only the sugars, I am anti-juice and pro-fiber, so I use the veggie itself. If I'm pressed for time, I'll splurge on store-bought precooked beets.

1 medium beet (6 ounces), steamed (see below), cooled, and quartered

1 cup frozen blueberries

2 tablespoons chia seeds

1 tablespoon grated fresh ginger or ginger juice

1½ cups unsweetened nondairy milk

Combine all the ingredients in your blender, adding the nondairy milk last. Blend until smooth, and drink right away!

Scorecard

✔
Other Veg

✔✔
Nuts and Seeds

THE RECIPES

Serves
2

HOW TO STEAM BEETS

I steam a bunch or two of beets at a time for the week, whether to use in this smoothie or for salads. Always buy beets with the greens still attached. Not only is it a sign of freshness, but the greens are a potassium powerhouse; save them after trimming the beets and sauté them as you would Swiss chard (see page 113).

To steam beets, fill a pot with 1 inch of water and put a steamer insert inside. Cover and bring the water to a simmer, add the beets, re-cover, and steam until you can stick a fork very easily into the center of a beet, 35 to 45 minutes, depending on the size of the beets. Slice ¼-inch off each end, then slip the skins off with your fingers (they should come off easily) or use a paring knife to remove them.

Immune-Boosting Super Smoothie

This is the kind of smoothie that many health books and "wellness" brands will tell you is doable every day. I know it's not, which is why the other smoothies in this chapter call for many fewer ingredients. Sometimes, though, getting some more plants in one package is worth the effort.

This recipe makes a big-ass smoothie to keep you full until lunch, with a little matcha green tea powder in there for an antioxidant and light caffeine boost. And yes, it's got a lot of ingredients. It's for the mornings where you have a little extra time. It's not sweet, but it packs in a meal's worth of dietary fiber, LGVs, and seeds.

1 cup frozen kale or spinach leaves

½ cup fresh or frozen berries (blueberries, raspberries, blackberries, or a mix)

½ cup sweet potato puree or mashed sweet potato (see page 335)

¼ ripe avocado

1 tablespoon melted or soft coconut oil

1 tablespoon flaxseeds

1 tablespoon grated fresh ginger

1 large, soft Medjool date, pitted (optional)

1 teaspoon culinary-grade matcha powder

1 teaspoon ground turmeric

¼ teaspoon freshly ground black pepper

2 cups unsweetened nondairy milk

Combine all the ingredients in your blender, adding the nondairy milk last. Blend until smooth, and drink right away!

Scorecard

✓
LGVs

✓
Other Veg

✓
Nuts and Seeds

Serves
2

Spinach and Squash Smoothie

A smoothie that's basically a salad, but tastes like breakfast. Amazing! For this recipe, any kind of pureed squash, like steamed kabocha (see page 209) or canned pumpkin, will work, as will sweet potato (see page 335). I just use what I have on hand, preferably something I've baked or steamed at home.

1 cup frozen chopped spinach

1 cup pureed squash, pumpkin, or sweet potato (see headnote)

1 tablespoon melted or soft coconut oil

1 tablespoon flaxseeds

1 large, soft Medjool date, pitted

Pinch of ground nutmeg or cinnamon

2 cups unsweetened nondairy milk

Combine all the ingredients in your blender, adding the nondairy milk last. Blend until smooth, and drink right away!

Scorecard

✓
LGVs

✓
Other Veg

✓
Nuts and Seeds

THE RECIPES

Serves

2

SEEDS

The reason I pulled these recipes out into their own special section is to showcase the incredible versatility of these tiny friends. One of the easiest ways to add fiber and nutrients like omega-3s, iron, and calcium to your diet is through seeds. Many people think seeds are a waste of money because they transit through your system too quickly for the nutrients to be absorbed by the body—but that's not true. Your friendly microbes feast on their indigestible plant fibers and synthesize them into vitamins and other chemicals that the body needs. I'm pro-seed, and your good bacteria are, too.

Dates,
Seeds, and
Peanut Butter
182

TIP It's so much easier (and more accurate) to make this recipe by using a digital scale, which is why I've included ingredient weights. If you don't have a scale or would rather use a cup measure, use the scoop-and-level method to get even, packed cups. With such a variety of ingredients it's more reliable than the spoon-and-level method.

Magic Seed-and-Nut Bread

When I started changing what I ate, one of my go-to breakfasts—thick, buttered toast with jam—was no longer available to me. Enter Sarah Britton's recipe for The Life-Changing Loaf of Bread, which she published on her blog, *My New Roots*. With the first bite, I felt a sense of relief—*Finally*, I thought, *I can eat breakfast in a way that feels like breakfast again.* In the end, I adapted the recipe quite a bit to a loaf that's based on nuts and seeds alone, swapping in almond flour and quinoa flour for the oats called for in Britton's original recipe. Psyllium seed husk is the key to getting a breadlike consistency without egg, flour, or gluten-free substitutes.

Scorecard

✔✔
Nuts and
Seeds

Makes

1

8½ by 4½-
inch loaf,
(12 slices)

1	cup raw hulled sunflower seeds (4.75 ounces)
¾	cup raw hulled pumpkin seeds (4.2 ounces)
½	cup flaxseeds (3.25 ounces)
½	cup raw almonds (2.25 ounces)
½	cup psyllium seed husk (1.5 ounces)
½	cup almond flour (2.1 ounces)
½	cup quinoa flour (2 ounces)
¼	cup chia seeds (1.4 ounces)
1½	teaspoons kosher salt
1½	cups water
3	tablespoons olive oil
1	tablespoon brown rice syrup or pure maple syrup
	Your favorite toast toppings, for serving

Oil an 8½-inch by 4½-inch loaf pan.

In a large bowl, stir together the sunflower seeds, ½ cup of the pumpkin seeds, the flaxseeds, almonds, psyllium seed husk, almond flour, quinoa flour, chia seeds, and salt.

In a small bowl, whisk together the water, oil, and brown rice syrup. Add the wet ingredients to the dry ingredients and stir until everything is well mixed and fully soaked. Scrape the batter into the prepared loaf pan and smooth it into an even layer, then sprinkle with the remaining ¼ cup pumpkin seeds. Let sit at room temperature for 4 hours or refrigerate for up to 24 hours.

Thirty minutes before baking, preheat your oven to 350°F with a rack in the center position.

Bake the loaf for 1 hour 30 minutes to 1 hour 45 minutes, rotating the pan front to back once, until the loaf is dark golden brown and sounds hollow when tapped. Remove from the oven and let cool completely in the pan, then turn the loaf out onto a cutting board and slice it into ½-inch-thick slices. Toast each slice individually to eat.

To Store

Freeze in a ziptop freezer bag for up to 2 months. (You can leave it at room temperature for a day or two, but since seeds can go rancid quickly, I recommend freezing it after any longer than this.)

STEP-BY-STEP
PHOTOS ON
THE NEXT PAGE

Measure out all your ingredients before getting started.

Combine the dry ingredients in a large bowl, and whisk the wet ingredients in a large measuring cup or small bowl.

Whisk the dry ingredients until combined.

Pour the wet ingredients into the dry ingredients.

Use a spatula to fold everything together until well combined.

Scrape the mixture into an oiled loaf pan and smooth the top.

Sprinkle with more pumpkin seeds to make the top pretty.

Cover the loaf with a clean dish towel. Let sit at room temperature for 4 hours or refrigerate for up to 24 hours and then bake.

TIP Toasting a slice of this dense bread from the freezer takes quite a bit of time, around 10 minutes in my toaster oven (flipping halfway through), to get it properly crispy and hot throughout. For faster and more even reheating, take a slice or two out of the freezer the night before you plan to eat the bread.

Top with:

Nut butter

100% fruit preserves or fresh fruit

Cultured cream cheese + smoked salmon
+ olive oil + squeeze of lemon juice +
flaky sea salt, natch

Avocado

Seed Shaker

In the past, I'd often choose one or two seeds to sprinkle over a grain bowl, blend into a smoothie, or garnish a dip because opening up a bunch of jars and containers is too much work. Since *Help Yourself* is not just about making gut-healthy eating delicious, but also smarter and easier, I thought, *Why choose just one or two seeds when you can easily reap the benefits of three or more?* Enter the Seed Shaker, a premixed blend of seeds that you can measure out 1 tablespoon at a time.

You can customize your own with any seeds you have on hand. I didn't include sesame or poppy here, because I find their flavors overwhelm whatever they touch, but you can definitely mix them into your batch. The point is to make eating seeds easier, so go with what tastes great to you! I like to use a jar large enough to store a tablespoon measure in for easy measuring. The oils in seeds can easily go rancid, so store this mix in the fridge or freezer to keep it fresher longer.

Scorecard

✓
Nuts and
Seeds

Hemp, Chia, and Flax Seed Shaker

Makes 1 cup (1 tablespoon per serving)

⅓ cup hemp seeds
⅓ cup chia seeds
⅓ cup flaxseeds

Mix the seeds together in a small bowl or shake in a jar until combined. Cover and store in the fridge or freezer for up to 6 months.

Five-Seed Shaker

Makes 2 cups (1 tablespoon per serving)

½ cup raw hulled pumpkin seeds
½ cup raw hulled sunflower seeds
⅓ cup hemp seeds
⅓ cup chia seeds
⅓ cup flaxseeds

Mix the seeds together in a medium bowl or shake in a jar until combined. Cover and store in the fridge or freezer for up to 6 months.

Ideas for Using Your Seed Shaker

Sprinkle on a steamed sweet potato.

Mix into nut butters.

Fold into cooked breakfast grains.

Mix with mashed fresh berries to top porridge.

Sprinkle over hummus.

Mix into cultured cream cheese and spread on a slice of whole-grain sourdough.

Dates, Seeds, and Peanut Butter

Candy-sweet dates are a great source of soluble fiber, as well as B vitamins, iron, potassium, and magnesium. This five-minute breakfast is one of my go-tos for mornings when I need to get to work quickly, and it's surprisingly filling, usually keeping me set until lunch.

2   tablespoons natural peanut butter

4   large, soft dates, preferably Medjool or Deglet Noor, with their pits

2   tablespoons Seed Shaker (page 180), or your favorite seeds

Spread the peanut butter over a small plate or in a shallow bowl. Remove the pits from the dates, tearing each date in half as you go and setting them on the peanut butter. Sprinkle the seeds on top and eat right away, with your fingers or a fork.

Scorecard

✔✔

Nuts and Seeds

Serves

1

Sesame Matcha Shakes

Something I discovered while developing these recipes is that time is its own ingredient in healthful cooking and can make up for the lack of shortcut ingredients like ice cream. That's the case in this plant-based take on a milk shake. To get that classically creamy texture, you'll freeze a can of coconut milk into ice cubes overnight. That keeps ice from watering down the taste of the shake. I love this recipe so much, I'm often tempted to have it for breakfast. When I want to do that, I add frozen spinach and cut down the dates to just two.

1	(13.5-ounce) can unsweetened light coconut milk
4	large, soft Medjool dates, pitted
2	tablespoons tahini
2	teaspoons culinary-grade matcha powder
¼	teaspoon pure vanilla extract
1½	cups nondairy milk
1	teaspoon black or white sesame seeds, or a mix

Pour the coconut milk into an ice cube tray and freeze for at least 4 hours.

In a blender, combine the frozen coconut milk cubes, dates, tahini, matcha, vanilla, and nondairy milk, adding the nondairy milk last. Blend until smooth and the consistency of a thick shake. Pour into two glasses and sprinkle with the sesame seeds.

Scorecard

✓

Seeds

Serves

2

TIP Keep a tray or two of frozen coconut milk cubes in your freezer to make this whenever you like.

LITTLE BITES: SNACKS, APPS, & DIPS

A good snack isn't just about being healthy for me, but also satiating on a psychological level, too. What I'm saying is, I do not want to just eat carrot sticks for my snack! My all-time favorite snack used to be cheese and tortilla chips—but sadly, they're not the favorite snacks of my gut microbiota. I wanted the snacks and apps in this section to be on the same level: there are sweet snacks to break up a morning slump, savory apps to start out a dinner party with style, and six dips, because dip is always welcome. Dig in.

Papaya and Mango Snack Salad
187

~~~

Sweet Snacks

A lot of the advice around healthful eating is to just "stop eating sweets," as though that could quench the craving in the moment. Fruit is one good option—and the salad of papaya and mango in this chapter answers the desire for something simple but not plain. The banana bread is as healthful as a loaf can get, thanks to a generous serving of oats and dates swapped in for granulated sugar. And finally, as an answer to the ubiquitous energy bar industry, I've included dense, matcha-spiked bites filled with the things you need to tide you over between meals, like seeds, nuts, and dates.

None of these three recipes is quite a meal, but they're not so slight that you will be rummaging in the pantry cabinets after enjoying them.

Papaya and Mango Snack Salad

How can you improve on perfection? With a lime–olive oil dressing. The citrus brightens the tropical fruit, while the olive oil adds healthy fat to increase satiety. Both papaya and mango are great sources of vitamin C, as well as soluble fiber— your microbes will thank you.

1   lime

1   teaspoon olive oil

¼   teaspoon kosher salt

1   small papaya, peeled, halved lengthwise, then seeded and cut into spears

1   just-ripe mango, pitted, peeled, and cut into spears

2   tablespoons unsweetened coconut flakes, toasted

2   tablespoons hemp seeds

    Flaky sea salt (optional)

Zest the lime onto your cutting board or a small plate and set aside. Squeeze 1 tablespoon of juice from the lime into a small bowl. Whisk in the oil and kosher salt until the salt dissolves.

Arrange the papaya and mango on a plate and drizzle with the lime–olive oil sauce. Sprinkle with the coconut flakes, hemp seeds, lime zest, and some flaky sea salt (if you want).

Scorecard

✔✔
Fruit

✔
Nuts and Seeds

Serves
2

THE RECIPES

To toast coconut flakes: Spread on a rimmed baking sheet and bake at 350°F for 3 to 5 minutes, until golden brown and fragrant. Keep an eye on them, as they turn from perfect to burnt in the blink of an eye.

Matcha-Raspberry Energy Bites

One of the easiest ways to get off track from healthful, gut-friendly eating is the snack arena. Most store-bought energy bars are essentially candy dressed up as a meal, not to mention that they contain additives that are harmful to the gut. One or two of these vibrant-colored energy bites will tide you over between meals (thanks to the fiber-rich oats, coconut, and peanut butter they contain) and won't cause a sugar crash. Since matcha has caffeine, though, I don't recommend eating these after two or three p.m. if you're sensitive.

- 1 (1.3-ounce) package freeze-dried raspberries
- ½ cup packed pitted soft Medjool dates (6 to 8 large/4 ounces)
- 1 cup unsweetened finely shredded coconut
- 1 cup packed rolled oats
- ¼ cup culinary-grade matcha powder
- ½ cup natural peanut butter
- ⅓ cup water
- 2 tablespoons chia seeds

Line a small baking sheet (one that will fit in your freezer) with parchment paper.

Place the freeze-dried raspberries in a food processor and process until you have a finely ground powder. Pour into a shallow bowl.

In the food processor (no need to rinse it), combine the dates, coconut, oats, matcha, and 3 tablespoons of the raspberry powder. Process until finely ground, about 1 minute. Add the peanut butter, water, and chia seeds and process until you have a dough that holds together.

Roll the dough into 16 balls (2 table-spoons/1.25 ounces each), then roll each in the remaining raspberry powder. Place on the lined baking sheet and freeze for at least 20 minutes before eating or storing.

To Make Ahead

Refrigerate in an airtight container (with parchment paper between the layers) for up to 4 days or freeze for up to 2 months. They are best right from the fridge or freezer, but you can pack them for an on-the-go snack. No matter what, a little raspberry powder will stick to your fingers, but you can just lick it off!

Scorecard

✔

Nuts and Seeds

Makes

16

THE RECIPES

Double Oat and Almond Banana Bread

In the age of the internet and social media, it's big bucks to call something healthy, whether that's true or not. But this banana bread *is* legitimately healthy: there's no added sugar, just sweetness from soft Medjool dates, plus a hefty serving of whole plant fiber in each slice thanks to the almond flour, bananas, and fiber-rich oats. It also happens to be gluten-free, without relying on a store-bought flour substitute (since those are packed with stabilizers that are hard on the gut). I toast slices until crispy and serve with cultured butter or peanut butter.

Scorecard

✔

Whole Grains

Makes

1

8½ by 4½-inch loaf (twelve ¾-inch thick slices)

½   cup mild-flavored oil or melted, unsalted butter, plus more for the pan

1¼   cups oat flour (6 ounces), plus more for the pan

⅓   cup packed pitted Medjool dates (3.75 ounces/about 5 large)

½   cup boiling water

2¼   packed cups mashed overripe bananas (1¼ pounds prepped)

3   large eggs, at room temperature

2   teaspoons pure vanilla extract

1   cup quick-cooking oats (4.5 ounces)

1   cup almond flour (4.5 ounces)

¼   cup arrowroot starch (1.25 ounces)

1½   teaspoons baking powder

1   teaspoon kosher salt

¼   teaspoon ground nutmeg

3   tablespoons rolled oats (or additional quick-cooking oats), for topping

Preheat your oven to 350°F. Brush an 8½ by 4½-inch loaf pan with oil. Line it with parchment paper across the wide side, then brush the parchment with oil, dust it with oat flour, and tap out any excess. I like to crease the paper so it doesn't curl into the batter as it bakes.

Combine the dates and boiling water in a blender. Let sit for 10 minutes..

Blend the dates a little to chop them, then add the bananas, oil, eggs, and vanilla to the blender and process on the lowest speed until just combined. Pour the banana mixture into a large bowl (use a flexible spatula to get every last bit).

In a medium bowl, whisk together the oat flour, quick-cooking oats, almond flour, arrowroot starch, baking powder, salt, and nutmeg. Fold the flour mixture into the wet ingredients until combined. Scrape the batter into the prepared pan and smooth out the top. Sprinkle the rolled oats evenly over the top of the batter.

Bake for 60 to 70 minutes, until a toothpick inserted into the center of the loaf comes out with just a few crumbs attached. Let cool in the pan for 15 minutes, then turn the loaf out onto a wire rack to cool completely. (Do not cut until fully cooled.) If the loaf is sticking to the pan, run a knife or an offset spatula around the edges to release.

STEP-BY-STEP PHOTOS ON THE NEXT PAGE

To Store

Store at room temperature, well wrapped, for up to 3 days. To freeze the loaf, cut it into twelve ¼-inch-thick slices and stack them in a zip-top bag with a piece of parchment paper between each slice; seal and freeze for up to 2 months.

Measure out all your ingredients before getting started.

Prep the pan.

Mash the bananas well in a bowl with a fork or potato masher.

Soak the dates and get your wet ingredients ready.

Blend the dates to chop them up a little, then blend in the rest of the wet ingredients.

Pour the mixture into a large bowl (use a flexible spatula to get every last bit out of the blender jar).

Whisk together the dry ingredients and pour over the banana mixture.

Fold until just combined.

Scrape the batter into the prepared pan. Sprinkle the rolled oats over the top.

10 Bake, cool completely, and then slice.

TIPS

• Bananas vary wildly in the amount they yield once mashed, especially as they move from yellow to overripe. My suggestion is to buy an entire bunch of bananas (6 or 7) and let them ripen at once. Whatever you don't use for this recipe, you can freeze and defrost for future batches.

• It's so much easier (and more accurate) to make this recipe by using a digital scale, which is why I've included ingredient weights. If you don't have a scale or would rather use a cup measure, use the scoop-and-level method to get even, packed cups. With such a variety of ingredients it's more reliable than the spoon-and-level method.

• I think rolled oats are much prettier for the top, but if you only have quick-cooking on hand, those will taste exactly the same!

• Do not blend the banana-egg mixture too long, or the bread will become rubbery and tough.

• Set the loaf pan on a rimmed baking sheet for easy transfer in and out of the oven.

~

Apps to Start a Meal

Could these pass the dinner party test? That was the criterion I kept in mind while creating the four recipes that follow. If I could present these recipes without the caveat of their healthful status and they were eaten with abandon by my guests, then I knew they were a keeper.

When all else fails, my go-to party app is cukes and Castelvetranos (pictured at right): Sprinkle spears of Persian cucumbers with flaky sea salt and serve them with a dish of unpitted Castelvetrano olives. If you can't find Castelvetranos, Cerignola olives are a decent substitute.

Chickpea Hush Puppies
with Herb Dip

Frequent fried food isn't great for your gut. But my approach is about long-term sustainability, which includes your sense of overall well-being, and sometimes that includes a crispy treat. When I want something that hits that craving for fried food, these hush puppies are a great option. Not to mention that you get over 6 grams of fiber in one serving, which your gut will thank you for. They have a tender interior thanks to the chickpea flour and a crisp crust from the cornmeal.

Serves
6 to 8
as an
appetizer

For the herb dip
½   cup packed fresh cilantro leaves and stems
½   cup vegan mayo
1   tablespoon lemon juice

For the hush puppies
1½   cups cooked chickpeas (see page 124), or 1 (15.5-ounce) can, drained and rinsed
1   large egg
½   cup cultured buttermilk, plus more if needed
½   cup finely chopped onion (from 1 small)
1   cup fine or medium cornmeal
½   cup chickpea (garbanzo bean) flour
2   teaspoons baking powder
1   teaspoon kosher salt
⅛   teaspoon cayenne pepper
3   cups grapeseed, vegetable, or canola oil, for frying

Make the herb dip Combine the cilantro, mayo, and lemon juice in a mini food processor or a blender. Process until smooth. Transfer to a bowl, cover, and refrigerate while you make the hush puppies.

Make the hush puppies Line a baking sheet with parchment paper.

Place the chickpeas in a large bowl and mash well with a potato masher until there are no large pieces remaining. Whisk in the egg, buttermilk, and onion.

In a separate medium bowl, whisk together the cornmeal, chickpea flour, baking powder, salt, and cayenne, then fold into the chickpea mixture until you have a thick dough. Form the dough into 22 heaping tablespoon-size balls and set them on the prepared baking sheet.

Fit a straight-sided medium pot with a candy thermometer. Pour in the oil and heat until it reaches 350°F. Working in batches, add the dough balls to the hot oil and fry until golden brown and crisp, 2 to 3 minutes, using a slotted spoon to turn them as they fry. Transfer the hush puppies to a paper towel–lined plate to drain. Repeat to fry the remaining hush puppies. Serve hot, with the herb dip alongside.

Get-Ahead TIP You can make the dough and shape the balls up to a day in advance. Just drape a clean dish towel over the baking sheet and store them in the refrigerator to fry and serve the next day.

THE RECIPES

Le Petit Aioli

Tucked behind an unassuming storefront in Cobble Hill, Brooklyn, is June, one of my favorite wine bars. The interior is dark enough for promising first dates; the backyard has string lights for long, wine-fueled catch-ups with friends; and it has a good vibe for business meetings. The rotating selection of natural wines is always on point, but while I vary what I drink at June, I never vary my food order. When they have it, I get their Le Petit Aioli—a colorful platter of cooked and raw seasonal vegetables with a generous pot of aioli for dipping. I'm hardly aware that I've eaten a platter of vegetables because the aioli is so sumptuous. This is my re-creation of that delicious meal, with my favorite dipping elements suggested on the next page.

Scorecard for appetizers

✔
LGVs

✔✔
Other Veg

**Serves
4 to 6**
as an
appetizer or
2 as a meal

1   small head cauliflower (about 1 pound), cut into small florets

1   tablespoon preferred cooking oil

½   teaspoon kosher salt

½   teaspoon freshly ground black pepper

1   pound fingerling potatoes

1   recipe Roasted Garlic Aioli (page 211)

1   head radicchio, quartered lengthwise and leaves separated

4   small, young carrots, scrubbed well and halved lengthwise

8   radishes, halved (or quartered, if large)

Plant-based Option

Doctor up your favorite vegan mayo with lemon juice and roasted garlic using the instructions on page 211.

To Store

The entire recipe (including the aioli) can be made up to 2 days in advance. Store the raw vegetables in a container loosely covered with a damp towel, and the cooked vegetables and aioli in separate airtight containers. When ready to serve, assemble as directed.

Preheat your oven to 400°F. On a rimmed baking sheet, toss the cauliflower with the, oil, salt, and pepper. Roast, tossing once, until golden brown and tender but not soft, 16 to 20 minutes. Remove from the oven and let cool.

Meanwhile, fill a large pot with 1 inch of water and put a steamer insert inside. Cover and bring the water to a simmer. Add the potatoes, re-cover, and steam until you can stick a fork easily into the center of a potato, 16 to 22 minutes, depending on the size of the potatoes. Let cool completely, then halve the potatoes lengthwise.

Spoon the aioli into a shallow bowl and set it on a platter. Arrange the vegetables around the bowl, nestling them in tightly so everything fits.

DIY Your Aioli Platter

My formula for the perfect vegetable platter is as follows: I like one steamed or blanched, one roasted, one raw, and one bitter lettuce-y-type thing like radicchio or endive (which are easy on the gut), plus radishes for their fresh, peppery bite. If turning on the oven feels like a chore, then just skip the roasted cauliflower and serve another raw veg. I don't use spices on the vegetables so nothing competes with the amazing homemade aioli.

Roasted Pepper and Aioli Flatbread

I never want my dinner guests to leave the party only to pick up food on the way home. But when I switched to a plant-focused way of eating, I worried that would be the case. So I set out to develop amazing, party-worthy recipes that are decadent, not subtle. Enter this flatbread recipe, slathered with homemade aioli and topped with smoky roasted peppers. People love how satisfyingly dense the flatbread is, and no one questions that it's a chickpea base, not a bread one.

Scorecard

✔
Other Veg

✔
Beans and
Legumes

Serves
8 to 10
as an
appetizer

2 pounds baby bell peppers

2 tablespoons preferred cooking oil

1½ teaspoons smoked paprika

1 teaspoon kosher salt

½ teaspoon freshly ground black pepper

1 cup Roasted Garlic Aioli (page 211) or vegan mayo

1 recipe Chickpea Flatbread (page 123)

2 tablespoons finely chopped fresh parsley

Flaky sea salt (optional)

Tip Start with flatbread fresh from the oven or reheated until hot while the peppers roast.

Preheat your oven to 425°F. Toss the peppers on a rimmed baking sheet with the oil, paprika, salt, and black pepper. Roast on the bottom rack, tossing once, until the peppers are tender and dark brown in spots, 30 to 35 minutes.

Remove the peppers from the oven. When they're cool enough to handle, pull off and discard the stems.

Spread the aioli over the flatbread, leaving a ½-inch border. Top with the roasted peppers in an even layer, then sprinkle with the parsley and some flaky sea salt (if you want). Cut into squares to serve.

THE RECIPES

Fork-and-Knife Wedge Salad
with Crispy Mushrooms and Faux Caesar

You might be surprised that a book that's about healthy eating isn't full of salad recipes, but this recipe is one of only three salads in this entire book. This is because lots of raw roughage can be difficult to digest as you shift to a plant-focused way of eating. So, most of the time, cooked vegetables are the name of the game, at least while you're adjusting to eating more dietary fiber.

I'm not going to pretend it's bacon, but slicing oyster mushrooms into planks and cooking them until crisp adds intense savory flavor to the dish, and the fish sauce in the Faux Caesar doubles down on the umami.

Scorecard

✓
LGVs

✓
Other Veg

Serves

4

as an
appetizer

3 tablespoons preferred cooking oil

1¼ pounds trumpet mushrooms, sliced lengthwise into ¼-inch-thick planks

1 teaspoon kosher salt

4 small heads Little Gem lettuce, or 2 heads Bibb lettuce, cut lengthwise into thin wedges

½ to ¾ cup Faux Caesar (page 135)

4 large radishes (4 ounces total), cut into matchsticks

1 tablespoon sesame seeds

Flaky sea salt (optional)

Freshly ground black pepper

In your largest nonstick skillet, heat half the oil over medium-high heat. Add half the mushrooms and ½ teaspoon of the salt. Cook, turning occasionally, until golden brown and deeply crispy, about 10 minutes total. Transfer to a paper towel–lined plate, then repeat with the remaining oil, mushrooms, and ½ teaspoon salt.

Divide the lettuce among four shallow bowls or large plates. Drizzle the dressing over the lettuce, then top with the mushrooms, radishes, and sesame seeds. Sprinkle with some flaky sea salt, if you want, and a few grinds of fresh pepper.

Six Delicious Dips

Strong opinion alert: The best person to be at any party is the dip bringer—a title I love to claim whenever I can. Rather than toting over a glorified tub of sour cream (which is delicious, don't get me wrong), I now create dips that celebrate their vegetable ingredients rather than masking them. And of course there is one classic, hot, bubbling baked dip in this section, but with a generous serving of artichokes to please your gut microbes, too.

I suggest serving these dips with your favorite crackers and a mixture of dipping vegetables. It's all about crunch when it comes to crudités. I like bitter but tender leaves like endive, Treviso, or radicchio, spears of Persian cucumbers, and segments of celery. Carrots and radishes also good dippers, but their flavor can overwhelm a dip.

As for crackers, the main concern is that they aren't ultraprocessed. Look for one made with ingredients you can pronounce, and no additives or stabilizers. Because so many people are sensitive to gluten when their guts are out of whack, I generally serve gluten-free crackers—there are so many good ones out there now. My favorites are the ones heavy on seeds, which add texture and can stand up to a hearty serving, or long, pretty mild-flavored planks that don't compete with the dip.

Beet, Avocado, and Pistachio Dip 210

Caramelized Onion Dip 208

Kabocha Squash and Tahini Dip 209

Baked Smoked Trout, Artichoke, and Chive Dip

Artichokes are a great source of prebiotic fiber, the beloved food of your gut microbes! This inspired me to make a healthyish take on classic artichoke dip—with double the normal quantity of artichokes, plus deliciously salty smoked trout (which also makes this dip quite high in vitamin D). While heat generally kills beneficial microbes in fermented food, I still call for cultured crème fraîche and cream cheese, just in case any of them survive the trek to your gut. If you want to maximize the benefit of the fermented dairy, omit the baking—this dip is quite tasty at room temperature.

Serves 10 to 12 as an appetizer

2   tablespoons olive oil, plus more for the baking dish

2   (14-ounce) cans quartered marinated artichoke hearts, drained

8   ounces smoked trout, skin removed, flaked fine

1   (8-ounce) package cultured cream cheese, at room temperature

1   cup cultured crème fraîche

⅓   cup chopped fresh chives, plus more for sprinkling

3   tablespoons lemon juice

½   teaspoon freshly ground black pepper, plus more as needed

¼   teaspoon flaky sea salt (optional)

Vegetables such as endive leaves, carrots, bell peppers, and celery, for serving

Get-Ahead TiP The dip can be prepared and transferred to the dish up to a day in advance. Just cover and store the unbaked dip in the fridge. If you bake it straight from the fridge, it'll take a bit longer in the oven.

Preheat your oven to 350°F with a rack in the center position. Brush a shallow 1-quart baking dish with oil.

In a medium bowl, fold together the artichoke hearts, smoked trout, cream cheese, crème fraîche, chives, lemon juice, and pepper until completely combined.

Scrape the artichoke mixture into the prepared baking dish and smooth the top. Set the baking dish on a rimmed baking sheet (to make it easy to maneuver). Bake until the dip is hot and the edges are golden brown, 35 to 40 minutes. Remove the dip from the oven and switch the oven to broil.

Brush the top of the dip with the 2 tablespoons oil. Sprinkle with the flaky sea salt (if you want) and grind some pepper over top. Return the dip to the oven and broil for 5 minutes, or until golden brown.

Sprinkle the dip with chives and serve with vegetables alongside.

THE RECIPES

Caramelized Onion Dip

I've seen a lot of plant-based recipes that call for tofu or cashews to make a healthy caramelized onion dip. I understand the goal, which is to approximate creaminess, but for me, the act of putting something decidedly UN-creamy like a cashew into a savory dip just doesn't appeal. Instead, I rely on my good friend vegan mayo to add creaminess, and for the traditional tang, lemon juice plays off the sweet onions. Of course, you can use cultured sour cream, too.

Properly caramelized onions take a bit of time to get to the ideal state, but if you don't have enough time to let them do their thing low and slow (a mostly hands-off approach), you can crank the heat up to high, stir constantly, and add water as needed to keep the onions from sticking and burning. This shortcut method should take 15 to 20 minutes.

Scorecard

✔

Other Veg

Serves

8 to 10

as an appetizer

2 tablespoons preferred cooking oil

3 pounds yellow onions (about 8 large), thinly sliced

1¾ teaspoons kosher salt

¾ teaspoon freshly ground black pepper, plus more for garnish

½ cup vegan mayo or cultured sour cream

¼ cup finely chopped fresh chives, plus a little extra for garnish

2 tablespoons lemon juice

⅛ teaspoon cayenne pepper

Your favorite dipping vegetables and seeded crackers, for serving

Get-Ahead Tip

You can cook the onions up to 3 days before serving and store them in an airtight container in the fridge. Stir in the remaining ingredients just before serving.

In a large pot, heat the oil over medium-high heat. Add the onions, 1 teaspoon of the salt, and ¼ teaspoon of the black pepper. Cook, stirring occasionally and making sure to scrape up any caramelized bits from the bottom of the pot, until the onions are incredibly soft and brown, 35 to 45 minutes. If the onions are starting to burn, add 1 tablespoon water at a time and stir and scrape well, adding up to ¼ cup water as needed over the course of cooking. Transfer the onions to a medium bowl and let cool slightly. You should have around 1¼ cups.

Add the mayo, chives, lemon juice, cayenne, remaining ¾ teaspoon salt, and remaining ½ teaspoon black pepper to the bowl with the onions and stir well to combine.

Spoon the dip into a serving dish, then top with some chives and a few grinds of black pepper. Serve with vegetables and crackers.

Kabocha Squash and Tahini Dip

The color of this gorgeous, bright orange dip tells you right away that it's high in beta-carotene, an essential component of vitamin A. You can also roast the squash as described on page 308. Keep any extra squash for a Spinach and Squash Smoothie (page 173).

Scorecard

✔

Other Veg

Serves

6 to 8

as an
appetizer

THE RECIPES

1 (2-pound) kabocha squash or baking pumpkin like kuri

5 tablespoons water

¼ cup tahini

2 tablespoons lemon juice

⅓ cup olive oil, plus more for drizzling

½ teaspoon Aleppo pepper flakes or crushed red pepper, plus a few flakes for garnish, if desired

1½ teaspoons kosher salt

Flaky sea salt (optional)

Your favorite dipping vegetables and crackers, for serving

Steam the squash Cut the squash in half, then scoop out the seeds (reserve the seeds, if you like to roast and eat them; otherwise, compost them). Cut the halves in half again.

Fill a large pot with 1 inch of water and put a steamer insert inside. Bring the water to a simmer, add the squash, and steam until you can stick a fork very easily into the flesh, 25 to 30 minutes.

Make the dip Scoop the flesh of the squash into a bowl (I don't use the skin for this dip, but you can if you don't mind the texture). Transfer 2 cups of the squash to a food processor and reserve the rest for another use.

Add the water, tahini, lemon juice, oil, Aleppo pepper, and salt to the food processor. Process until smooth and well combined.

Transfer the dip to a serving bowl. Drizzle with some more oil and sprinkle with flaky sea salt and more Aleppo pepper, if you want. Serve warm or at room temperature, with vegetables and crackers.

To Store

Refrigerate the dip in an airtight container for up to 3 days. Bring to room temperature before serving.

Beet, Avocado, and Pistachio Dip

This dip is a creamy wonder, thanks to the steamed beets and avocado, which both have a puddinglike texture when pureed. I was surprised that this dip just might my favorite of the bunch in this book—not only is the vivid magenta color appealing, the taste is complex and modern.

You can also make this dip with store-bought steamed beets. Microwave them until warm before pureeing.

10 ounces beets (about 2 small), scrubbed well

1 large avocado

½ cup raw unsalted pistachios, plus a few for sprinkling

3 tablespoons olive oil, plus more for drizzling

3 tablespoons lime juice

1 tablespoon water

½ teaspoon kosher salt

Your favorite dipping vegetables and crackers, for serving

Fill a large pot with 1 inch of water and put a steamer insert inside. Cover and bring the water to a simmer. Add the beets, re-cover, and steam until you can stick a fork very easily into the center of a beet, 35 to 45 minutes, depending on the size of the beets. Let the beets cool slightly, then slip the skins off.

In a blender or food processor, combine the beets, avocado, pistachios, oil, lime juice, water, and salt. Blend on high until smooth.

Spoon the dip into a serving dish, then top with pistachios and a drizzle of olive oil. Serve with vegetables and crackers.

To Store

Refrigerate the dip in an airtight container for up to 3 days. Bring to room temperature before serving.

Scorecard

✓
Other Veg

✓
Nuts and Seeds

Serves

8

as an appetizer

Roasted Garlic Aioli

Ooooh, aioli. Is there a better food in this world? This isn't the most traditional rendition—I've zinged it up with some lemon, but I like it here to balance the oil, and it also results in a silkier texture. While most dips are better at room temperature, I prefer the aioli cold, which makes this recipe even better for making ahead. Roasting the garlic makes it easier on your digestion, while still preserving the prebiotic fiber that the microbes in your gut love.

Makes
1½
cups
(2 tablespoons
per serving)

2   large heads garlic

½   cup grapeseed oil

1¼ teaspoons kosher salt

    Freshly ground black pepper

2   large egg yolks

½   cup olive oil

2   tablespoons lemon juice

Roast the garlic Preheat your oven to 400°F.

Pull any loose, papery peels from the outside of the garlic heads, then trim ¼ inch off the top of each with a serrated knife. Pull 1 large clove out and save it for later. Set the garlic heads cut-side up on a sheet of aluminum foil. Drizzle them with 1 tablespoon of the grapeseed oil and sprinkle with ¼ teaspoon of the salt. Wrap the foil around the garlic to enclose the heads and stick them right on a rack in the oven or place them on a baking sheet. Roast for 45 minutes to 1 hour, until the cloves are deep golden brown and very soft. Let cool.

Make the aioli Place a damp kitchen towel underneath a medium bowl. Slip the roasted garlic cloves out of their skins into the bowl; discard the skins. Chop the reserved raw garlic clove and add it to the bowl. Add the remaining 1 teaspoon salt and use a fork to mash everything together into a smooth paste.

Whisk the egg yolks into the paste. While whisking continuously, very slowly drizzle in the remaining grapeseed oil (it's helpful to ask someone else to drizzle in the oil, if you can) and whisk until you have a thick emulsion (it'll look like mayo). While whisking, steadily stream in the olive oil. Finally, whisk in the lemon juice. Season to taste with salt and pepper.

To Store

Refrigerate the aioli in an airtight container for up to 2 days.

Plant-based option

Roast the garlic according to the recipe, then whisk in 1 cup vegan mayo and the lemon juice, and season with salt and pepper.

THE RECIPES

Whipped Cauliflower and Harissa Dip **with Herb Oil and Sesame Seeds**

I brought this dip to a few potlucks and didn't mention that it was 100% plant-based. Even placed next to a cheese-and-meat board, it was gone first! The key to the deep flavor is roasting the cauliflower until it's deeply caramelized and soft. This gives the florets a delicious umami flavor, which infuses the dip with that "why the heck is this so delicious?" taste.

Scorecard
✔
Other Veg

Serves
6 to 8
as an appetizer

For the cauliflower dip

- 6 cups (1¾ pounds) small cauliflower florets (from 1 medium head)
- 2 tablespoons preferred cooking oil
- 2 teaspoons ground coriander
- 1¼ teaspoons kosher salt, plus more as needed
- ½ teaspoon freshly ground black pepper, plus more as needed
- 2 tablespoons lemon juice
- ¼ cup tahini
- 2 tablespoons water
- 1 teaspoon harissa paste

For the herb oil

- 2 tablespoons chopped fresh parsley
- 2 tablespoons chopped fresh cilantro
- 2 tablespoons olive oil
- 2 tablespoons lemon juice
- 1 tablespoon sesame seeds
- 1 tablespoon toasted sesame oil
- 1 garlic clove, mashed into a paste
- ¼ teaspoon kosher salt

To serve

- Flaky sea salt
- Your favorite dipping vegetables and crackers

Make the cauliflower dip Preheat your oven to 425°F.

Toss the cauliflower on a rimmed baking sheet with the olive oil, coriander, 1 teaspoon of the salt, and the pepper. Roast, tossing once, until the cauliflower is very soft and golden brown, 30 to 35 minutes. Transfer all but a few of the prettiest florets to a food processor.

Add the lemon juice, tahini, water, ½ teaspoon of the harissa, and remaining ¼ teaspoon salt to the food processor and process until smooth, at least 1 minute. Taste and adjust the seasoning.

Transfer the cauliflower dip to a serving bowl, then use a pastry brush to spread the remaining ½ teaspoon harissa over the dip.

Make the herb oil In a small bowl, stir together the parsley, cilantro, olive oil, lemon juice, sesame seeds, sesame oil, garlic, and salt. (If you want a smoother sauce, combine the ingredients in a mini food processor and process until smooth.)

Assemble the dip Drizzle the dip with the herb oil, top with the reserved cauliflower florets, and sprinkle with flaky sea salt. Serve with vegetables and gluten-free crackers.

Get-Ahead

Tip

You can make the dip up to 3 days ahead and refrigerate it in an airtight container (the herb oil must be prepared just before serving). Bring the dip to room temperature and top it with the herb oil before serving.

SOUPS & STEWS

Soups are a sort of healthful meal in disguise—chock-full of vegetables while also signaling comfort. That's why they're such a great option to start with when you're adjusting to more plant-focused eating.

Since these soups are loaded with lots of plant fiber, I like to give my gut a hand with extra fiber-loving microbes from miso: Just before eating, place 1 tablespoon miso paste in a small bowl, then ladle in 2 tablespoons of your soup. Whisk until smooth, then pour the mixture over your bowl. This allows the microbes to stay alive, since adding them to the hot pot would kill them off. (If you do this, check off one Fermented Food box on your scorecard, page 342.)

Vegetarian Chili with Poblanos and Hominy 216

Vegetarian Chili
with Poblanos and Hominy

This recipe started with a question: How do you make a plant-focused chili that satisfies as much as any meat version would? My solution was to use some Tex-Mex elements: charred poblanos, canned chiles, and hominy. I love the nutty flavor that hominy adds, but some people don't tolerate corn well. If this is the case for you, substitute beans or canned tomatoes for the hominy. (This will change the consistency of the chili a fair amount.)

As any true chili lover knows, it's equally important to go big on the toppings. I've listed my favorites, including a splash of cultured sour cream or kefir to get some beneficial microbes, but you can skip that if you want a 100 percent plant-based meal.

Scorecard

✔
Beans and Legumes

✔
Other Veg

Serves
4 to 6

For the chili

- 3 poblano peppers
- 3 tablespoons olive oil
- 2 large onions, chopped
- 5 garlic cloves, chopped
- 2 teaspoons chili powder
- 1 teaspoon dried oregano
- 1 teaspoon ground cumin
- 1½ teaspoons kosher salt, plus more as needed
- 1½ teaspoons freshly ground black pepper, plus more as needed
- ¼ cup tomato paste
- 2 (4-ounce) cans chopped green chiles
- 6 cups Trash or Treasure Broth (page 129) or high-quality store-bought broth
- 3 cups hominy (from one 25-ounce can), drained and rinsed
- 3 cups cooked pinto beans (see page 124), or 2 (15.5-ounce) cans, drained and rinsed
- 2 tablespoons lime juice

For serving

Ripe avocado

Cultured sour cream or kefir (omit if you're eating plant-based)

Pickled hot peppers or jalapeños

Fresh cilantro

Lime wedges

Flaky sea salt (optional)

Use tongs to char the poblanos over a gas flame until blistered and black, turning to get every side, 8 to 10 minutes total. (If you don't have a gas stove, preheat your broiler to high and char the peppers on a baking sheet, turning them to char all sides.) Place the peppers in a bowl and cover with plastic wrap; let steam for 5 minutes. Slip the skins off, halve the peppers, discard the seeds, and chop.

In a large pot, heat the oil over medium-high heat. Add the peppers, onions, garlic, chili powder, oregano, cumin, 1 teaspoon of the salt, and 1 teaspoon of the black pepper. Cook, stirring occasionally, until the onions are golden brown and tender, 10 to 12 minutes.

Stir in the tomato paste and chiles and cook, stirring continuously and scraping any caramelized spices off the bottom of the pot, until any excess moisture has evaporated, about 2 minutes.

Stir in the broth, bring to a boil, then reduce the heat to maintain a simmer. Add the hominy, beans, and the remaining ½ teaspoon each salt and black pepper. Cook until heated through and the liquid is thick and chili-like, about 30 minutes. Stir in the lime juice. Taste the soup and season with salt and black pepper.

Serve the chili topped with avocado, sour cream, pickled peppers, and cilantro, with a squeeze of lime juice and some flaky sea salt, if you want.

To Store

Refrigerate the soup in an airtight container for up to 4 days, or freeze for up to 2 months.

Spiced Carrot Soup
with Coconut Cream

This recipe turns the humblest of kitchen ingredients—carrots, onions, and celery—into a spicy, delicious soup that's greater than the sum of its parts. Coconut milk complements the sweetness of the carrots, while ginger adds a fiery kick to ground the flavors. Get artsy and decorate the top of each bowl with a pretty swoosh of coconut milk and a sprinkling of pumpkin seeds.

- 2 tablespoons coconut oil
- 2 pounds carrots, scrubbed and sliced (you can use a food processor to slice them)
- 1 large onion, chopped
- 2 celery stalks, thinly sliced
- ¼ cup peeled and chopped fresh ginger (2 ounces)
- 1¼ teaspoons kosher salt, plus more as needed
- ½ teaspoon freshly ground black pepper, plus more as needed
- 2 teaspoons ground turmeric
- 2 teaspoons ground cumin
- 2 teaspoons ground coriander
- 6 cups Trash or Treasure Broth (page 129) or high-quality store-bought broth
- 1 (13.5-ounce) can unsweetened coconut milk
- 2 tablespoons lime juice
- ¼ to ⅓ cup raw hulled pumpkin seeds
- 2 tablespoons canned coconut cream
  Flaky sea salt (optional)

In a large pot, melt the coconut oil over medium-high heat. Add the carrots, onion, celery, ginger, ¾ teaspoon of the salt, and the pepper. Cook, stirring occasionally with a flexible spatula and scraping the bottom, until the vegetables are soft, 12 to 14 minutes. You should hear gentle sizzling; if you don't, the heat is too low.

Add the turmeric, cumin, and coriander and cook until the spices are fragrant, about 2 minutes. Stir in the broth, coconut milk, and remaining ½ teaspoon salt. Bring to a boil, then reduce the heat to maintain a simmer. Cook until the carrots are very soft, about 20 minutes. Working in batches, transfer to a blender and puree, or use an immersion blender directly in the pot. Stir in the lime juice. Taste and season with salt.

Ladle the soup into bowls and top with the pumpkin seeds, coconut cream, and a few grinds of pepper. Sprinkle with flaky sea salt, if you want, and serve.

To Store

Refrigerate the soup in an airtight container for up to 4 days, or freeze for up to 2 months.

Scorecard

✓
Other Veg

✓
Nuts and Seeds

Serves
4 to 6

TIP

If you want, you can toast the pumpkin seeds in a skillet over medium heat until golden brown and nutty-smelling, 3 to 5 minutes.

To Store

I recommend eating this soup right away, but if you do have leftovers, remove the meatballs from the liquid and store the meatballs and soup in separate airtight containers in the fridge for up to 3 days.

Spiced Lamb Meatball and Escarole Soup

This soup was inspired by the flavors of intensely spiced lamb shawarma and the components of Italian wedding soup (subbing beans for the traditional pasta). If you prefer another green like Swiss chard, collards, or beet greens, use those instead.

Scorecard

✔

LGVs

Serves

4 to 6

1¼ pounds ground lamb

3 large garlic cloves, minced

1 tablespoon ground coriander

1 tablespoon ground cumin

2 teaspoons dried oregano

2 teaspoons ground turmeric

½ teaspoon paprika

2¾ teaspoons kosher salt, plus more as needed

1¼ teaspoons freshly ground black pepper

2 tablespoons preferred cooking oil

2 large onions, sliced

¼ cup tomato paste

8 cups Trash or Treasure Broth (page 129) or high-quality store-bought broth

1 large head escarole, torn into 2-inch pieces

1½ cups cooked gigante or cannellini beans (see page 124) or 1 (15.5-ounce) can, drained and rinsed

Flaky sea salt (optional)

Lemon wedges, for serving

Make the meatballs In a large bowl, mix the lamb, garlic, coriander, cumin, oregano, turmeric, paprika, 1 teaspoon of the salt, and 1 teaspoon of the pepper. Pinch off 1 ounce (2 scant tablespoons) of the lamb mixture at a time and gently roll it into a ball with your hands. Place on a plate and repeat with the remaining lamb mixture.

Sear the meatballs In a large pot, heat the oil over medium-high heat. Add the meatballs and cook until golden brown and crispy on all sides, 7 to 9 minutes. Transfer to a plate. Pour off 3 tablespoons of the fat from the pan.

Get the soup going Add the onions, ¼ teaspoon of the salt, and the remaining ¼ teaspoon pepper to the fat remaining in the pot. Cook over medium high heat, stirring often, until the onions are golden and everything is softened, 8 to 10 minutes. Add the tomato paste and cook, stirring continuously, for 1 minute to cook off the raw tomato flavor. Add the broth and 1 teaspoon salt and bring to a boil.

Finish the soup Add the escarole, beans, meatballs, and remaining ¼ teaspoon salt and return the soup to a simmer. Cook until the escarole has wilted and the meatballs have cooked through, 4 to 6 minutes more. Taste and season with salt and pepper.

Serve Ladle into bowls, sprinkle with flaky sea salt (if you want), and serve with a lemon wedge alongside.

THE RECIPES

Fennel, Parsnip, and Apple Soup

Softly sweet, comforting, and delicious—that's what this easy soup is all about. If you're just getting used to eating lots of vegetables or are repairing a sensitive gut, this is a great recipe to start with because the process of deeply cooking and then pureeing breaks down a lot of the tough plant fibers, but the good microbes in your gut still get the indigestible carbohydrates they need to thrive.

3 tablespoons olive oil, plus a little for drizzling

2 large fennel bulbs (1½ pounds total), chopped small, a few fronds reserved for garnish

4 parsnips (1½ pounds total), chopped small

3 small apples (1 pound total), cored and chopped small

1 cup water

2 tablespoons fresh sage leaves

1 tablespoon grated fresh ginger

1½ teaspoons ground coriander

2 teaspoons kosher salt

¾ teaspoon freshly ground black pepper, plus more as needed

8 cups Trash or Treasure Broth (page 129) or high-quality store-bought broth

3 tablespoons apple cider vinegar

Flaky sea salt (optional)

In a large pot, heat the oil over medium-high heat. Add the fennel, parsnips, apples, water, sage, ginger, coriander, 1 teaspoon salt, and the pepper. Cook, stirring occasionally, until the apples are mushy and the liquid has evaporated, 6 to 8 minutes.

Stir in the broth, bring to a boil, then reduce the heat to maintain a simmer and cook until the parsnips are completely soft, about 20 minutes more.

Working in batches, transfer to a blender and puree, or use an immersion blender directly in the pot. Stir in the vinegar and remaining 1 teaspoon salt. Adjust the seasoning to taste.

Ladle into bowls and top with a drizzle of oil, a few fennel fronds, a couple grinds of pepper, and some flaky sea salt (if you want).

To Store

Refrigerate the soup in an airtight container for up to 4 days, or freeze for up to 2 months.

Scorecard

✔✔
Other Veg

Serves

4 to 6

THE RECIPES

Cauliflower and Sunchoke Soup

There's a beige-on-beige soup situation going on here, but don't let that deter you. A long simmer with nutmeg coaxes out maximum flavor from these humble ingredients.

The sunchoke skins are a great source of fiber for the friendly creatures in your gut, so don't peel them—just scrub them well to remove any dirt before cooking. Sunchokes have a reputation for causing some gastrointestinal distress in people who are adjusting to eating more plant fiber. Skip this one if your digestion is sensitive.

Scorecard

Other Veg

Serves
4 to 6

- 2 tablespoons preferred cooking oil
- 4 garlic cloves, minced
- 1 medium head cauliflower (1½ pounds), cut into very small florets
- 1¼ pounds sunchokes, well scrubbed and thinly sliced
- 2 large onions, chopped
- 3 celery stalks, thinly sliced
- ¼ teaspoon freshly grated nutmeg
- 1½ teaspoons kosher salt, plus more as needed
- 1 teaspoon freshly ground black pepper, plus more as needed
- 8 cups Trash or Treasure broth (page 129) or high-quality store-bought broth
- 3 tablespoons lemon juice

For serving

Chopped toasted hazelnuts

Fresh parsley leaves

Flaky sea salt

Lemon wedges

Heat the oil in a large pot over medium-high heat. Add the garlic and cook until fragrant, 30 seconds to 1 minute.

Add the cauliflower, sunchokes, onions, celery, nutmeg, salt, and pepper. Cook, stirring occasionally, until the vegetables are soft, 12 to 14 minutes. Add the broth and bring to a boil. Reduce the heat to maintain a simmer and cook until everything can be easily mashed with a fork, 15 to 20 minutes more.

Working in batches, transfer to a blender and puree, or use an immersion blender directly in the pot. Stir in the lemon juice. Taste and season with salt and pepper to your liking.

Serve topped with hazelnuts, parsley, and a sprinkling of flaky sea salt, with lemon wedges alongside.

To Store

Refrigerate the soup in an airtight container for up to 4 days, or freeze for up to 2 months.

Lemony Chicken and Quinoa Soup with Pesto

Think of this recipe as "Chicken Soup for the Gut." It still hits that delicious, homey chicken soup note, but with quinoa instead of noodles, and leeks—which are prebiotic fiber superstars—for happy microbes. Leftovers soak up the stock, so add some more when you reheat if you want the soup to be brothy.

1	tablespoon olive oil
10	garlic cloves, sliced
3	large leeks, white and light green parts only, halved lengthwise, rinsed well, and sliced into half-moons
2	teaspoons kosher salt, plus more as needed
1	teaspoon freshly ground black pepper, plus more as needed
6	cups Trash or Treasure Broth (page 129) or high-quality store-bought broth
1	cup quinoa, soaked, sprouted, or rinsed (see page 124)
1	to 1¼ pounds boneless, skinless chicken breasts
3	tablespoons fresh lemon juice
4	to 6 tablespoons Parsley, Kale, and Pumpkin Seed Pesto (page 132) or your favorite store-bought pesto
¼	cup grated or shaved Parmesan cheese
¼	cup snipped fresh chives
	Lemon wedges, for serving

In a large pot, heat the oil over medium-high heat. Add the garlic and cook, stirring continuously, until golden and fragrant, about 2 minutes. Add the leeks, 1 teaspoon of the salt, and the pepper. Cook, stirring often, until soft, 8 to 10 minutes.

Add the broth and bring to a boil. Stir in the quinoa and chicken and reduce the heat to maintain a simmer. Cover and cook until an instant-read thermometer inserted into the thickest part of the chicken reads 165°F, 12 to 14 minutes.

Transfer the chicken to a plate and shred the meat with two forks. Return the meat to the soup and stir in the lemon juice and remaining 1 teaspoon salt.

Divide the soup among serving bowls and stir 1 tablespoon of the pesto into each bowl. Top with the Parmesan and chives, dividing them evenly. Serve with a lemon wedge and salt and pepper alongside.

To Store

Refrigerate the soup in an airtight container for up to 3 days, or freeze for up to 2 months.

Scorecard

✔

Whole Grains

Serves

4 to 6

THE RECIPES

Brothy Tomatoes, Spinach, and Chickpeas with Herbs

Little did I know when creating this quick recipe that it would turn out to be so good for you, and your microbes, too. My goal was to make a pantry dinner that comes together quickly, but still feels fresh. With staples like canned tomatoes, chickpeas, and shallots on hand, all you'll have to buy day-of are the spinach and herbs. I like a combination of basil, parsley, cilantro, and dill, but you can choose just one favorite to keep it easy. Chives would be delicious, too.

I call for whole peeled tomatoes, which you crush as you add them to the pan so there are big chunks of juicy tomato in each bite. Of course, if you have diced tomatoes on hand instead, those will work, too.

2 tablespoons olive oil, plus more for drizzling, if desired

1 shallot, thinly sliced

1 teaspoon dried oregano

½ teaspoon kosher salt

½ teaspoon freshly ground black pepper

1 (28-ounce) can whole peeled tomatoes

2 cups Trash or Treasure Broth (page 129) or high-quality store-bought broth

1½ cups cooked chickpeas (see page 124), or 1 (15.5-ounce) can, drained and rinsed

6 cups baby spinach

2 large avocados, sliced, for serving

2 tablespoons chopped mixed fresh herbs (see headnote), for serving

Flaky sea salt (optional)

In a large, straight-sided skillet, heat the oil over medium heat. Add the shallot, oregano, salt, and pepper. Cook, stirring often, until the shallot is soft, 4 to 5 minutes.

Add the tomatoes and their juices using your hands to crush them as you add them. Stir in the broth and bring the mixture to a simmer. Cook until the liquid has reduced by half, 6 to 8 minutes.

Add the chickpeas and cook until just enough liquid is left for a sauce, 6 to 8 minutes more, then add the spinach and remove from the heat. Toss with tongs until the spinach is wilted.

Serve topped with the avocado, fresh herbs, a drizzle of olive oil, and sprinkling of flaky sea salt, if you want.

To Store

Once the spinach hits the hot broth, it wilts and needs to be eaten right away. If you anticipate having leftovers, I recommend only adding the spinach to what you plan to eat. The rest can be stored in an airtight container in the refrigerator for up to 4 days. Reheat and fold in the spinach just before serving.

Scorecard

✓
LGVs

✓
Other Veg

✓
Beans and Legumes

Serves

4

To Store
Refrigerate the soup in an airtight container for up to 3 days, or freeze for up to 2 months.

Coconut Chicken and Rice Stew

They say that necessity is the mother of invention, but with my job as a cookbook writer, it's more like cravings are the mother of the best recipes. Case in point: this recipe, which I dreamed up while on a cold winter walk. I was chilled to the bone, and as I trudged home through the snow, all I could think about was a spicy chicken-and-rice stew made with coconut milk. To bump up the plant fiber, I simmer cauliflower rice alongside the brown rice, and stir in a whole head of napa cabbage, too.

8   cups Trash or Treasure Broth (page 129) or high-quality store-bought broth

1   (13.5-ounce) can unsweetened coconut milk

¼   cup red curry paste

3   tablespoons fish sauce, plus more for seasoning

2   cups short-grain brown rice, rinsed

1   (12-ounce) bag riced cauliflower (2½ cups)

1   pound boneless, skinless chicken thighs, or 4 cups shredded cooked chicken (from Slow-Roasted Chicken, page 276)

1   large head napa cabbage (2 pounds), quartered lengthwise and thinly sliced

½   cup chopped fresh cilantro leaves

Kimchi, for serving (I like about ½ cup in my bowl)

In a large pot, combine the broth, coconut milk, curry paste, and fish sauce. Bring to a boil over high heat and then add the rice and cauliflower. Return the mixture to a boil, then reduce the heat to maintain a gentle simmer.

If you're cooking the chicken thighs: Simmer the rice for 18 minutes, then add the chicken thighs to the pot. Simmer until the chicken is cooked through and opaque throughout, 14 to 18 minutes. Transfer the chicken to a bowl and use two forks to shred the meat into bite-size pieces. The rice should be cooked through by now as well. Stir in the cabbage and shredded chicken; remove from the heat.

If you're using already cooked, shredded chicken: Simmer the rice for 24 to 28 minutes, until there's a little bite remaining to the grain. Add the shredded chicken to the pot. Cook until the chicken is heated through, about 3 minutes. The rice should be perfectly cooked through by now. Stir in the cabbage and remove from the heat.

Serve Divide the soup among serving bowls and top with the cilantro. Serve with kimchi and season to taste with more fish sauce.

Scorecard

✓
LGVs

✓
Other Veg

✓
Whole Grains

✓
Fermented Food

THE RECIPES

Serves
8

VEGETARIAN MAINS

When it comes to eating more vegetables and less meat, I've learned that one of the biggest roadblocks is the idea of what "dinner" should be. This is especially true for people whose partners or families are vocally wary of healthful food. But the recipes in this chapter satisfy in an emotional, psychological way. If the dish felt luxurious and I craved the leftovers, then I knew it was right.

These recipes are hearty vegetable- and plant-forward dishes to satiate a variety of palates. My hope is that they convince even the biggest skeptics that the idea of dinner can stretch in multiple dimensions, welcoming the meat eater and the vegetable pusher to the same table with grace. All this without the plate screaming "VEGGIES" in your face.

Toasted Corn, Mushroom, and Kale Quiche with a Millet Crust 236

Olive Tapenade and Onion Quinoa Quiche

One of my go-to spots in my favorite city, Berlin, serves a delicious vegetable quiche with a quinoa base instead of a pastry crust. I like to serve my riff on this concept with roasted broccoli rabe (see page 110) or sautéed Swiss chard (see page 113), but any vegetable will pair nicely.

- 2 tablespoons preferred cooking oil, plus more for brushing
- 1 cup quinoa, sprouted or rinsed (see page 124)
- 12 large eggs
- 1¾ teaspoons kosher salt
- 1 teaspoon freshly ground black pepper
- 2 large onions, thinly sliced
- 1 teaspoon smoked paprika
- 1 teaspoon ground turmeric
- 1 teaspoon dried oregano
- ⅓ cup store-bought olive tapenade

Preheat your oven to 375°F. Brush a 9-inch (ideally nonstick) springform pan with oil, then line it with a parchment paper round. Oil the parchment and then set the pan on a rimmed baking sheet.

Cook the quinoa Bring a large pot of water to a boil. Add the quinoa and cook until very tender, about 18 minutes. Drain and transfer to a large bowl.

Make the crust Beat 1 of the eggs in a small bowl, then stir it into the quinoa, along with ¼ teaspoon each of the salt and pepper. Scoop the quinoa mixture into the prepared pan. Use a flat-bottomed measuring cup to press the mixture evenly over the bottom and 1 inch up the sides of the pan. Bake for 20 minutes.

Meanwhile, sauté the onions In a large straight-sided skillet, heat the oil over medium-high heat. Add the onions, paprika, turmeric, oregano, 1 teaspoon of the salt, and ½ teaspoon of the pepper. Cook, stirring often, until the onions are very soft, about 15 minutes.

Assemble the quiche Beat the remaining 11 eggs with the remaining ½ teaspoon salt and ¼ teaspoon pepper.

Pile the onions into the baked crust, then smooth them to the edges and push them up the sides slightly so they create a barrier. Pour in the eggs and then dollop the tapenade over the eggs.

Bake until the eggs are just barely set in the center, 60 to 70 minutes. Let cool completely before cutting into wedges and serving.

To Store

Refrigerate leftover quiche in an airtight container for up to 3 days.

Toasted Corn, Mushroom, and Kale Quiche with a Millet Crust

In the past, I've stayed away from giving multistep recipes because quick and easy was the name of the game. But when creating genuinely healthy food, sometimes an extra step or two is the difference between blah and amazing. That's the case with this recipe, which calls for roasting mushrooms, sautéing kale, and toasting corn in three separate steps. It's worth it for the distinct flavors and textures, and while it takes some time, the payoff is breakfast or lunch for days. However, you can cut down on the cook time significantly by using whatever cooked vegetables you have on hand.

Makes

1

9-inch quiche, to serve 8

1	pound button mushrooms, quartered
4	tablespoons preferred cooking oil, plus more for the pan
1¾	teaspoons kosher salt
1¼	teaspoons freshly ground black pepper
1	cup millet, soaked overnight, or rinsed (see page 124)
1	teaspoon fresh thyme leaves
1½	cups fresh corn kernels, or 1 (15.25-ounce) can, drained
8	cups torn lacinato or curly kale leaves (from 2 bunches)
12	large eggs, beaten
¼	cup water
½	cup tightly packed grated Parmesan cheese (optional)

Roast the mushrooms Preheat your oven to 450°F with racks in the top and bottom positions.

Toss the mushrooms, 3 tablespoons of the oil, ½ teaspoon of the salt, and ½ teaspoon of the pepper on two rimmed baking sheets. Roast on the top rack, tossing once, until golden brown and crispy, 20 to 25 minutes.

While the mushrooms roast, cook the millet Meanwhile, bring a large pot of water to a boil. Add the millet and cook until very soft, 25 to 30 minutes. Drain well in a fine-mesh strainer. (Rinse out the pot and set it aside.)

Bake the crust Brush a 9-inch springform pan with oil and set it on a rimmed baking sheet. Add the cooked millet, thyme, and ½ teaspoon of the salt. Toss with a flexible spatula to mix and then press into an even layer over the bottom of the pan. Bake on the bottom rack for 30 minutes, or until dry and pulled away slightly from the sides.

Meanwhile, toast the corn In the pot you used to cook the millet, heat the remaining 1 tablespoon oil over medium-high heat. Add the corn and ½ teaspoon each salt and pepper. Cook, stirring often, until the corn is golden and toasty smelling, 6 to 8 minutes. Remove the corn from the pot (you can scrape it onto the pan with the mushrooms if they're done roasting).

Cook the kale Return the pot to the heat and add the kale and ¼ cup water. Cook, scraping the bottom to get the toasted corn bits up and tossing frequently, until the water has evaporated and the kale is tender but still has a bite, 5 to 7 minutes. Add the kale to the corn and mushrooms and toss to combine.

Assemble the quiche In a medium bowl, whisk together the eggs, ¼ cup of the Parmesan (if using), and the remaining ¼ teaspoon each salt and pepper.

Layer the vegetable mixture on top of the crust. Pour the egg mixture over the top, then sprinkle with the remaining ¼ cup Parmesan (if using).

Bake the quiche on the top rack until the eggs are set and there's no jiggle in the center, 45 to 55 minutes. The top should be golden brown. Remove from the oven and let cool slightly.

Run a spatula around the edge of the pan, release the sides, and remove the springform ring. Cut the quiche into wedges and serve.

To Store
Refrigerate leftover quiche in an airtight container for up to 3 days.

Millet and Black Bean Cakes

I was inspired to create these bean cakes after suffering through a cardboard-like patty at a popular vegan restaurant. My goal: to create something truly delicious that didn't scream "health food" as you ate it. Black beans are particularly great because they have a higher skin-to-flesh ratio, so there's more texture and less mush. Combined with spiced scallions, fragrant cilantro, and chewy millet, the result is unbelievably delicious.

- 3 tablespoons preferred cooking oil
- 2 bunches scallions, thinly sliced (1 cup total)
- 6 garlic cloves, chopped
- 2 teaspoons chili powder
- 2 teaspoons ground cumin
- 1½ teaspoons kosher salt
- ½ teaspoon freshly ground black pepper
- 3 cups cooked black beans, rinsed (see page 124), or 2 (15.5-ounce) cans, drained and rinsed
- 2 cups cooked millet (see page 124), at room temperature
- ½ packed cup fresh cilantro leaves and stems
- ¼ cup flaxseed meal

My favorite way to eat these is with a drizzle of Cheater's Romesco (page 133) and a tablespoon of pumpkin seeds (as pictured), but they do well with any combination of creamy and crunchy.

Preheat your oven to 425°F. Line a baking sheet with parchment paper.

In a nonstick skillet, heat 2 tablespoons of the oil over medium heat. Add the scallions, garlic, chili powder, cumin, 1 teaspoon of the salt, and the pepper. Cook, stirring often, until the scallions are soft, 4 to 6 minutes. Let cool to room temperature.

In a food processor, combine the beans, millet, cilantro, flaxseed meal, and the cooked scallions. Pulse, stirring a couple of times between pulses, until the mixture is just combined and sticks together. You don't want it to be too paste-like.

Divide the mixture into eight ½-cup (4-ounce) portions and shape them into 1-inch-thick patties (about 3 inches wide), placing them on the prepared baking sheet as you go. Brush with the remaining 1 tablespoon oil and sprinkle with the remaining ½ teaspoon salt.

Bake for 35 to 40 minutes, rotating the baking sheet front to back halfway through, until the cakes are crispy, browned, and cooked through. Serve hot.

To Store

Cool the cakes and then store in an airtight container in the refrigerator for up to 2 days or in the freezer for up to 2 months. Reheat in a toaster oven or microwave.

Scorecard

✔
Whole Grains

✔
Beans and Legumes

Makes
8
cakes

THE RECIPES

Lentil and Chard Cakes

All the ingredients in these cakes would be amazing piled into a bowl—and you can use the recipes in Prep City (see page 92) to do just that. But for the sake of variety in texture and format, these hearty patties are a great way to mix up a standard dinner, so that every meal doesn't feel like a pile of plants in a bowl.

My favorite way to eat these cakes is on a bed of greens with avocado and some crumbled feta.

Scorecard

✓
LGVs

✓
Beans and Legumes

✓
Whole Grains

Makes
8
cakes

2	teaspoons kosher salt, plus more if needed
½	cup short-grain brown rice, soaked overnight or rinsed (see page 124)
¾	cup Puy lentils, rinsed
2	tablespoons preferred cooking oil
1	small onion, chopped
4	garlic cloves, minced
1	teaspoon ground cumin
½	teaspoon freshly ground black pepper
1	large bunch Swiss chard or beet greens (1 pound), stems sliced ½ inch thick, leaves shredded into 1-inch strips
2	tablespoons water
1¼	cups quinoa flakes (see Tip, opposite)
1	tablespoon lemon juice
2	large eggs

Preheat your oven to 375°F with a rack in the center position.

Bring a large pot of water to a boil. Add ¼ teaspoon of the salt and the rice. Cook for 10 minutes, then add the lentils. Cook for 20 to 22 minutes more, until the lentils and rice are tender but not mushy. Drain and let cool.

Meanwhile, in large nonstick skillet, heat 1 tablespoon of the oil over medium-high heat. Add the onion, garlic, cumin, ½ teaspoon of the salt, and the pepper. Cook for 3 minutes, then add the chard stems. Cook until the onions and chard stems are very soft, 10 to 12 minutes more. Add the chard leaves, water, and ¼ teaspoon of the salt and cook, tossing with tongs, until very soft, 5 minutes more. Let cool.

Line a baking sheet with parchment paper. In a food processor, combine the lentils and rice, chard, quinoa flakes, lemon juice, eggs, and ¾ teaspoon of the salt. Pulse until just combined. Divide the mixture into eight ½-cup (4-ounce) portions and shape them into 1-inch-thick patties (about 3 inches wide), placing them on the prepared baking sheet as you go.

Brush the patties with the remaining 1 tablespoon oil and sprinkle with ¼ teaspoon salt. Bake for 20 to 25 minutes, flipping halfway through, until the cakes are crispy, browned, and cooked through. Serve hot.

To Store

Cool the cakes and then store in an airtight container in the refrigerator for up to 2 days or in the freezer for up to 2 months. Reheat in a toaster oven or microwave.

 **TIP**

Quinoa flakes are made from a dried, rolled quinoa seeds. Think of them as the quinoa equivalent of quick-cooking oats. Find them near the specialty flours in your grocery store.

Brown Rice Burrito Bowls
with Spicy Black Beans and Onions

Yes, you can have a delicious burrito bowl without meat and cheese! I actually loved this dish so much I ate it day after day after day until I got sick of it. Oh wait, I never got sick of it. I'm eating it right now. That's how good it is.

2	tablespoons preferred cooking oil
2	large onions, chopped
½	teaspoon ground cumin
½	teaspoon dried oregano
	Pinch of cayenne pepper
¾	teaspoon kosher salt
¼	teaspoon freshly ground black pepper, plus more if needed
2	tablespoons tomato paste
1½	cups cooked black beans (see 124), or 1 (15.5-ounce) can, drained and rinsed
1	cup Trash or Treasure Broth (page 129) or high-quality store-bought broth
4	cups cooked short-grain brown rice (see page 124)
2	ripe avocados, sliced
	Plain kefir (optional; omit if eating plant-based), torn fresh cilantro leaves, hot sauce, and lime wedges, for serving
	Flaky sea salt (optional)

In a medium nonstick skillet, heat the oil over medium-high heat. Add the onions, cumin, oregano, cayenne, and ½ teaspoon each salt and black pepper. Cook, stirring often, until the onions are golden brown and soft, 10 to 12 minutes. Add the tomato paste and cook, stirring continuously, until it starts to caramelize and is dry, about 2 minutes. Stir in the beans, broth, and remaining ¼ teaspoon salt. Cook until the beans are hot and the sauce has thickened slightly, about 3 minutes more.

Divide the rice among serving bowls, then top with the beans and avocado. Drizzle with a little kefir (if you want) and sprinkle with cilantro leaves. Serve with hot sauce and lime wedges alongside. I always finish with a sprinkling of flaky sea salt and a few grinds fresh pepper, but that's up to you.

Scorecard

✔✔
Other Veg

✔
Beans and Legumes

✔
Whole Grains

Serves
4

For an extra decadent upgrade, swap in guac for the sliced avocado.

Saucy Coconut Collards
with Crispy Sweet Potato Rounds and Millet

Sometimes you need a meal with big, gorgeous payoff—especially when you're eating gut-friendly all the time—that's where this dish comes in. Oh, and it's high in fiber for your microbe friends, and plant-based, too. Here I turn to one of my favorite tricks—roasting chickpeas until they're chewy—then combine them with sweet potato rounds (also roasted, to caramelize their naturally present sugars), millet (for its ability to soak up flavors without competing), and saucy, turmeric-spiced collards to bring it all together.

- 3 cups cooked chickpeas (see page 124), or 1 (29-ounce) can or 2 (15.5-ounce) cans, drained and rinsed
- 4 tablespoons preferred cooking oil
- 2¾ teaspoons kosher salt
- 1 teaspoon freshly ground black pepper
- 2 long, skinny sweet potatoes (1 pound total), sliced into ½-inch-thick rounds
- 1 cup millet, rinsed, soaked overnight, or sprouted (see page 124)
- 1 recipe Quick-Braised Coconut Collard Greens (page 313), hot

  Toasted unsweetened coconut flakes and red pepper flakes, for serving

  Flaky sea salt (optional)

Preheat your oven to 400°F with racks in the top and bottom positions.

Spread the chickpeas in an even layer on a rimmed baking sheet. Bake on the top rack until the chickpeas are very dry, about 10 minutes. Remove the pan from the oven and drizzle the chickpeas with 2 tablespoons of the oil, then season with 1 teaspoon of the salt and ½ teaspoon of the black pepper. Return the baking sheet to the top rack of the oven and bake, tossing once, until the chickpeas are crispy, 25 to 30 minutes more.

Arrange the sweet potatoes on a separate baking sheet. Brush them on both sides with the remaining 2 tablespoons oil and season with ¾ teaspoon of the salt and remaining ½ teaspoon black pepper. Roast on the bottom rack, flipping halfway through baking, until golden brown and you can easily insert a fork in the center, 25 to 30 minutes.

Meanwhile, bring a large pot of water to a boil. Add the millet and remaining 1 teaspoon salt. Return to a boil, then reduce the heat to maintain a simmer and cook until tender but with a small bite, 24 to 28 minutes. Drain and divide among four serving bowls.

Ladle the collards and sauce over the millet, then top with the sweet potato slices and chickpeas. Sprinkle with coconut, red pepper flakes, and flaky sea salt (if you want).

Scorecard

✓
LGVs

✓
Beans and Legumes

✓
Other Veg

✓
Whole Grains

THE RECIPES

Serves
4 to 6

Crispy Tofu Steaks
with Broccoli Rabe and Romesco

One of the funny things about writing a cookbook with over 125 recipes is that people will ask you the same question every time: What's your favorite recipe? As though I could choose! But if I were pressed to name my top ten, this recipe would be in the group. It's flavorful, easy to make, and packed with plant-based protein.

1 (14-ounce) package extra-firm tofu, halved through the center horizontally, then halved again to make 2 wide planks

2 tablespoons preferred cooking oil

½ teaspoon kosher salt

1 large bunch broccoli rabe or Broccolini (about 12 ounces), halved lengthwise through the stems if thick

½ cup Cheater's Romesco (page 133)

2 tablespoons chopped roasted almonds

   Flaky sea salt (optional)

I like to use a small lid that fits in the pan to press down on the tofu, which will help you press the full surface area. Wear an oven mitt to prevent oil from splattering your forearm.

Line a small rimmed baking sheet with a clean dish towel or paper towels. Place the tofu on top in a single layer, then top with another towel. Top with a second baking sheet and place something on top to weight the tray down, like two cans of beans. Let sit for at least 30 minutes or refrigerate up to overnight.

In a large nonstick skillet, heat the oil over medium-high heat. (You can do this in a smaller skillet in batches; just add 1 tablespoon of the oil at a time.) Pat the pressed tofu dry and season on both sides with the salt. Add the tofu to the hot oil and press down on it very firmly with a flat-bottomed spatula or a pot lid for the first minute. Cook, turning once, until golden brown and crispy, 5 to 6 minutes per side, pressing again with the pot lid for the first minute after flipping.

Meanwhile, fill a large pot with 1 inch of water and put a steamer insert inside. Cover and bring the water to a simmer. Add the broccoli rabe, re-cover, and steam until tender but with a little bite, 6 to 8 minutes.

Serve the tofu and broccoli rabe dolloped with the romesco and sprinkled with the almonds and flaky sea salt (if you want).

Scorecard

✔
LGVs

✔
Beans and Legumes

✔
Nuts and Seeds

Serves
2

Brussels Sprout and Peanut Butter Curry Bowl

It can be hard to find genuinely healthful meals on the go in New York City. So I was happy to discover Le Botaniste, a plant-based, fast-casual restaurant. My standing order is the Tibetan Mama bowl, a delicious peanut curry served over your choice of grain, with herbs and veggies on top. I re-created my own version for you (okay, for me), but my version has a heck of a lot more kimchi on top to keep your gut happy, and Brussels sprouts instead of broccoli. It's so good, I might never go out to eat again.

Scorecard

✔
LGVs

✔
Whole Grains

✔
Fermented Food

✔
Nuts and Seeds

Serves
4

THE RECIPES

1½ cups short-grain brown rice, sprouted, soaked, or rinsed (see page 124)

2 pounds Brussels sprouts, halved

3 tablespoons preferred cooking oil

1 teaspoon kosher salt, plus more if needed

¼ teaspoon freshly ground black pepper

2 (13.5-ounce) cans unsweetened coconut milk

1½ cups water

½ cup natural peanut butter

4 garlic cloves, minced fine

1 tablespoon plus 1 teaspoon curry powder

½ teaspoon Aleppo pepper flakes or crushed red pepper, plus more for serving

2 tablespoons lime juice

Kimchi, for serving (I like about ½ cup on my bowl)

½ cup fresh cilantro leaves

Lime wedges, for serving

You can toss the sprouts on the baking sheets to save a dish but they won't be evenly coated.

Preheat your oven to 425°F with racks in the top and bottom positions.

Bring a large pot of water to a rolling boil. Add the rice. Cook until just tender, 26 to 30 minutes. Drain and keep warm.

Meanwhile, in a large bowl, toss the Brussels sprouts, oil, salt, and black pepper. Divide between two rimmed baking sheets. Roast, tossing once and switching the baking sheets from top to bottom halfway through, until golden brown and tender, 24 to 28 minutes.

In a small pot, combine the coconut milk, water, peanut butter, garlic, curry powder, and Aleppo pepper. Bring to a boil over medium-high heat. Reduce the heat to maintain a simmer and cook, whisking occasionally, until slightly thickened, about 10 minutes. Remove from the heat and stir in the lime juice. Taste and season with salt (if you want).

Divide the rice among serving bowls. Top with the curry, Brussels sprouts, kimchi, and cilantro. Sprinkle with more Aleppo pepper, if you want, and serve with lime wedges alongside.

Trumpet Mushroom "Scallops"
with Cauliflower, Red Pepper, and Miso Puree

This recipe was inspired by a lunch at Prado in Lisbon, which ranks as one of my all-time favorite meals. The dish was just a simple mushroom sauté atop a house-fermented red pepper miso, sprinkled with toasted buckwheat.

Rather than ask you to ferment anything yourself, I call for store-bought miso add beneficial bacteria. As for the mushrooms, I'm borrowing from myself: In my first cookbook, *Healthyish*, I created a method of cooking trumpet mushrooms like scallops. This might count as a light dinner for some and an appetizer for others, so gauge your hunger before making your shopping list.

Scorecard

✔✔
Other Veg

✔
Fermented Food

Serves

4

½ cup buckwheat groats

5 tablespoons preferred cooking oil

1½ teaspoons kosher salt

1¼ teaspoons freshly ground black pepper

4 cups small cauliflower florets (from a 1¼-pound head)

1½ pounds 2-inch-wide trumpet mushrooms, cut into ¾-inch-thick rounds

1⅓ cups packed roasted red peppers (12 ounces, from a 1-pound jar, drained), microwaved until warm

2 tablespoons white miso paste

2 tablespoons fresh lemon juice

2 tablespoons chopped fresh parsley

Flaky sea salt (optional)

Toast the buckwheat Preheat your oven to 350°F. Toss the buckwheat, 2 tablespoons of the oil, ½ teaspoon of the salt, and ¼ teaspoon of the pepper on a rimmed baking sheet. Bake, tossing once, until dark brown (almost maroon) and crisp, 18 to 24 minutes. Remove from the oven and let cool.

Steam the cauliflower Meanwhile, fill a large pot with 1 inch of water and put a steamer insert inside. Bring the water to a simmer, add the cauliflower, cover, and steam until very soft, about 15 minutes.

Cook the mushrooms While the cauliflower steams, in a large skillet (ideally nonstick), heat 1 tablespoon of the oil over medium-high heat. Add a third of the mushrooms and season with ¼ teaspoon each of the salt and pepper.

Cook the mushrooms, stirring a few times, until golden brown on both sides, 5 to 7 minutes. You want them to brown nicely, so avoid stirring too much. Transfer the mushrooms to a plate and cover to keep warm. Repeat in two batches with the remaining 2 tablespoons oil and mushrooms.

Make the puree In a blender or food processor, combine the steamed cauliflower, roasted peppers, miso paste, lemon juice, and remaining ¼ teaspoon each salt and pepper. Process until smooth.

Divide the puree among serving plates and top with the mushrooms and buckwheat. Sprinkle with the parsley and flaky sea salt (if using), then serve.

TiP Choose the fattest possible mushrooms for the most scallop-y effect.

Roasted Eggplant and Chickpeas
with Herbed Oat Pilaf

This is a dish to reform eggplant haters. Trust me! The eggplant is roasted until meltingly tender, then topped with a chickpea-studded pilaf and a blanket of tahini sauce. Oat groats are oats in their whole form, with just the inedible outer hull removed. They have a texture similar to that of barley and are wonderful tossed into savory dishes.

Scorecard

✔
Other Veg

✔
Whole Grains

✔
Beans and Legumes

Serves

4

with leftovers

1 cup oat groats, preferably soaked overnight (see page 124), rinsed

3 cups cooked chickpeas (see page 124), or 2 (15.5-ounce) cans, drained and rinsed

3 tablespoons preferred cooking oil

1 teaspoon kosher salt, plus more as needed

¾ teaspoon freshly ground black pepper, plus more as needed

2 long, thin medium eggplants (12 to 14 ounces each and about 8 inches long), halved lengthwise, flesh scored crosswise on an angle

1 teaspoon smoked paprika

¼ teaspoon ground cardamom

3 tablespoons lemon juice

1 tablespoon olive oil

¼ cup chopped fresh parsley, plus more for garnish

½ teaspoon Aleppo pepper flakes, plus more for garnish

½ cup White Tahini Sauce (page 134)

Flaky sea salt (optional)

Preheat your oven to 450°F. Bring a large pot of water to a boil over high heat. Add the oats and cook for about 50 minutes, until the grains are tender but with a bite.

Meanwhile, toss the chickpeas, 1 tablespoon of the oil, and ¼ teaspoon each of the salt and black pepper on a large rimmed baking sheet. Bake for 5 minutes to dry them off.

Drizzle the eggplant halves on both sides with the remaining 2 tablespoons oil. In a small bowl, stir together the paprika, cardamom, ½ teaspoon of the salt, and the remaining ½ teaspoon black pepper. Sprinkle the spice mixture on both sides of the eggplant halves. Nestle the halves cut-side down among the chickpeas, leaving at least ½ inch of space around each eggplant. Roast, tossing the chickpeas and turning the eggplants cut-side up after 30 minutes, until the eggplants are meltingly tender and the chickpeas are crispy, 45 to 50 minutes.

Drain the oats and transfer to a large bowl. Add the lemon juice, olive oil, parsley, Aleppo pepper, ¼ teaspoon salt, and a few grinds of black pepper. Fold in most of the roasted chickpeas, saving a few for the top of the bowls. Taste and adjust the seasoning.

Divide the eggplant halves among serving bowls. Top each bowl with a scoop of the oat pilaf. Drizzle with the tahini sauce and top with the reserved crispy chickpeas, some parsley, Aleppo pepper, and flaky sea salt (if you want).

SEAFOOD MAINS

Seafood is a great source of omega-3 polyunsaturated fatty acids—an essential nutrient for the gut microbiota and human health overall. Omega-3s may contribute to the integrity of the intestinal lining and promote production of anti-inflammatory molecules like short-chain fatty acids. Humans can't make them on their own—and rather than get them from a supplement, it's better to get them from food. Two types—known in shorthand as EPA and DHA—come mainly from fish.

The biggest issue with fish and other seafood is not one of human gut microbial health. Rather, the challenges are chemicals in the seafood due to pollution, a strain on the environment from overfishing, and unethical fishing practices.

Sustainable fishing comes from waters that have healthy populations and uses practices that don't impact the ecosystem. Enjoying fish twice a week is enough to reap the benefits without contributing to overtaxing the oceans.

Loaded Baked Potatoes with Tomatoey Swiss Chard, White Beans, and Arctic Char 256

Loaded Baked Potatoes
with Tomatoey Swiss Chard, White Beans, and Arctic Char

Many people who are trying to eat healthfully have a strict "no white potatoes" rule. This is generally because people overeat highly processed, fried white potatoes, giving russets a particularly bad rap. While I don't recommend loading up on French fries all the time, an organic russet potato here and there is not only fine, it's an amazing source of potassium! The more I learned about potassium and how important it is for metabolizing sodium, the more I prioritized getting it into my diet through food (not supplements).

2   large russet potatoes (about 1 pound each)

2   tablespoons plus 1 teaspoon olive oil

1   teaspoon kosher salt, plus more as needed

1   small onion, very thinly sliced

1   large bunch Swiss chard (1 pound), leaves torn and stems thinly sliced

½   teaspoon dried oregano

¾   teaspoon freshly ground black pepper, plus more as needed

3   tablespoons tomato paste

1   cup water, plus more if needed

1½   cups great northern or cannellini beans (see page 124), or 1 (15.5-ounce) can, drained and rinsed

1   tablespoon fresh lemon juice

1   (1-pound) wild-caught Arctic char or salmon fillet (at least 1 inch thick, skin-on or skinless—whatever you can get works)

    Flaky sea salt (optional)

Bake the potatoes Preheat your oven to 400°F with racks in the top and bottom positions.

Set each potato in a piece of foil large enough to wrap around it. Rub the potatoes all over with 1 tablespoon of the oil and sprinkle with ¼ teaspoon of the salt. Wrap each tightly in the foil and place on a rimmed baking sheet.

Bake on the lower rack for 1 hour 15 minutes to 1 hour 25 minutes, until you can very easily stick a fork into the center of the potato.

Meanwhile, make the tomatoey beans and chard In a large pot, heat 1 tablespoon of the oil over medium-high heat.

Add the onion, chard stems, oregano, and ½ teaspoon each of the salt and pepper. Cook, stirring often, until very soft and golden brown, 10 to 12 minutes.

Stir in the tomato paste and cook, stirring often, until the paste is caramelized and starting to turn golden brown in parts, 1 to 2 minutes. Stir in the water and use a flat-edged spatula to scrape the tomato paste off the bottom of the pot.

Add the chard leaves, stirring to coat all the leaves. Cook, stirring often, until the leaves are tender, about 5 minutes. Stir in the beans and cook until heated through, about 2 minutes more. (If the bottom of the pan is browning too much, add up to ¼ cup more water.) Stir in the lemon juice. Taste and season with salt and pepper.

Cook the fish Fifteen minutes before the potatoes are done, place the fish on a separate rimmed baking sheet. Rub the fish with the remaining 1 teaspoon oil, then season with the remaining ¼ teaspoon each salt and pepper. Place the fish skin-side up (if it has skin) and roast on the top rack until opaque throughout, 12 to 14 minutes. Peel off any skin and discard. Use a fork to gently flake the fish.

Slice the potatoes in half lengthwise. Divide the halves among serving bowls and use a fork to fluff up the potato flesh. Pile the chard and beans on top and then finish with the fish. Season with flaky sea salt (if you want) and serve.

BUYING SUSTAINABLE SEAFOOD

Ask the person at the fish counter (aka the fishmonger) if the fish you're interested in is sustainable (if you're eating at a restaurant, ask your waiter). The species isn't necessarily the best indication of whether or not it's sustainable; it will also depend on how it was fished in your region.

Look for labels like "Certified Sustainable Seafood— MSC," the Marine Stewardship Council's seal of approval.

Monterey Bay Aquarium's website Seafood Watch and its app are good resources for choosing what to buy in your area.

Summer Swordfish
with Grilled Pineapple Salsa

Quick, easy, and smart strategy—that's what great weeknight dinners are all about. I like swordfish for its vitamin D and potassium. But if you can't find sustainably sourced swordfish, ask at the fish counter for an alternative like sea bass or halibut—a variety of different fish will work; the key is a thick fillet that can stand up to grilling. See page 257 for sustainable fish-sourcing tips.

1 pineapple (about 3 pounds), cored and quartered

¼ large red onion, cut into 2 wedges with the root intact

2 limes—1 halved, 1 peeled and chopped (see page 296)

3 tablespoons olive oil

1¾ teaspoons kosher salt

¼ cup chopped fresh cilantro

Pinch of cayenne pepper

1½ pounds swordfish steaks, about 1 inch thick each

1 teaspoon freshly ground black pepper, plus more as needed

Tip This makes the onions easier to manage on the grill and prevents any petals from falling through the grill grates.

Heat a grill to high. (Place a mesh grilling mat on your grill if you have one.)

Put the pineapple wedges, onion, and halved lime on a rimmed baking sheet and brush with 1 tablespoon of the oil. Season with ½ teaspoon of the salt. Grill, covered, until charred and tender throughout, 10 minutes for the lime and 20 minutes for the pineapple and onion.

Chop the pineapple and onion into bite-size pieces and transfer to a medium bowl. Add the chopped lime, cilantro, 1 tablespoon of the oil, the cayenne, ½ teaspoon of the salt, and a few grinds of black pepper. Squeeze the grilled lime over. Set aside to marinate while you cook the fish.

Brush the swordfish with the remaining 1 tablespoon oil and season with the remaining ¾ teaspoon salt and the black pepper. Grill the swordfish until just opaque throughout, 4 to 5 minutes per side. Serve hot with the pineapple salsa spooned over the top.

Scorecard

✓
Fruit

Serves
4

THE RECIPES

Shrimp, Black Bean, and Kimchi Tacos with Romaine Salad

I do my best to eat fermented foods at least once, if not twice, during my day, but piling kimchi directly on top of a taco can have the effect of diminishing the other flavors. Instead, I add it to a quick shrimp-and-bean sauté, cooking it just long enough for it to meld with the other flavors but not so long that the heat kills all the good microbes.

2	romaine hearts, thinly sliced
3	large radishes, thinly sliced
2	tablespoons lime juice
2	tablespoons olive oil
¼	teaspoon kosher salt
¼	teaspoon freshly ground black pepper
1	bunch scallions, thinly sliced, some dark green parts reserved for garnish
1½	cups cooked black beans (see page 124), or 1 (15.5-ounce) can, drained and rinsed
1	cup packed chopped kimchi
2	tablespoons fish sauce
½	cup water
1	pound peeled and deveined medium shrimp, tails removed
½	cup chopped fresh cilantro, plus more leaves for serving
8	sprouted or regular corn tortillas, microwaved or toasted over a gas flame
	Lime wedges, for serving

In a large bowl, toss the romaine, radishes, lime juice, 1 tablespoon of the oil, the salt, and the pepper.

In a large skillet, heat the remaining 1 tablespoon oil over medium heat. Add the scallions and cook, stirring often, until soft, 4 to 6 minutes. Stir in the beans, kimchi, fish sauce, and water. Cook, stirring frequently, until just bubbling, 2 to 3 minutes. Stir in the shrimp, cover, and cook until the shrimp are pink and opaque throughout, 2 to 3 minutes. Stir in the cilantro.

Divide the filling among the warm tortillas and sprinkle with the reserved scallion greens. Serve the tacos with lime wedges and the salad.

Scorecard

✔ LGVs

✔ Beans and Legumes

✔ Fermented Food

Serves
4

Oven-Poached Salmon
with Roasted Cauliflower Salad

This recipe is deceptively easy, thanks to smart strategy: You'll use a foil-covered water bath to steam the salmon in the oven and, at the same time, roast the cauliflower until crispy. A side of salmon is prettiest for serving family-style, but you can also use an equal weight of fillets.

Serves
4 to 6

- 2 medium cauliflower heads (3½ pounds total), cut into small florets
- 1 large red onion, sliced
- ¼ cup plus 1 tablespoon olive oil
- 1 teaspoon ground coriander
- 2½ teaspoons kosher salt
- 1 teaspoon freshly ground black pepper, plus more for serving
- 1 (1½-pound) salmon fillet (one intact piece)
- ¼ cup water
- ¼ cup golden raisins
- 3 tablespoons sherry vinegar
- 2 tablespoons capers
- ¼ cup chopped fresh parsley, plus more for garnish
- Lemon wedges, for serving
- Flaky sea salt, for serving (optional)

NOTE If you only have two oven racks and you can't fit everything in the oven at once, roast the cauliflower first, then the salmon. The cauliflower is fantastic at room temperature, and will only increase in flavor as it sits.

Preheat your oven to 425°F with racks spaced evenly in the top, bottom, and center positions.

In a large bowl, toss the cauliflower, onion, ¼ cup of the olive oil, the coriander, 1½ teaspoons of the salt, and ¾ teaspoon of the pepper. Divide between two rimmed baking sheets (keep the bowl for later) and roast on the top and bottom racks until golden brown, 35 to 40 minutes. Toss once and switch the pans front to back and top to bottom halfway through.

Place the salmon in an ovenproof baking dish (if it has skin, place it skin-side down). Season with the remaining 1 teaspoon salt and ¼ teaspoon pepper. Drizzle with the remaining 1 tablespoon oil and pour ¼ cup water around the edges of the salmon. Cover tightly with foil and bake on the middle rack until the salmon is opaque, 25 to 30 minutes.

In the same large bowl you tossed the cauliflower in, combine the raisins, vinegar, and capers. Add the roasted cauliflower to the bowl with the parsley and toss to combine. Pile into a serving bowl.

Place the salmon on a serving platter. Set the lemon wedges alongside and garnish the salmon with more parsley leaves and flaky sea salt (if you want). Serve with the cauliflower salad.

Garlicky Shrimp and Quinoa "Grits"

I love shrimp and grits, but I wanted a lighter, gut-friendlier version than the standard recipe. Quinoa stands in for the grits here, and after cooking for a long time with the onions, it all breaks down into something comforting and delicious.

Serves
4

4	tablespoons unsalted butter, ghee, or preferred cooking oil
2	large onions, very thinly sliced
¼	teaspoon paprika
2	teaspoons kosher salt
½	teaspoon freshly ground black pepper, plus more as needed
1½	cups quinoa, rinsed
8	cups Trash or Treasure Broth (page 129) or high-quality store-bought broth
10	garlic cloves, mashed into a paste (use a garlic press if you have one)
½	teaspoon crushed red pepper
1	pound peeled and deveined medium shrimp
2	tablespoons lemon juice
¼	cup chopped fresh chives
	Flaky sea salt (optional)

In a large pot, heat 2 tablespoons of the butter over medium heat. Add the onions, paprika, 1 teaspoon of the salt, and the black pepper. Cook, stirring occasionally, until the onions are soft, 10 to 12 minutes. Add the quinoa and cook for 5 minutes to toast the seeds a bit. Pour in the broth and bring to a boil. Reduce the heat to maintain a generous simmer and cook until the quinoa has broken down into a smooth, grits-like texture, 25 to 30 minutes more. You can keep cooking it over low heat for up to 1 hour total, adding water to adjust the consistency if it's getting too thick.

Ten minutes before serving, in a large skillet (ideally nonstick), heat the remaining 2 tablespoons butter over medium-high heat. Add the garlic and crushed red pepper and cook until the garlic is golden brown and fragrant, 30 seconds to 1 minute. Add the shrimp, remaining 1 teaspoon salt, and a few grinds of black pepper. Cook, tossing continuously, until the shrimp are pink and opaque throughout, 2 to 3 minutes. Stir in 1 tablespoon of the lemon juice.

Stir the remaining 1 tablespoon lemon juice into the grits. Divide the grits among shallow bowls, then top with the shrimp. Make sure to scrape all that garlicky chile oil out of the pan and onto the grits. Top with the chives and some flaky sea salt (if you want), then serve.

Salmon with Broccoli-Pea Puree
and Cucumber-Grape-Dill Salsa

I always keep frozen peas and broccoli in my freezer and crisp-skinned Persian cucumbers in my fridge (a favorite healthy snack). With those on hand, a fresh dinner like this one can come together without much planning—all I have to buy day-of is the fish and an ingredient or two. Of course, if you'd rather use fresh broccoli and peas, those work just as well.

- 3 Persian cucumbers, chopped
- 1½ cups halved red grapes
- 4 tablespoons lemon juice
- 2 tablespoons preferred cooking oil
- 2 tablespoons chopped fresh dill
- ⅛ to ¼ teaspoon crushed red pepper
- 1¼ teaspoons kosher salt, plus more if needed
- 1 teaspoon freshly ground black pepper
- 1 large onion, chopped
- 2 (10-ounce) bags frozen broccoli florets
- 1 (10-ounce) bag frozen peas
- 1 cup water, plus more if needed
- 4 (4-ounce) skin-on salmon or Arctic char fillets
  Flaky sea salt (optional)

Preheat your broiler to high with a rack in the top position.

In a medium bowl, combine the cucumbers, grapes, 1 tablespoon of the lemon juice, 1 tablespoon of the oil, the dill, crushed red pepper, and ¼ teaspoon each of the salt and black pepper. Let sit, tossing occasionally, while you make the puree and cook the salmon.

In a large pot, heat the remaining tablespoon oil over medium heat. Add the onion and ½ teaspoon each of the salt and black pepper and cook, stirring often, until the onion is golden brown and soft, 10 to 12 minutes. Add the broccoli, peas, water, and ¾ teaspoon of the salt. Cover and bring to a simmer. Cook until you can easily stick a fork in the center of a floret, 4 to 6 minutes depending on the thickness. Transfer to a blender and puree into a thick mash. Or use an immersion blender right in the pot. Stir in the remaining 3 tablespoons lemon juice. If you want it a little looser, add up to ¼ cup more water. Season to taste with salt.

Meanwhile, place the salmon on a rimmed baking sheet and season on both sides with the remaining ¼ teaspoon each salt and black pepper. Broil until opaque throughout, 8 to 12 minutes, depending on the thickness of the fillet.

Divide the broccoli-pea puree among plates or shallow bowls. Top with the salmon, cucumber salsa, and a sprinkling of flaky sea salt (if you want).

Scorecard

 ✔
LGVs

 ✔✔
Other Veg

Serves
4

THE RECIPES

Poached Shrimp Caesar Salad

Shrimp Caesar has always been one of my favorites, and here it gets a microbe-friendly boost from the crispy chickpeas and more vegetables than the Caesar-standard romaine. If you don't have time to roast the chickpeas, you can use them straight from the can (but rinse them first).

For the shrimp

10	cups water
5	whole sprigs parsley leaves
1	bay leaf
1	tablespoon kosher salt
1	lemon, thinly sliced
1	pound small peeled and deveined shrimp, tails removed

For the salad

1	small head radicchio (8 ounces), halved and thinly sliced
4	cups baby arugula
¾	cup halved cherry tomatoes
2	Persian cucumbers, thinly sliced
½	cup Faux Caesar (page 135)
	Kosher salt and freshly ground black pepper (optional)
1	cup Crispy Roasted Chickpeas (page 100) or canned chickpeas (rinsed, if canned), for serving

In a large pot, combine the water, parsley sprigs, bay leaf, and salt and bring to a boil over high heat. Remove from the heat, then stir in the lemon and the shrimp. Cover and let sit until the shrimp are just cooked through, about 3 minutes. Drain the shrimp in a colander and let cool while you prepare the salad. Discard the poaching ingredients.

In a large bowl, toss the radicchio, arugula, tomatoes, cucumbers, and half the dressing until the leaves are well coated. Taste and season with salt and pepper. Top with the shrimp and chickpeas and drizzle with the remaining dressing.

Scorecard

✓
LGVs

✓✓
Other Veg

✓
Beans and Legumes

Serves
4

This method for poaching shrimp is also great for making shrimp cocktail.

Five-Minute Tuna and Kimchi Bowl

This tangy, savory salad struggled to find a home as I was finishing this book. I shifted this recipe back and forth between various chapters—first it was in the seafood mains, then in breakfast, next in the seeds chapter, and finally back here. That "belongs everywhere and nowhere" identity is a testament to how versatile this dish is. I like it at any time of day, and I'll eat it whenever I'm pressed for time but still want to eat a healthful meal that's heavy on vegetables and long on flavor.

These ingredients are all staples in my kitchen—I keep olive oil–packed tuna and sesame seeds in my pantry, I always have a jar of kimchi in the fridge, and cucumbers and avocados are on my weekly fresh ingredients shopping list.

Scorecard

Other Veg

Fermented Food

Serves
1

THE RECIPES

2   Persian cucumbers, thinly sliced
1   avocado, halved
⅛   teaspoon kosher salt
½   cup kimchi
⅓   cup oil-packed drained tuna (3 ounces)
1   tablespoon sesame seeds
    Flaky sea salt (optional)
    Freshly ground black pepper

Pile the cucumbers on a plate and top with the avocado halves. Season both with the kosher salt. Pile the kimchi and tuna on top, then sprinkle with the sesame seeds, flaky sea salt (if you want), and a few grinds of black pepper. Eat with a fork and knife.

Oil-packed tuna is tastier, but you can use water-packed, too. Drizzle some of the oil from the can or jar over the dish to make it richer, or refrigerate it to use in salad dressings.

271

MEAT & POULTRY MAINS

While we don't strictly need meat on a regular basis to be healthy, and the essential nutrients that meat and poultry provide can be derived from other foods, I do eat occasional, small amounts of meat because, for me, there's an X factor that satisfies in a psychoemotional way.

From the perspective of both the planet and your gut microbes, too much red meat is a problem. Not only is industrial farming a contributor to global warming, too much red meat is one of the main dietary contributors to a prevalence of harmful bacteria in the gut.

You probably know by now that I am not a fan of extremes—they don't work long-term, and to approach life with rigid rules often sets people up for failure. If you like to eat meat, chicken, or turkey, there is a role for eating these foods occasionally without it harming your health.

As with all animal products, it's important to buy sustainable meat and poultry if you can afford it. This is important for the planet as well as the animals. Do what you can to buy products from animals that were pasture-raised without hormones or antibiotics and fed organic feed without GMOs. For beef, look for 100 percent grass-fed.

Special
Occasion
Short Ribs
274

Special Occasion Short Ribs
with Olive Oil–Kefir Mashed Potatoes

"Special occasion" takes on new meaning when it comes to keeping gut health in mind. Too much red meat tips the balance toward carcinogen-producing microbes. But occasional red meat from well-raised cows can be a delicious treat. When I serve these, I splurge on the best-raised beef, and since I buy meat once a week or less, I can justify the expense.

Many short rib recipes call for discarding the vegetables after braising, but I keep them in. Not only have they absorbed all the delicious flavor from the pot, they're especially gut-friendly when they've been cooked for so long.

For the short ribs

5½ to 6 pounds bone-in short ribs, 1½ to 2 inches thick

1 teaspoon dried thyme

1 teaspoon dried oregano

1 teaspoon crushed fennel seeds

3 teaspoons kosher salt

1½ teaspoons freshly ground black pepper

1 tablespoon preferred cooking oil

2 tablespoons mashed garlic (from 5 to 7 cloves)

3 celery stalks, very thinly sliced

2 large onions, cut into eighths (1½-inch-thick wedges)

4 large, thick carrots, scrubbed and cut into 2-inch chunks

¼ cup tomato paste

2 cups dry red wine, such as pinot noir or merlot

8 cups Trash or Treasure Broth (page 129) or high-quality store-bought broth

5 sprigs parsley

2 bay leaves

For the kefir mashed potatoes

4 to 4½ pounds fingerling potatoes, scrubbed

½ cup olive oil

1 teaspoon freshly ground black pepper

1 cup plain kefir

1 tablespoon kosher salt

For the chive gremolata

¼ cup olive oil

1 tablespoon lemon zest

¼ cup lemon juice

½ teaspoon kosher salt

½ teaspoon freshly ground black pepper

1 cup finely snipped fresh chives

Flaky sea salt (optional)

Save the fat from searing the short ribs for scrambled eggs or roasting vegetables (or discard it).

Preheat your oven to 300°F with a rack in the bottom position, with enough space above it to fit a large pot.

Start the short ribs Place the short ribs on a rimmed baking sheet. In a small bowl, mix the thyme, oregano, fennel seeds, 2 teaspoons of the salt, and 1 teaspoon of the pepper and sprinkle the seasoning mixture evenly over all sides of the short ribs.

In a large, heavy-bottomed pot, heat the oil over medium-high heat. Add the short ribs and cook until golden brown on all sides, 2 to 3 minutes per side. (Do this in batches if necessary.) Return the browned meat to the baking sheet. (Don't worry about the raw meat juices since the meat will cook for a long time in the oven.)

Pour off 2 tablespoons of the fat from the pot. You should have a slick of oil left in the pot for the vegetables.

Sauté the vegetables Return the pot to medium-high heat and add the garlic and celery. Cook until softened, 3 minutes. Add the onions, carrots, 1 teaspoon salt, and the remaining ½ teaspoon pepper. Cook, stirring often, until the onions are starting to soften and the edges are golden, 7 to 9 minutes. Add the tomato paste and cook, stirring continuously and scraping the bottom of the pot with a flat-edged spatula, until caramelized, about 1 minute.

Pour in the wine and scrape the bottom of the pot well. Bring to a simmer and cook until reduced by half, 4 to 5 minutes. Add the broth, parsley sprigs, and bay leaves and bring to a boil. Remove from the heat and return the short ribs to the pot. Nestle the meat in the liquid. Use tongs to pile the vegetables on top of the ribs.

Braise the short ribs Cover the pot and transfer to the oven. Cook until the meat is falling apart and meltingly tender, at least 3 hours and ideally 4½ to 5 hours. Let sit, covered, for 30 minutes before serving. Skim some fat off the broth, and discard along with the bay leaves and parsley sprigs.

Make the kefir mashed potatoes While the meat rests, fill a large pot with 1 inch of water and put a steamer insert inside. Bring the water to a simmer, add the potatoes, cover, and steam until you can insert a fork into a potato with just a little resistance, 18 to 22 minutes. Transfer the potatoes to a large bowl, then pour in the olive oil and kefir. Season with the salt and pepper. Mash until smooth.

Make the gremolata In a small bowl, whisk together the olive oil, lemon zest, lemon juice, salt, and pepper until smooth. Gently stir in the chives.

Serve Ladle the short ribs, cooking liquid, and vegetables over the mashed potatoes, then top with the gremolata and some flaky sea salt (if you want).

THE RECIPES

Slow-Roasted Chicken
with Extra-Crispy Skin

I wasn't trying to rethink classic roast chicken when I went about developing this dish, but in the end, I came up with a new go-to recipe that's quite nearly foolproof, especially for those scared of carving a chicken. Slow roasting makes the meat fall-off-the-bone tender—read: easy to neatly pull off every piece with your fingers.

Then there's the other goal of a great roast bird: crispy skin. Too often the meat ends up overcooked for the sake of the skin. Not here. After roasting the meat, you'll slip the skin off and crisp it up in the oven until it's as crunchy as a chip. Save the bones for making broth.

Serves

6 to **8**

1 **(4-pound) whole chicken, patted dry with paper towels**

1 **lemon, quartered, plus additional wedges for serving**

1 **large sprig rosemary**

1½ **teaspoons kosher salt**

Freshly ground black pepper

1 **tablespoon chopped fresh parsley leaves**

Flaky sea salt (optional)

Preheat your oven to 300°F with a rack in the center position.

Stuff the cavity of the chicken with the quartered lemon and the rosemary. Season the chicken all over with the salt and grind pepper generously over the top. Set the chicken breast-side up on a rimmed baking sheet or in a small roasting pan.

Roast until an instant-read thermometer inserted into the thickest part of a chicken thigh registers 165°F, 2½ to 3 hours. Remove from the oven and let cool just enough to handle. Crank the oven up to 425°F.

Pull the skin off the entire chicken. It helps to use a paring knife to cut the skin; if it's too hot to touch, use tongs to pull the skin back. (Don't forget the skin on the bottom of the chicken.) Place the chicken skin on a clean rimmed baking sheet and roast until the skin is deeply golden brown and crispy, 14 to 18 minutes.

While the skin roasts, carve the chicken—it should be quite easy to slice or pull apart. Arrange the chicken on a serving platter. (Save the bones for Trash or Treasure Broth, page 129.) Pour off any juices from the pan into a small bowl or saucepan, and cover to keep warm.

Pull the crispy skin out of the oven. Crumble the crispy skin over the sliced chicken and drizzle with the juices from both pans. Sprinkle with the parsley, some freshly ground black pepper, and some flaky sea salt (if you want). Serve with lemon wedges alongside.

Serving Ideas

Because this chicken is lightly seasoned, it plays well with just about any vegetable. (And if you're worried about flavor clashes, you can omit the lemon and rosemary.) A few of my favorite combinations are:

White Wine–Braised Endive with Mustardy Pan Sauce (page 292) + Slow-Roasted Shallots (page 109)

Grilled Romaine (page 116) + Faux Caesar (page 135)

Brown Rice, Roasted Carrot, and Avocado Salad (page 310)

Fingerling Potato Salad with Warm Chive-Bacon Vinaigrette and Sauerkraut (page 301) + Blanched Haricots Verts (page 114)

TiP

I save my stems and sauté them in olive oil with salt and pepper for breakfast tacos or grain bowls.

Crispy Chicken Thighs
with Kale and Black-Eyed Peas

There are a lot of ways to get people on board with eating more vegetables, which is one of the most essential ways to prioritize gut health. For me, the way was through "gateway health food" like this crispy chicken recipe. If I felt like I could never have bacon again, I would probably respond by eating an entire package in a single sitting. Instead, I use a few slices here or there, like in this recipe or in the tacos on page 142, to help me feel less restricted (read: less depressed). While I now strive for a 75-percent plant-based way of eating (aka what I call plant-focused), it's dishes like this one that make it easier to eat more fiber.

Scorecard

✔✔
LGVs

✔
Beans and Legumes

Serves
4

THE RECIPES

- 8 **small bone-in, skin-on chicken thighs (2 pounds total)**
- 2 **teaspoons onion powder**
- 1 **teaspoon smoked paprika**
- 1 **teaspoon celery salt**
- 1½ **teaspoons kosher salt**
- ¾ **teaspoon freshly ground black pepper**
- 3 **slices no-sugar-added bacon**
- 8 **cups torn curly or lacinato kale leaves (from 2 large bunches)**
- 3 **cups cooked black-eyed peas (see page 124), or 2 (15.5-ounce) cans, drained and rinsed**
- 2 **cups Trash or Treasure Broth (page 129) or high-quality store-bought broth**
- 2 **tablespoons lemon juice**
- 2 **tablespoons chopped fresh chives**
  Lemon wedges, for serving

Preheat your oven to 425°F with a rack in the top position.

Put the chicken thighs on a rimmed baking sheet. In a small bowl, mix the onion powder, paprika, celery salt, 1 teaspoon of the kosher salt, and ½ teaspoon of the pepper in a small bowl. Sprinkle the spice mixture on both sides of the chicken thighs. Roast until an instant-read thermometer inserted into the thickest part of the largest thigh registers 165°F, 25 to 30 minutes. The skin should be golden brown and crispy.

Meanwhile, place the bacon strips in your largest skillet (ideally nonstick). Cook over medium-high heat, turning once, until crispy, 3 to 4 minutes per side. Use tongs to pull the strips out and set them aside on a cutting board. Leave the fat in the pan.

Return the pan to medium-high heat. Add the kale leaves, tossing them in the fat to coat. Add the black-eyed peas, broth, remaining ½ teaspoon kosher salt, and remaining ¼ teaspoon pepper. Cover the skillet and cook, stirring a couple of times, until the kale is tender and the beans are hot, 4 to 6 minutes. Chop the cooked bacon into pieces and stir it into the kale. Stir in the lemon juice. Cover and keep warm until the chicken is ready.

Divide the kale among shallow bowls (to catch any broth), set the chicken thighs on top, sprinkle with the chives, and serve with lemon wedges alongside.

Southwestern Chicken Burgers
with Sweet Potato Fries

My god, these were difficult to get right. I wanted a chicken burger that was high in both whole-food vegetable fiber *and* flavor. Turns out, that required five tries. Too gluey, falling apart, too many patties—you name it, I went through it. But now I have a keeper: a recipe that hits a satisfying burger note while packing in prebiotic-rich oats and chickpea flour. I keep a batch in my freezer at all times to easily defrost whenever I don't feel like cooking.

Scorecard

✔✔
Other Veg

Serves
4 to **6**

For the sweet potatoes

2½ to 3 pounds sweet potatoes, cut into 1-inch-thick wedges

3 tablespoons preferred cooking oil

2 teaspoons ground cumin

½ teaspoon kosher salt

½ teaspoon freshly ground black pepper

For the burgers

⅓ cup Trash or Treasure Broth (page 129) or high-quality store-bought broth

1 cup quick-cooking oats

½ cup chickpea flour

1 large egg, beaten

1 tablespoon lemon juice

3 tablespoons preferred cooking oil

1 small onion, finely chopped

1 bell pepper, finely chopped

½ cup corn kernels (from 1 cob fresh or one 15.25-ounce can, drained)

2 teaspoons chili powder

1½ teaspoons kosher salt

1 teaspoon freshly ground black pepper

½ pound ground chicken or turkey

⅓ cup chopped fresh cilantro leaves

For the Dijonnaise

⅓ cup vegan mayonnaise

1 tablespoon Dijon mustard

For serving

1 large ripe avocado, mashed

Toasted burger buns, lettuce, and tomato

Roast the sweet potato fries Preheat your oven to 425°F. Toss the sweet potatoes, oil, cumin, salt, and black pepper on a rimmed baking sheet. Roast, tossing after 15 minutes, until the sweet potatoes are golden brown and you can easily insert a fork into a wedge, 25 to 30 minutes.

Meanwhile, make the burgers In a large bowl, whisk together the broth, oats, chickpea flour, egg, and lemon juice until well mixed. Set aside.

In a large nonstick skillet, heat 1 tablespoon of the oil over medium-high heat. Add the onion, bell pepper, corn, chili powder, 1 teaspoon of the salt, and ½ teaspoon of the black pepper. Cook, stirring occasionally, until softened, 12 to 14 minutes.

Add the sautéed vegetables and remaining 1/2 teaspoon each salt and black pepper to the oat mixture and stir until evenly combined. Add the chicken and cilantro and use your hands to gently mix until just combined. Shape the chicken mixture into six 1/2-cup (4.75-ounce) patties.

Cook the burgers In a large nonstick skillet, heat 1 tablespoon of the oil over medium-high heat. Add 3 of the patties and cook, flipping once halfway through cooking, until golden brown and cooked through, 6 to 8 minutes. Transfer the patties to a plate Repeat with the remaining 1 tablespoon oil and 3 patties.

Make the Dijonnaise In a small bowl, whisk together the mayonnaise and mustard.

Assemble the burgers Spread the mashed avocado on the bottom buns, then top each with lettuce, a burger patty, some Dijonnaise, and sliced tomato. Serve the burgers with the sweet potato fries and the remaining Dijonnaise alongside.

Stuffed Zucchini
with Ground Turkey and Millet

As I was working hard to get more and more vegetables in my diet, it became essential to mix up the format to keep things interesting. Enter stuffed zucchini, which had always seemed Pinterest-healthy (more about clever ideas than taste), but intrigued me with their all-in-one format. I've packed these with layers of flavor—garlic and chili powder and parm—and just enough juicy turkey to make this feel hearty.

Scorecard

✓
Other Veg

✓
Whole Grains

Serves
4 to 6

½ cup millet, preferably soaked overnight, rinsed

6 medium zucchini (3½ to 4 pounds total)

3 teaspoons kosher salt

2 tablespoons preferred cooking oil

½ pound lean ground turkey

4 garlic cloves, minced

1 teaspoon chili powder

¾ teaspoon freshly ground black pepper

1 (14.5-ounce) can diced tomatoes, drained

½ cup finely grated Parmesan cheese (2 ounces)

2 tablespoons chopped fresh parsley

¼ cup water

Preheat your oven to 400°F with a rack in the center position.

Cook the millet Bring a medium pot of water to a boil. Add the millet and cook until tender, 20 to 24 minutes. Drain and set aside.

Meanwhile, prep the zucchini shells Slice ½ inch off the top lengthwise. Use a melon baller to scoop out the insides, leaving a ¼-inch-thick shell. Chop the insides of the zucchini and reserve. Set the scooped-out shells in an ovenproof baking dish.

Sprinkle the insides of the zucchini shells with 1 teaspoon of the salt and leave to sweat out any excess moisture while you make the filling.

In a large nonstick skillet, heat the oil over medium-high heat. Add the garlic and cook until fragrant, 30 seconds to 1 minute. Add the turkey, chili powder, 1 teaspoon of the salt, and ¼ teaspoon of the pepper. Cook, occasionally breaking up the meat with a flat-edged spatula, until golden brown and cooked through, about 5 minutes. Use a slotted spoon to transfer the meat to a plate, leaving the fat behind in the pan. Add the chopped zucchini to the pan and cook over

CONTINUES

THE RECIPES

medium-high heat, stirring, until the liquid has evaporated and the zucchini is very soft and golden brown, 14 to 16 minutes.

In a large bowl, combine the cooked millet, turkey, cooked chopped zucchini, tomatoes, ¼ cup of the Parmesan, the parsley, remaining 1 teaspoon salt, and remaining ½ teaspoon pepper. Stir until evenly mixed.

Stuff the zucchini shells The zucchini shells should have released a fair amount of liquid after salting—wipe it out with a paper towel, then fill each zucchini with the turkey filling, dividing it evenly. Press firmly to make sure the zucchini are filled as much as possible.

Bake the zucchini Pour ¼ cup water into the bottom of the baking dish and cover tightly with foil. Bake for 15 to 20 minutes, until a paring knife can easily be inserted through the side of a zucchini shell. Remove the foil and sprinkle with the remaining ¼ cup Parmesan. Bake for about 15 minutes more, until the cheese is melted and golden. Serve hot.

You might have extra filling; it's delicious on its own, or with a fried egg or chopped avocado on top.

Long-Braised Lamb
with Greens and Spicy Schmear

This recipe is impressive enough for having people over and can be made entirely the day ahead. In fact, the braise even benefits from some resting time. The recipe is written with kale, but you can use Swiss chard or collards, or even sub in steamed broccoli rabe. Whatever you choose, it's essential that it's a bitter vegetable, to balance the rich lamb.

For the lamb

- 1 (3½- to 4-pound) bone-in leg of lamb, shoulder, or neck
- 2 teaspoons kosher salt
- 1½ teaspoons freshly ground black pepper
- 4 tablespoons olive oil
- 2 large onions, thinly sliced
- 2 large fennel bulbs, halved and thinly sliced
- 2 tablespoons mashed garlic (from 5 to 7 cloves)
- 2 teaspoons paprika
- 2 teaspoons ground cumin
- ¼ teaspoon ground cardamom
- 4 cups Trash or Treasure Broth (page 129) or high-quality store-bought broth, heated
- 1 (28-ounce) can whole peeled tomatoes
- 1⅓ cups packed roasted red peppers (12 ounces, from a 1-pound jar, drained), sliced
- 1 bay leaf

For the greens

- 4 large bunches curly or lacinato kale, leaves sliced into 1-inch strips and washed and dried thoroughly
- ⅓ cup olive oil
- 8 garlic cloves, chopped
- 1 teaspoon crushed red pepper
- 2 teaspoons kosher salt
- 1 teaspoon freshly ground black pepper
- ¼ cup lemon juice

For the spicy feta sauce

- 1 cup Greek yogurt
- 2 tablespoons harissa paste
- 2 tablespoons olive oil, plus more for serving
- 1 tablespoon lemon juice
- ¾ teaspoon kosher salt
- ¼ teaspoon freshly ground black pepper
- 4 ounces feta cheese, crumbled into chunks

  Flaky sea salt (optional)

For serving

- 6 cups cooked short-grain brown rice (see page 124)

  Flaky sea salt (optional)

Scorecard

✔
LGVs

✔
Other Veg

✔
Fermented Food

Serves
8 to 10
(with leftovers)

THE RECIPES

TIP Save the kale stems to sauté for a breakfast scramble or whatever you like.

→

CONTINUES

Preheat your oven to 325°F with a rack in the bottom position, with enough space above it to fit a large pot.

Sear the lamb Season the lamb with 1 teaspoon of the salt and ½ teaspoon of the black pepper. In a large pot or Dutch oven, heat 2 tablespoons of the oil over medium-high heat. Add the lamb and cook until well browned on all sides, 10 to 12 minutes. Transfer the lamb to a plate.

Sauté the vegetables Add the onions, fennel, garlic, paprika, cumin, cardamom, and remaining 1 teaspoon each salt and black pepper to the pot. Cook, stirring often and scraping up any bits that have caramelized on the bottom of the pot, until the vegetables are starting to soften and have some color on them, 12 to 14 minutes.

Get the braise going Add the broth, tomatoes and their juices (crushing them gently with your fingers as you add them to the pot), roasted peppers, and bay leaf and stir to combine. Bring to a boil, then remove from the heat and nestle the lamb in the liquid. Use tongs to pile the veg over the lamb.

Cover and transfer the pot to the oven. Cook until the lamb is falling apart and meltingly tender, 4 to 4½ hours. Let sit for 30 minutes before serving.

Cook the kale Twenty minutes before serving, in a large nonstick skillet, heat the oil over medium-high heat. Add the garlic and crushed red pepper and cook until fragrant, 30 seconds to 1 minute. Add as much kale as you can fit, tossing with tongs and adding more as the previous additions wilt. Season with the salt and black pepper and cook until all the kale is cooked but still has a bite to it, 8 to 10 minutes. Stir in the lemon juice.

Make the spicy feta sauce In a small bowl, whisk together the yogurt, harissa, oil, lemon juice, salt, and black pepper. Fold in the feta. Just before serving, top with a drizzle of oil and a little flaky sea salt (if you want).

Serve Use two forks to gently pull the meat into large chunks and stir them into the cooking liquid. (Save the bone for Trash or Treasure Broth or discard.)

Serve the lamb over the rice, topped with a scoop of sautéed kale and a dollop of the spicy feta sauce. Sprinkle with flaky sea salt, if you want, and serve.

THE RECIPES

VEGETABLE SIDE DISHES

I never really cared about side dishes until I started trying to eat more vegetables. At a dinner party I'd fill up on cheese and dessert, and when I did eat vegetables, they were tucked alongside other foods in the name of "balance."

Thanks to these recipes, I've come to realize that eating a rainbow of vegetables is more than just healthful. A beautiful pile of veg is also delicious and interesting and can introduce people (like me) to things they wouldn't have tried before. No matter which recipe you choose, the colors in this section are lush and the flavors are vibrant.

These recipes make enough to serve a group, but I also love picking one or two as part of my weekly meal prep—with their deep, complex flavors, adding just a grain and half an avocado is enough to make a satisfying meal.

Roasted Kabocha Squash with Gochujang and Cilantro 308

Smoky White Beans and Brussels Sprouts 302

Beets with Scallions and Creamy Dill Dressing 304

Tikka Masala–Inspired Cauliflower with Kefir Raita
293

Crispy Roasted Broccoli with Toasted Sunflower Seeds
297

White Wine–Braised Endive
with Mustardy Pan Sauce

When cooked, endive goes from bitter and crunchy to meaty and sweet. Here it's incredible with browned butter, white wine, and a little Dijon mustard. It's sophisticated and a little bit French, just how I wish to be.

- 3 tablespoons unsalted butter, ghee, or preferred cooking oil
- 1 pound small endives (about 5), halved lengthwise through the core
- ½ teaspoon kosher salt
- ½ teaspoon freshly ground black pepper, plus more as needed
- ¾ cup dry white wine, such as savignon blanc or pinot grigio
- 1 tablespoon Dijon mustard
- 1 tablespoon chopped fresh chives
  Flaky sea salt (optional)

In a large nonstick skillet, melt 2 tablespoons of the butter over medium-high heat. Add the endives, cut-side down, and sprinkle with the salt and pepper. Cook until golden brown and slightly softened, about 4 minutes. (The butter should be browned by now.)

Turn the endives cut-side up and add the wine. Cover and cook until the endive is tender but with a bit of bite, 7 to 10 minutes. Use tongs to transfer the endives to a serving platter, then stir the Dijon and remaining 1 tablespoon butter into the pan sauce.

Pour the sauce over the endives and sprinkle with the chives. Grind some pepper over the top and finish with flaky sea salt (if you want). Eat hot.

Scorecard

✔

LGVs

Serves

4

as a side

WHY I LOVE RAW ENDIVE

I almost always have a head or two of endive in my fridge, to serve with dips or to add a bit of fresh veg to a winter grain bowl. I find endive easier on a sensitive gut than most raw vegetables, which makes it a winner in my book.

Tikka Masala–Inspired Cauliflower
with Kefir Raita

Cauliflower pairs well with complex spices, so it makes a great stand-in for chicken in this tikka masala–inspired side dish. Without the original's standard cream sauce, it's not as indulgent, but the kefir raita still adds a generous dose of richness (along with good bacteria).

Scorecard

Other Veg

Fermented Food

Serves
6 to 8
as a side

For the raita

1	large hothouse cucumber, chopped small
½	teaspoon kosher salt
¾	cup plain kefir
¼	cup chopped fresh cilantro leaves
2	tablespoons lime juice
	Pinch of cayenne pepper

For the cauliflower

3	pounds cauliflower (about 2 medium or 1 extra-large head), cut into big florets
¼	cup preferred cooking oil
1½	teaspoons kosher salt
1¼	teaspoons freshly ground black pepper
¼	cup tomato paste
1	tablespoon ghee or unsalted butter, melted
2	teaspoons ground coriander
2	teaspoons ground cumin
1	teaspoon ground ginger
½	teaspoon ground cardamom
1	teaspoon paprika
1	tablespoon water

Preheat your oven to 425°F. Place the cucumber in a fine-mesh strainer set over a bowl. Toss with the salt and let sit, shaking the strainer and stirring the cucumber occasionally, for at least 10 minutes and up to the entire time you're roasting the cauliflower.

In a large bowl, toss the cauliflower, oil, and 1 teaspoon each of the salt and black pepper. Divide between two rimmed baking sheets and roast until just tender, switching the sheets from top to bottom and rotating them front to back halfway through roasting, 14 to 16 minutes.

In the bowl used to toss the cauliflower, whisk together the tomato paste, ghee, coriander, cumin, ginger, cardamom, paprika, water, remaining ½ teaspoon salt, and remaining ¼ teaspoon black pepper.

Pull the cauliflower out of the oven and use tongs to transfer it to the bowl with the sauce. Toss to coat each floret evenly, then return the cauliflower to the baking sheets. Bake until the sauce has coated the cauliflower and is somewhat dry to the touch, about 20 minutes more.

Transfer the drained cucumber to a small bowl and stir in the kefir, cilantro, lime juice, and cayenne.

Serve the cauliflower with the raita alongside.

THE RECIPES

Cauliflower and Quinoa "Tabbouleh" with White Beans and Herbs

Cauliflower rice and quinoa stand in for bulgur in this tabbouleh-inspired side dish, which I originally developed to serve alongside roasted chicken or grilled steak. The reality is, it's so filling and flavorful that I eat leftovers as a meal by itself. When I'm feeling extra hungry, I'll add a fried egg or chopped avocado.

- 2 tablespoons preferred cooking oil
- 5 garlic cloves, chopped
- 1 teaspoon chili powder
- 2½ cups riced cauliflower (from one 12-ounce bag), defrosted
- 1 cup quinoa, rinsed (and preferably sprouted or soaked; see page 124)
- 1 teaspoon kosher salt, plus more as needed
- ½ teaspoon freshly ground black pepper, plus more as needed
- 2 cups Trash or Treasure Broth (page 129), high-quality store-bought broth, or water
- 1½ cups cooked white beans (see page 124), or 1 (15.5-ounce) can, drained and rinsed
- 1 cup chopped mixed fresh herbs (I like chives, parsley, and cilantro)
- 1 large lemon, peeled and finely chopped (see page 296)
- 2 tablespoons lemon juice
- ⅛ teaspoon crushed red pepper (optional)

In a large skillet, heat the oil over medium heat. Add the garlic and chili powder and cook until fragrant, 30 seconds to 1 minute. Add the cauliflower, quinoa, salt, and black pepper. Cook, stirring often, until the cauliflower is brown but not soft, about 5 minutes.

Add the broth and bring to a boil, then reduce the heat to maintain a simmer, cover, and cook until all the liquid has been absorbed and the quinoa is tender but with a little bite, about 15 minutes. Stir in the white beans and let cool to room temperature.

Stir in the herbs, chopped lemon, and lemon juice. Taste and season with the crushed red pepper, salt, and black pepper.

Scorecard

✓
Other Veg

✓
Whole Grains

✓
Beans and Legumes

Serves
4 to 6
as a side

CLOCKWISE FROM TOP LEFT

Cauliflower and Quinoa "Tabbouleh" *opposite*

Brown Rice, Roasted Carrot, and Avocado Salad *310*

White Wine–Braised Endive with Mustardy Pan Sauce *292*

Delicata Rings with Kefir-Ranch Dip *309*

How to Chop a Lemon (or Other Citrus)

Cut both ends off the lemon.

Stand the lemon flat on one end. Following the contour of the lemon, cut off the peel. (Save the ends and any plump rinds to squeeze over food like you would a lemon wedge.)

Continue cutting the peel off the entire lemon.

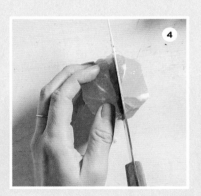

Cut the lemon in half through the center.

Slice into vertical segments. Pull out and discard any seeds. Finely chop the lemon.

Continue until the entire lemon is chopped into small pieces.

Crispy Roasted Broccoli
with Toasted Sunflower Seeds

This recipe is my love letter to roasted broccoli. It's intensely savory thanks to a generous amount of oil and a long roast. If you have long stems left over after cutting the florets, you can slice them using your food processor. Feed them through the slicing blade and then sauté them like you would onions. I like to make a quick frittata with these and some goat cheese or mix them into a grain bowl. You can also save them for Trash or Treasure Broth (page 129).

Scorecard

✔
LGVs

✔
Nuts and Seeds

Serves
6 to 8
as a side

THE RECIPES

5	large heads broccoli, cut into florets (16 cups/2¾ to 3 pounds)
½	cup olive oil
2	teaspoons ground coriander
⅛	teaspoon cayenne pepper
2	teaspoons kosher salt
¾	teaspoon freshly ground black pepper
1	head garlic
½	cup raw hulled sunflower seeds
1	large lemon, peeled and finely chopped (see opposite page)
2	tablespoons lemon juice
½	cup chopped fresh cilantro leaves
	Flaky sea salt (optional)

Preheat your oven to 425°F.

In a large bowl, toss the broccoli, ¼ cup of the oil, the coriander, cayenne, 1½ teaspoons of the salt, and ½ teaspoon of the black pepper, taking care to rub the oil into the scrubby broccoli tops. Divide between two rimmed baking sheets (set the bowl aside to use later).

Pull any loose, papery peels from the outside of the garlic, then trim ¼ inch off the top of the head with a serrated knife.

Set the head cut-side up on a piece of foil large enough to completely enclose the head. Drizzle the cut cloves with 1 tablespoon of the oil and sprinkle with ¼ teaspoon of the salt. Wrap the garlic in the foil and nestle it among the broccoli on one of the baking sheets.

Roast until the broccoli is golden brown and crispy and the garlic is very tender, switching the baking sheets top to bottom and rotating them front to back halfway through roasting, about 45 minutes.

Meanwhile, in a dry skillet, toast the sunflower seeds over medium heat until golden brown and fragrant, 2 to 3 minutes. Transfer to a plate and let cool completely.

Squeeze the roasted garlic cloves from their skins into the bowl you used for the broccoli and mash. Stir in the toasted sunflower seeds, chopped lemon, lemon juice, cilantro, remaining 3 tablespoons olive oil, and remaining ¼ teaspoon each salt and black pepper.

Add the broccoli and toss to combine. Arrange on a serving platter and sprinkle with flaky sea salt (if you want).

Shaved Turnip, Celery, and Kohlrabi Salad 306

Marinated Cucumber-Tomato Salad 303

Salt-Massaged
Napa Cabbage
and Kimchi
Slaw
311

Roasted
Brussels Sprouts
with Toasted
Hazelnuts and
Pomegranate
307

Fingerling Potato Salad
with Warm Chive-Bacon Vinaigrette and Sauerkraut

I'm going to be real with you—this is the only recipe in the book that uses sauerkraut. In my opinion, sauerkraut doesn't blend as well with vegetable-forward food as other fermented ingredients like kimchi, miso, and kefir, so I tend to eat it piled on grain bowls or mixed into salads. But when paired with steamed potatoes and some strips of bacon, well, sauerkraut is a revelation. If you'd rather use Yukon Gold or new potatoes, see page 120 for adjusted cooking times.

1½ pounds fingerling potatoes, scrubbed

5 slices no-sugar-added bacon

1 cup chopped sauerkraut, plus ¼ cup liquid from the jar

½ cup finely chopped fresh chives

¼ teaspoon kosher salt

¼ teaspoon freshly ground black pepper

Flaky sea salt (optional)

Fill a large pot with 1 inch of water and put a steamer insert inside. Bring the water to a simmer, add the potatoes, cover, and steam until you can insert a fork into a potato with just a little resistance, 14 to 18 minutes. Let cool to room temperature, then slice the potatoes in half lengthwise and put them in a large, shallow bowl.

Place the bacon strips in a large nonstick skillet. Cook over medium-high heat, turning once, until crispy, 6 to 8 minutes total. Use tongs to pull the strips out and set them aside on a cutting board, leaving the fat in the pan.

Whisk the sauerkraut juice, all but a few of the chives, the salt, and pepper into the bacon fat in the pan. Pour the dressing over the cooled potatoes, add the sauerkraut, and toss to mix everything evenly.

Chop the bacon into small pieces and sprinkle it over the potatoes, along with the reserved chives. Season with flaky sea salt, if you want, and serve.

Scorecard

✔
Other Veg

✔
Fermented Food

Serves
6
as a side

THE RECIPES

Smoky White Beans and Brussels Sprouts

This was another gateway dish to my more plant-focused lifestyle. I initially started making this combination with sautéed ground chicken. (I've been judged for my love of ground chicken, but honestly, just try it added to this dish.) I also love adding a fried egg or two to leftovers to make a quick meal, or I'll throw on a heap of kimchi for its beneficial microbes.

2 tablespoons preferred cooking oil

2 garlic cloves, chopped

1 pound Brussels sprouts, halved

¾ teaspoon smoked paprika

⅛ teaspoon crushed red pepper

1 teaspoon kosher salt, plus more as needed

Freshly ground black pepper

1½ cups cooked white beans such as cannellini or great northern (see page 124), or 1 (15.5-ounce) can, drained and rinsed

¾ cup water

2 tablespoons lemon juice

2 tablespoons chopped fresh chives

In a large nonstick skillet, heat the oil over medium-high heat. Add the garlic and cook until fragrant, 30 seconds to 1 minute.

Add the Brussels sprouts, paprika, crushed red pepper, salt, and a few grinds of black pepper. Use tongs to flip the sprouts so they're cut-side down. Cook, turning after 5 minutes, until they're golden brown and just barely tender, 2 to 3 minutes more.

Add the beans and water and cook, stirring often, until the beans are heated through and almost all the water has evaporated, 3 to 4 minutes. The sprouts should be perfectly cooked by now. Stir in the lemon juice and chives, taste, and season with salt and black pepper. Eat hot!

Scorecard

✓
LGVs

✓
Beans and Legumes

Serves

4

as a side

Marinated Cucumber-Tomato Salad

No doubt, it's better to buy your vegetables at your local farmers' market, picked at peak freshness. When you can do that, wonderful—this salad really shines in August when juicy tomatoes and crisp cucumbers are on the stands. But in the winter, when I crave a chopped salad, this is the recipe I use, since small tomatoes and Persian cucumbers have a better skin-to-flesh ratio than their larger counterparts. This means they are crunchier and taste fresher even in the depths of February. For an easy upgrade, I'll toss in a few chunks of feta cheese and some chopped olives.

1   pint cherry tomatoes, quartered

2   Persian cucumbers, halved lengthwise and thinly sliced

2   tablespoons lemon juice

2   tablespoons olive oil

1   teaspoon kosher salt

¼   teaspoon freshly ground black pepper

2   tablespoons sesame seeds

2   tablespoons chopped fresh cilantro leaves

1   tablespoon torn fresh small mint leaves

In a medium bowl, toss the tomatoes, cucumbers, lemon juice, oil, salt, and pepper. Let sit, stirring occasionally, for at least 20 minutes and up to 2 hours. Just before serving, fold in the sesame seeds, cilantro, and mint leaves.

Scorecard

✔

Other Veg

Serves

4

THE RECIPES

Beets with Scallions
and Creamy Dill Dressing

This side dish is deceptively simple for how elegant it looks. Plus, it can be prepped a day ahead, perfect for easier dinner organization.

1½ pounds beets (about 3 medium), scrubbed well

1 bunch scallions

½ cup plain Greek yogurt

2 tablespoons chopped fresh dill, plus more for garnish

3 tablespoons olive oil

2 tablespoons lemon juice

½ teaspoon kosher salt

¼ teaspoon freshly ground black pepper

½ cup roasted unsalted pistachios, coarsely chopped

Flaky sea salt (optional)

Get-Ahead Tip The scallion-dill dressing intensifies as it sits, so it only benefits from an overnight rest in the fridge—if you really like scallion flavor! Otherwise, make the dip as written, but stir in the scallions just before serving. Store the beets and dressing separately until you're ready to serve.

Steam the beets Fill a large pot with 1 inch of water and put a steamer insert inside. Bring the water to a simmer, add the beets, cover, and steam until you can stick a fork very easily into the center of a beet, 35 to 45 minutes, depending on the size of the beet.

Make the dressing While the beets steam, slice some of the dark green scallion tops on an angle and set them aside to use as a garnish. Slice the remaining scallions lengthwise, then finely chop them and transfer to a small bowl. Add the yogurt, dill, 2 tablespoons of the oil, the lemon juice, salt, and pepper. Spread on a serving platter.

Peel and chop the beets Let the beets cool slightly, then slip the skins off. Slice the beets into 1-inch-thick wedges. Let cool to room temperature, then nestle them into the dill dressing.

Assemble the platter Drizzle the salad with the remaining 1 tablespoon oil, then sprinkle with the reserved scallions, pistachios, and flaky sea salt (if you want).

Shaved Turnip, Celery, and Kohlrabi Salad

This light and refreshing salad was inspired by chef Joshua McFadden's amazing vegetable cookbook, *Six Seasons*, and a rendition Instagrammed by fellow cookbook author Susan Spungen. The original uses white turnips, and Susan reworked it with kohlrabi and daikon radish. My version takes a little of both—combining kohlrabi with white turnips—and adds celery for balancing bitterness.

2   medium kohlrabi (1 pound), ends trimmed, thinly shaved on a mandoline

4   small white turnips (8 ounces total), thinly shaved on a mandoline

2   large celery stalks (4 to 5 ounces), thinly shaved on a mandoline

3   tablespoons olive oil

1   teaspoon kosher salt

¼   cup plain kefir

1   tablespoon poppy seeds

1   tablespoon chopped fresh dill

   Freshly ground black pepper

   Flaky sea salt (optional)

 Buy a bunch with pretty greens and steam or sauté them (see page 113).

In a large bowl, toss the kohlrabi, turnips, celery, 2 tablespoons of the oil, and the salt. Let sit at room temperature for 30 minutes, tossing occasionally, until the vegetables are almost translucent and very pliable.

Pile the marinated vegetables on a large serving platter. Drizzle with the kefir and the remaining 1 tablespoon oil. Sprinkle with the poppy seeds and dill. Grind fresh pepper over the platter and sprinkle with flaky sea salt, if you want.

Scorecard

✔

Other Veg

✔

Fermented Food

Serves

4 to 6

as a side

Roasted Brussels Sprouts
with Toasted Hazelnuts and Pomegranate

I used to make a version of this salad with shredded raw Brussels sprouts, but those can be quite hard on a sensitive digestive system. Roasting the Brussels makes them easier on your gut, and the bright lemon and tart pomegranate seeds complement the caramelized sprouts nicely. If you like, shaved Parmesan really takes this up a notch.

2 pounds Brussels sprouts, halved

3 tablespoons preferred cooking oil

1¼ teaspoons kosher salt

¼ teaspoon freshly ground black pepper

½ cup chopped toasted hazelnuts

½ cup pomegranate seeds

¼ cup fresh lemon juice

¼ cup chopped fresh parsley

Flaky sea salt (optional)

Preheat your oven to 425°F with racks in the top and bottom positions.

In a large bowl, toss the Brussels sprouts, oil, 1 teaspoon of the salt, and the pepper. Divide the sprouts between two rimmed baking sheets and keep the bowl on hand. (It's worth taking the time to arrange each sprout so it's cut-side down to ensure extra crispiness.)

Roast, tossing once and switching the baking sheets from top to bottom halfway through, until golden brown and tender, 24 to 28 minutes.

Transfer the Brussels sprouts to the bowl you used earlier and add the hazelnuts, pomegranate seeds, lemon juice, parsley, and remaining ¼ teaspoon salt. Toss to combine. Scoop into a serving bowl and sprinkle with flaky sea salt if you want.

Scorecard

✔
LGVs

Serves
6 to 8
as a side

THE RECIPES

Roasted Kabocha Squash
with Gochujang and Cilantro

For years, every time I visited Gjusta Bakery in LA, I'd spend about $12 on their delicious wedges of roasted squash with pumpkin seeds and cilantro. That stopped the day I re-created the combination in my own kitchen—made spicy thanks to gochujang, a Korean fermented chile paste. If you buy shelf-stable gochujang, it will work here, but the beneficial microbes will no longer be alive. That's why I seek out refrigerated gochujang from my local Korean market.

- 1 (4- to 4½-pound) kabocha or kuri squash, halved, seeded, and cut into 1½-inch-thick wedges
- ¼ cup plus 2 tablespoons preferred cooking oil
- 1¼ teaspoons kosher salt
- 1 teaspoon freshly ground black pepper, plus more as needed
- 1 tablespoon gochujang (fermented Korean chile paste)
- 2 tablespoons lime juice
- ½ cup raw hulled pumpkin seeds
- ¼ cup packed fresh cilantro leaves
- Flaky sea salt (optional)

Kuri squash has a flourier texture than kabocha. I still like it, but for some people it's too starchy.

Preheat your oven to 425°F with racks positioned in the top and bottom thirds.

Divide the squash between two rimmed baking sheets. Drizzle with 2 tablespoons of the oil and sprinkle with the salt and pepper. Roast, turning the wedges once and switching the pans from top to bottom and rotating front to back, until you can easily insert a fork into the squash, 24 to 28 minutes.

Transfer the squash to a serving platter, then use a pastry brush to coat the slices on one side with the gochujang. Drizzle with the remaining ¼ cup oil and the lime juice. Sprinkle with the pumpkin seeds, cilantro, some flaky sea salt (if you want), and a few grinds of pepper.

Scorecard

✓
Other Veg

✓
Nuts and Seeds

Serves
4 to 6
as a side

Delicata Rings
with Kefir-Ranch Dip

Hi, hello. It's the reality police here, sending out a bulletin to all healthy recipe writers: please stop comparing rings of roasted delicata squash to deep-fried onion rings! If you want onion rings once in a while, just go get them—and make sure they're the crispiest, saltiest ones out there.

I'd rather enjoy these caramelized delicata rings for what they are—perfectly crispy rounds of squash that hit an ideal savory-sweet balance. The tangy ranch dip has beneficial microbes for your gut thanks to the fermented kefir.

For the delicata rings

- 3 delicata squash (3 pounds total), sliced ½ inch thick and seeds/center cut out with a biscuit cutter or paring knife
- 3 tablespoons preferred cooking oil
- 1½ teaspoons kosher salt
- 1 teaspoon freshly ground black pepper

For the kefir ranch dip

- ½ cup plain full-fat kefir
- ½ cup finely chopped fresh chives, plus a few for garnish
- 2 tablespoons chopped fresh dill
- 2 teaspoons onion powder
- ½ teaspoon kosher salt
- ¼ teaspoon freshly ground black pepper

 Delicata skin is edible!

Preheat your oven to 425°F.

Divide the squash rings between two rimmed baking sheets. Use a pastry brush to coat both sides of the rings with the oil. Season with the salt and pepper, making sure to get both sides.

Roast until golden brown and just tender, 30 to 35 minutes, flipping the squash after 20 minutes and switching the baking sheets from top to bottom and rotating them front to back.

Meanwhile, in a small bowl, stir together the kefir, chives, dill, onion powder, salt, and pepper.

Set the bowl of dip on a serving platter and arrange the squash rings around it. Sprinkle with a few chives to make it pretty.

Scorecard

✔
Other Veg

✔
Fermented Food

Serves
4 to 6
as a side

THE RECIPES

Brown Rice, Roasted Carrot, and Avocado Salad

This is intentionally a room-temperature rice salad, since cooked and cooled rice qualifies as resistant starch—one of the top sources of food for your beneficial microbes. You can always swap in quinoa or millet if you'd rather use a grainlike seed.

- 1 **pound carrots (7 small to medium), well-scrubbed, thick ones halved lengthwise**
- 2 **tablespoons preferred cooking oil**
- 1 **teaspoon smoked paprika**
- 1 **teaspoon ground cumin**
- 2¾ **teaspoons kosher salt**
- 1 **teaspoon freshly ground black pepper, plus more as needed**
- 1 **cup short-grain brown rice, sprouted, soaked, or rinsed (see page 124)**
- 1½ **cups loosely packed watercress or pea shoots (2 ounces)**
- 2 **tablespoons olive oil, plus more for drizzling**
- 2 **tablespoons lemon juice**
- ½ **teaspoon Aleppo pepper flakes or crushed red pepper, plus more for sprinkling**
- 2 **ripe avocados, sliced**
- ¼ **cup fresh cilantro leaves**
- 3 **tablespoons raw hulled pumpkin seeds, toasted**

  Flaky sea salt (optional)

Toast in a skillet over medium heat until golden brown and nutty-smelling, 3 to 5 minutes.

Roast the carrots Preheat your oven to 400°F. On a rimmed baking sheet, toss the carrots with the cooking oil, paprika, cumin, ¾ teaspoon of the salt, and ½ teaspoon of the black pepper. Roast, tossing once and rotating the baking sheet front to back, until golden brown and you can just barely insert a fork into the center of the thinnest carrot, 24 to 28 minutes. Remove from the oven and let cool to room temperature.

Cook the rice Meanwhile, bring a large pot of water to a boil. Add 1 teaspoon of the salt and the rice. Reduce the heat to maintain a simmer and cook until the rice is just tender, 24 to 28 minutes. Drain and let cool to room temperature.

Assemble the salad In a large bowl, combine the cooked rice, watercress, olive oil, lemon juice, Aleppo pepper, remaining 1 teaspoon salt, and remaining ½ teaspoon black pepper and toss until evenly mixed. Pile onto a serving platter and smooth into an even layer. Lay the carrots and avocado on top, alternating so they're all mixed in together. Sprinkle with the cilantro and pumpkin seeds, drizzle with olive oil and finish with some Aleppo pepper, flaky sea salt (if you want), and a few grinds of black pepper.

Scorecard

Other Veg

Whole Grains

Serves

8

Salt-Massaged Napa Cabbage and Kimchi Slaw

I created this simple slaw to play off the napa cabbage in kimchi—it's mellower and less intense, flavor-wise, than pure kimchi, and has even more veg for your gut to love.

1 large head napa cabbage (about 2 pounds), quartered and sliced ¼ inch thick

1 teaspoon kosher salt

1 cup chopped kimchi

2 tablespoons lime juice

2 tablespoons fish sauce

½ cup chopped fresh cilantro

2 tablespoons sesame seeds

Toss the cabbage with the salt in a large bowl. Let sit for 30 minutes to 1 hour, tossing occasionally. Fold in the remaining ingredients and serve.

Scorecard

LGVs

Fermented Food

Serves
6 to 8

THE RECIPES

Quick-Braised Coconut Collard Greens

I would never want to mess with classic long-braised collards with ham. But collards don't always have to be stewed into submission—I actually like them best when they're cooked until soft yet still have a slight bite.

Here I pair them with coconut milk, which tames the bitterness of the greens, and golden raisins, which echo coconut's inherent sweetness. This recipe forms the backbone of the Saucy Coconut Collards with Crispy Sweet Potato Rounds and Millet (page 245), but I also love it spooned over brown rice with shredded chicken, or with a white-fleshed fish like cod poached right in the broth.

2   tablespoons coconut oil

1   large bunch collard greens (1¼ pounds), stems removed, leaves sliced ½ inch thick

1   teaspoon ground turmeric

1   teaspoon kosher salt, plus more as needed

½   teaspoon freshly ground black pepper

1   (13.5-ounce) can unsweetened coconut milk

2   cups water

¼   cup golden raisins

1   tablespoon lime juice

¼   cup large unsweetened coconut flakes, toasted

¼   teaspoon crushed red pepper

In a large pot or straight-sided skillet, melt the coconut oil over medium-high heat. Add the collards, turmeric, salt, and black pepper. Cook, tossing frequently with tongs, until softened, about 5 minutes. Add the coconut milk, water, and raisins. Bring to a boil over high heat, then reduce the heat to maintain a simmer. Cook, uncovered, for 10 to 14 minutes, until the greens are tender but with a slight bite. Remove from the heat and stir in the lime juice. Taste and season with salt.

Pour the coconut collards into a shallow serving dish and sprinkle with the coconut flakes and some crushed red pepper. Serve hot.

Scorecard

✓

LGVs

Serves

4

as a side

THE RECIPES

DRINKS

Rather than create an exhaustive guide to drinks that are gut-friendly, I'm showcasing three recipes that can each serve as a sort of template for your own creations. There's a spiced coconut milk latte—easily tweaked with your favorite warm baking spices (try it with cinnamon, nutmeg, or even steeped black tea)—an easy infusion of aromatic herbs and ginger, and a lightly sweetened cocktail. In general, I stick with natural wine or cocktails with no sugar added. Moderation (to manage inflammation) and not drinking on an empty stomach (to manage blood sugar) are both key.

Turmeric-
Coconut-
Ginger Latte
318

Ginger, Lemongrass, and Fennel Infusion

This delicious infusion is full of anti-inflammatory ingredients, but most important, it soothes an upset stomach. I keep a jar full of these ingredients in my fridge all winter to easily brew up a batch—even if I don't have a stomachache, I've come to love the herbal taste as an alternative to tea.

When I have leftover fennel stalks from Fennel, Parsnip, and Apple Soup (page 223) or another recipe, I use them here. But I love the stronger taste of dried fennel seeds just as much; either works in this recipe.

4   cups water

¼   cup thinly sliced fresh ginger

¼   cup chopped fresh lemongrass (from two 6-inch stalks)

A large handful of mint sprigs, rinsed

1   teaspoon fennel seeds, or about 5 fresh fennel stalks, sliced

½   teaspoon whole black peppercorns

I call for sliced fresh ginger since it's faster than grating it. But if you have the time and the will, grated will have a stronger fiery kick!

Combine all the ingredients in a small pot. Bring to a boil over high heat, then reduce the heat to maintain a gentle simmer. Cook for about 1 minute, then remove from the heat and let steep until the tea is the right temperature to drink. (For me, that's at least 20 minutes, but a little over or under is fine.)

Strain into a mug and drink up! Keep the rest hot in the pot to sip steadily or save in a jar. You can add more boiling water and re-steep the infusion if desired.

Makes
a big pot to
serve

1 or 2

THE RECIPES

Turmeric-Coconut-Ginger Latte

The paste in this recipe is a long-standing Lindsay special, which I created many years ago as a sort of "healing tonic." It's true that citrus, ginger, and turmeric are all anti-inflammatory foods. However, I know now that the last thing you want to put in your body when you're under the weather is any sort of added sugar. So skip the honey when you're sick; when you're in good health, the sweetened version is the perfect occasional afternoon treat.

Makes
3/4
cup paste
(about
6 lattes)

For the spicy paste

¼ cup freshly squeezed lemon juice

¼ cup peeled and grated fresh ginger

¼ cup ground turmeric

3 tablespoons raw, local honey

1½ teaspoons black pepper

For each latte

½ cup unsweetened nondairy milk

½ cup unsweetened canned coconut milk

2 tablespoons Spicy Paste

Make the paste Whisk all the ingredients for the paste together in a small bowl. Transfer to an airtight jar and keep refrigerated for up to 10 days.

To make 1 latte In a small pot, heat the nondairy milk and the coconut milk over medium-high heat until gently simmering (alternatively, heat them in the microwave). Scoop 2 tablespoons of the paste into a large mug. While whisking, slowly pour in the hot milk; whisk until smooth. Drink right away.

Hibiscus and Mezcal Sparklers

At the beginning of my quest to feel better via food, I went to the depths of the no-grain lifestyle, which in its most extreme state means no corn- or grain-derived spirits like vodka, bourbon, or gin. Instead I opted for mezcal—which is derived from agave. I've since gone back to grains, but mezcal remains a favorite. Here it's paired with gorgeous fuchsia-hued hibiscus tea in a big-batch recipe.

Serves

6

4 cups water

¼ cup loose hibiscus tea

1 large bunch mint leaves (3 ounces), washed, plus a sprig per glass for serving

2 tablespoons raw honey (optional)

¾ cup mezcal or tequila (6 ounces)

⅔ cup lime juice (from 5 to 6 limes)

Ice

1 lime, thinly sliced, for serving

3 cups cold soda water

Bring the water to a boil. Place the hibiscus, mint, and honey (if using) in a heatproof bowl or pitcher and pour the boiling water over. Let steep for 30 minutes, then strain into a serving pitcher. Stir in the mezcal and lime juice.

To serve, fill large glasses with ice. Slide a few slices of lime down the edge of the glasses (because it looks pretty) and stick a sprig of mint between the cubes. Divide the hibiscus-mezcal mixture among the glasses (¾ cup per drink), then top with the soda water and serve.

NATURAL WINE

I am a big fan of natural wine, which I see as the wine equivalent of shopping at my local farmers' market. It matters to me how my beef was raised and processed, so why wouldn't it be the same for what I drink?

Natural wine is a general term that encompasses an organic winemaking style of minimal intervention in how the grapes are grown, harvested, fermented, or bottled. This process excludes things that conventional winemakers do like adding sugar, unfermented grape juice, or other chemicals during the fermentation process. While some organic wines are natural, "organic" alone doesn't mean that the winemaker didn't intervene in the growing or fermentation processes.

Even though wine is made from grapes, which contain fructose (the sugar found in fruit), the fermentation process reduces the sugar content significantly. Red wine is lower in sugar than white wine, and drier wines are lower than sweeter ones. Makes sense, right? You can literally taste the sugar content.

TREATS & DESSERTS

These sweets may not taste quite like the sugar-laden baked goods or desserts you're used to—without the same amount of butter and sugar, they simply can't—but they'll satisfy your sweet tooth without leaving you feeling inflamed or tired. They taste great and look gorgeous, too.

What's the difference between a treat and a dessert? Not much in taste, but to me, it's about the format. A treat is a casual affair, eaten on its own, while a dessert is the follow-up to a meal. The point is—this chapter runs the gamut between small treats to make-ahead to enjoy when you like, like miso-infused caramels, to more involved recipes like a three-vegetable take on pumpkin pie.

Sweet Potato, Squash, and Carrot Pie 334

Miso-Date Butterscotchy Sauce

Making a caramel-like sauce with miso and dates isn't a revolutionary idea—I've seen versions in many different places. But what's different about mine is that the only sweetness comes from the dates, with no refined sugar. You can use it as you would caramel or another dessert sauce, or (since it's not loaded with added sugar) even enjoy a spoonful over a yogurt bowl. I also use it to top steamed sweet potato (see page 152) and in the parfait on page 331.

⅔ packed cup pitted large, soft Medjool dates (about 10 dates/ 7 ounces pitted), chopped

¾ cup just-boiled water

¾ cup unsweetened canned coconut milk

¼ cup white miso paste

2 tablespoons lemon juice

1 teaspoon pure vanilla extract

¼ teaspoon kosher salt

⅛ teaspoon ground cinnamon

Combine the dates and water in a blender or mini food processor. Let sit for 10 minutes to soften the dates, then add the coconut milk, miso paste, lemon juice, vanilla, salt, and cinnamon. Blend until smooth. Transfer to an airtight container and refrigerate for up to 10 days.

Scorecard

✔ Fermented Food

Makes

2

cups

Coconut Whipped Cream

Coconut whipped cream is hot s#!t in the plant-based blogosphere, so naturally I wanted to try it as well. I found a lot of versions out there, but none that felt like a decent replica of real whipped cream. After many tries and an obsessive attention to detail, I figured it out. You have to chill the cans overnight, upside down. This allows the water to fully separate from the cream so you can pour it off. Also, I was in the habit of buying "simple" coconut milk that has no guar gum added to it, since gum extracts can be hard on the gut. But cream without guar gum doesn't perform quite right. Since you're only having a little bit, I think the exception to the rule is fine here.

2   (13.5-ounce) cans unsweetened coconut milk (buy one with guar gum)

1   teaspoon pure vanilla extract

Pinch of kosher salt

 NOTE   You have to chill the cans of coconut milk overnight before making this recipe.

How to use it:

Mash up raspberries with lemon juice and fold them into the cream to make a quick fool.

Stir in some Miso-Date Butterscotchy Sauce (page 325) for something pudding-esque.

Use in place of the yogurt in Roasted Pineapple Parfaits (page 331).

Refrigerate the cans of coconut upside-down overnight.

Scoop the hardened coconut cream out of the cans into the bowl of a stand mixer or a large metal bowl (about 1¾ cups total). Keep the coconut liquid on hand. Add the vanilla and salt to the coconut cream.

Beat on high speed with the stand mixer (fitted with the whisk attachment) or a handheld mixer until fluffy and smooth, about 2 minutes. Add the reserved coconut water 1 tablespoon at a time to get to the consistency of whipped cream (around 3 tablespoons total). Save any extra coconut water in an airtight container in the fridge to use in smoothies.

Serve right away, or store in an airtight container in the fridge for up to 1 week.

Makes

2

cups (¼ cup per serving)

Chocolate-Chunk Peanut Butter–Banana "Nice" Cream

In my decade of testing and developing recipes, I've rolled my eyes at anything that sounded too much like a hack—think one-ingredient ice cream. But when seeking a healthful plant-focused alternative to ice cream, I turned to the internet-famous method for blending frozen bananas into "nice cream." It really works! Blending the banana with peanut butter adds richness that's lost when you don't use dairy, and the ribbon of chocolate chunks makes this appropriately decadent. To ensure this is 100 percent plant-based, make sure to buy vegan chocolate.

Serves
6 to 8

9   ripe bananas, sliced and frozen overnight (8½ cups)

⅔   cup natural smooth peanut butter

1½   teaspoons pure vanilla extract

½   teaspoon kosher salt

4   ounces 85% dark chocolate, broken into small pieces

3   tablespoons coconut oil, melted

     Flaky sea salt

Make the nice cream Place the bananas and peanut butter in a food processor. Process until the banana breaks down and the mixture becomes a smooth puree, 5 to 7 minutes. Stop every minute or so to scrape down the sides with a spatula. Blend in 1 teaspoon of the vanilla and the salt.

Make the chocolate chunks Place the chocolate and coconut oil in a microwave-safe bowl. Microwave in 15-second bursts, stirring after each, until melted. (You can also do this in a heatproof bowl set over a pan of simmering water.) Stir in the remaining ½ teaspoon vanilla.

Layer the two mixtures Scrape the banana mixture into a 9-inch square pan and smooth it out. Drizzle the chocolate mixture over the top, then swirl with an offset spatula or knife to create small chunks of chocolate. (It will solidify as you stir it into the banana mixture.)

Serve right away, sprinkled with flaky sea salt (it will be soft). To make it scoopable like ice cream, cover the pan and freeze for at least 1 hour. Store in an airtight container for up to 1 month; let it soften at room temperature for 20 to 30 minutes before serving.

THE RECIPES

STEP-BY-STEP
PHOTOS ON
THE NEXT PAGE

After freezing the bananas overnight, grab the rest of the ingredients.

Process the bananas and peanut butter until smooth.

Blend in the vanilla and salt.

Place the chocolate and coconut oil in a microwave-safe bowl.

Microwave until melted. Stir in the remaining vanilla.

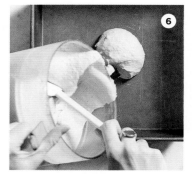

Scrape the banana mixture into the pan.

Drizzle the chocolate mixture over the top.

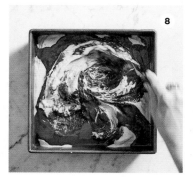

Swirl with an offset spatula or knife to create small chunks of chocolate.

Roasted Pineapple Parfaits

I don't know what it is about a parfait, but I just love them. I think it's the distinct layers that make me think I'm eating a more extravagant dessert than I am. In this recipe, roasting the pineapple takes out some of the moisture, resulting in chewy, caramelized bites of heaven.

For dinner parties, I assemble this dish family-style on a big platter and let everyone serve themselves. (See page 89 for a photo.) Here's how to do it: Spread the yogurt on a serving platter, then pile the roasted pineapple on top. Dollop with the Miso-Date Butterscotchy Sauce, then sprinkle with the pistachios, mint, and coconut flakes.

Scorecard

✔
Fermented Food

✔
Fruit

Serves

4

THE RECIPES

1 pineapple (4 pounds), peeled, quartered, cored, and chopped into 1-inch chunks

1 tablespoon preferred cooking oil

½ teaspoon ground cardamom

½ teaspoon kosher salt

½ cup unsweetened large coconut flakes

1 cup plain Greek yogurt or Coconut Whipped Cream (page 326)

½ cup Miso-Date Butterscotchy Sauce (page 325)

¼ cup chopped roasted pistachios

2 tablespoons torn fresh mint leaves (optional)

Flaky sea salt (optional)

Preheat your oven to 450°F.

Toss the pineapple, oil, cardamom, and kosher salt on a rimmed baking sheet. Roast, turning once, until the pineapple is golden brown and caramelized, about 30 minutes. Let cool to room temperature.

While the pineapple cools, toast the coconut on a rimmed baking sheet until golden, 3 to 5 minutes. Keep an eye on it, because it can burn quickly.

Assemble the parfaits in the glasses, making two layers of each component, starting with the yogurt, then the butterscotchy sauce, pineapple, coconut, and pistachios. Top each off with the mint and a sprinkle of flaky sea salt (if you want).

Pistachio Butter Thumbprints
with Raspberry-Chia Filling

In my original version of these cookies, I didn't use any sweetener at all. I loved the taste, but the texture was somewhat . . . breakfast-y. That's because one of the essential things sugar does in a cookie is make it crisp. So, here I use just 3 tablespoons added sugar, which I discovered is the minimum threshold for these to taste dessertlike. To get the cookies exactly evenly sized, use a baking scale to measure out the dough into 0.8-ounce balls.

For the cookie dough

- 2 tablespoons flaxseed meal
- ⅓ cup water
- 1¼ cups pistachios (6.5 ounces)
- 1 cup packed quick-cooking oats
- 3 tablespoons coconut or other fine sugar
- 1 teaspoon lemon zest
- 1 teaspoon pure vanilla extract
- 1 teaspoon kosher salt
- ¼ teaspoon ground cardamom

For the jam filling

- ⅓ cup 100% fruit no-sugar-added raspberry jam
- 1 tablespoon chia seeds (white ones are prettiest here)

Preheat your oven to 375°F. Line a baking sheet with parchment paper.

Mix the flaxseed meal and water in a small bowl. Let sit for 5 minutes to thicken while you measure the remaining ingredients.

Blitz the pistachios in a food processor until finely ground with just some small chunks remaining. Pull out ¼ cup of the pistachios and smooth into a single layer on a plate. Set the plate aside.

Add the oats, coconut sugar, lemon zest, vanilla, salt, and cardamom to the food processor and process until finely ground. Pulse in the flaxseed mixture until you have a thick dough.

Divide the dough into 16 heaping-tablespoon balls and roll them in the reserved pistachios to coat, pressing to adhere the nuts to the dough and placing them on the prepared baking sheet as you go. Flatten each ball into a ¾-inch-thick disc. Use a round-bottomed ½-teaspoon measuring spoon to press a divot into the center of each disc. (It helps to wrap your thumb and forefinger around the disc as you press the teaspoon into the dough.)

Stir the jam and chia seeds together, then divide the filling evenly among the divots in the cookies.

Bake, rotating the baking sheet halfway through, until the cookies are golden brown around the edges and the filling is set, 14 to 18 minutes. Let cool to room temperature before eating.

To Store

The cookies will keep in an airtight container at room temperature for up to 3 days.

Sweet Potato, Squash, and Carrot Pie

This pie was my Everest. I had a vision: a dessert that tasted like pumpkin pie, was legitimately healthy—thanks to a ton of vegetables—and was sexy enough to compete with sugar-laden classic pies. Nine tries later, the resulting pie checks all those boxes, boasting a sweet, smooth filling bolstered by warm holiday spices. It's healthy enough that I feel great about eating what's left for breakfast—if there are any leftovers, that is.

Soft Medjool dates are key for this recipe. If yours are too dry, soak them in boiling water to soften them up first, then drain and proceed with the recipe. This recipe is time-consuming, so I recommend making it a day before you plan to serve it.

Scorecard

Other Veg

Serves
8 to 10

For the crust

- ⅓ cup coconut oil, melted, plus more for the pan
- 1 cup quick-cooking or old-fashioned oats
- ¾ cup unsweetened shredded coconut
- ½ cup raw hulled pumpkin seeds, toasted and cooled, plus more for garnishing
- 2 tablespoons flaxseed meal
- 1 teaspoon kosher salt
- ½ teaspoon baking powder
- ½ packed cup pitted soft Medjool dates (6 ounces/7 or 8 large), chopped
- 1 large egg
- 1 teaspoon pure vanilla extract

For the filling

- 14 ounces carrots (4 or 5 medium), scrubbed and cut into 2-inch lengths
- 1 sweet potato (12 ounces), cut into 1-inch pieces
- 1 butternut or kabocha squash (12 ounces), peeled, seeded, and cut into 1½-inch-thick wedges

- 1 cup unsweetened canned coconut milk
- ¼ cup tightly packed pitted soft Medjool dates (3 ounces/about 4 large), chopped
- 1½ teaspoons ground cinnamon
- 1 teaspoon ground ginger
- ¼ teaspoon ground allspice
- ¼ teaspoon ground nutmeg
- ½ teaspoon kosher salt
- 3 large eggs
- 2 teaspoons pure vanilla extract

For serving

Whipped heavy cream or Coconut Whipped Cream (page 326)

Make the crust Preheat your oven to 350°F. Brush a 9-inch springform pan with coconut oil and set it on a rimmed baking sheet.

In a food processor, combine the oats, coconut, pumpkin seeds, flaxseed meal, salt, and baking powder. Process until finely ground. Add the dates and pulse until well incorporated, then pulse in the egg, coconut oil, and vanilla until it all holds together.

Press the dough evenly over the bottom of the springform pan and 2 inches up the sides. (It helps to use a flat-bottomed measuring cup to get into the edges of the pan so you don't get a thick edge.) Prick the bottom all over with a fork (about 20 times). Bake for about 30 minutes, until dry and golden brown. Remove from the oven and let cool to room temperature. Keep the oven on.

Meanwhile, make the filling Fill a large pot with 2 inches of water and put a steamer insert inside. Bring the water to a simmer and place the carrot, sweet potato, and squash in separate thirds of the pot. Cover and steam until you can stick a fork very easily into the center of each, about 25 minutes. Divide the carrot, sweet potato, and squash into separate bowls, then mash them. Measure out 1 packed cup (8 ounces) of each and transfer to a food processor or blender. (Save any extra in an airtight container in the fridge for a smoothie.)

Add the coconut milk, dates, cinnamon, ginger, allspice, nutmeg, and salt. Puree until completely smooth. Add the eggs one at a time, processing until incorporated after adding each, then add the vanilla.

Bake the pie Pour the filling into the baked crust and smooth the top. Bake until the filling is almost entirely set, with just a small quarter-size bit in the center still jiggling when you shake the pan, 45 to 50 minutes.

Chill the pie Let the pie cool to room temperature, then refrigerate for at least 6 hours and up to overnight.

Serve the pie Release the sides of the pan and remove the springform ring. Spread the whipped cream over the top and sprinkle with pumpkin seeds.

Chocolate-Dipped Peanut Butter, Miso, and Date Caramels

I love to serve these caramels without announcing their healthful status. They're pretty enough to entice almost anyone, and it's always fun to reveal that there are a generous amount of seeds and miso packed into the "caramel" center.

If it's important to you that these are 100 percent plant-based, make sure to buy vegan chocolate.

- 1 tablespoon coconut oil, melted, plus more for brushing
- 1½ cups tightly packed pitted soft Medjool dates (14 ounces)
- ½ cup natural peanut butter
- 2 tablespoons chia seeds
- ¼ cup flaxseed meal
- 2 tablespoons white miso paste
- ¼ teaspoon ground nutmeg
- 1 teaspoon pure vanilla extract
- 3.5 ounces 85% dark chocolate, broken into chunks
- 1 teaspoon flaky sea salt

Brush an 8½ by 4½-inch loaf pan with oil and line it with a sheet of parchment paper that hangs over each side by 1 inch.

In a food processor or blender, combine the dates, peanut butter, chia seeds, flaxseed meal, miso, nutmeg, and vanilla. Process on high until you have a smooth paste and the mixture forms a ball.

Scrape the date paste into the prepared pan and pat until smooth. Fold the overhanging parchment down and press down with a second loaf pan. (If you don't have one, no worries—the caramels will turn out fine!) Freeze for 1 hour.

Brush a wire rack with coconut oil and set it over a rimmed baking sheet. Line a cutting board with parchment. Turn the caramels out of the pan onto the cutting board so the bottom is face up. Top with the parchment from the pan and roll out to ½ inch thick. Cut the caramels into 36 (1-inch) squares.

Place the chocolate in a microwave-safe bowl and microwave in 15-second bursts, stirring after each, until melted. Stir in the melted coconut oil. Use a fork to dip a caramel into the melted chocolate. Place it on the prepared rack, let set for 5 seconds, then sprinkle with sea salt. Repeat to coat the remaining caramels, re-melting the chocolate if needed. Freeze for 1 hour before serving.

Get-Ahead Tip Freeze the caramels in airtight container with parchment between the layers for up to a month.

Scorecard

✔ Nuts and Seeds

✔ Fermented Food

Makes

36

caramels

THE RECIPES

Spiced Vanilla Pear Crumble

This is what you want from a crumble—almost equal parts topping and fruit filling. It's my go-to winter dessert, and I'm not mad when there are leftovers for breakfast. I heat them up in a bowl and drizzle kefir over the top.

I'm loath to eat a bowl of crumble without ice cream on top. When I go for it, I always seek out a locally made vanilla bean ice cream that has the least amount of added sugar. Or, I serve it with just-barely-frothed heavy cream or Coconut Whipped Cream (page 326).

Scorecard

✔
Whole Grains

✔
Fruit

Serves
10 to 12

For the pears

¼ cup brown coconut or other fine sugar

¼ cup arrowroot starch

3 tablespoons coconut oil, melted

2 teaspoons pure vanilla extract

1 teaspoon ground cardamom

¼ teaspoon kosher salt

8 firm but ripe Bosc or Anjou pears (3¾ pounds total), cored and sliced very thin (¼ inch or thinner)

½ cup water

For the topping

3 cups rolled oats

1½ cups unsweetened coconut flakes

1 cup raw hulled pumpkin seeds

1 tablespoon ground cinnamon

2 teaspoons kosher salt

1 teaspoon baking powder

¼ cup brown coconut or other fine sugar

1 cup coconut oil, melted

Bake the pears Preheat your oven to 375°F. Line a baking sheet with parchment paper, then use a permanent marker to trace the outline of a 9 by 13-inch baking dish on the parchment. Flip the parchment so the marker side is face-down. Set aside. Brush the baking dish with 1 tablespoon of the coconut oil.

In a large bowl, whisk together the sugar, arrowroot starch, remaining 2 tablespoons coconut oil, the vanilla, cardamom, and salt until evenly combined. Add the pears and toss until evenly coated. Transfer to the prepared dish and smooth it out. Pour the water over the pears, cover the baking dish tightly with foil, and bake for 40 minutes.

Meanwhile, make the topping In a food processor, combine 2 cups of the oats, 1 cup of the coconut flakes, ½ cup of the pumpkin seeds, the cinnamon, salt, baking powder, and sugar until evenly ground. Add the coconut oil and pulse until incorporated, then add the remaining 1 cup oats and ½ cup each coconut flakes and pumpkin seeds and pulse until just combined. (You want to keep big pieces for textural difference.) Scrape the topping onto the outlined rectangle on the parchment-lined baking sheet and pat it into a slightly smaller rectangle, leaving a ¼-inch border between the topping and the marker line. Freeze for 30 minutes while the filling bakes.

Remove the pears from the oven and carefully lift off the foil (there will be a lot of steam). Discard the foil. Lift the frozen crumble topping off the parchment (it should be solid) and place it on the top of the pears. Return the baking dish to the oven and bake for 20 to 25 minutes more, until the topping is golden brown, the filling is bubbling, and there's a thick sauce coating the pears. Let cool to room temperature before serving.

Seeded Chocolate-Tahini Bark

I honestly can't be left alone in the house when I know there's a batch of this bark in my freezer. It's everything I love about a peanut butter cup, but with a generous serving of seeds, which beneficial microbes love. I also love how pretty the bark looks—particularly when made with golden flax and white chia. When I have friends over, I bring out the whole slab on a platter and let everyone break off their own pieces.

1 pound 85% dark chocolate

½ cup tahini

3 tablespoons flaxseeds

3 tablespoons chia seeds

3 tablespoons hemp seeds

½ cup raw hulled pumpkin seeds

1 teaspoon flaky sea salt

Line a baking sheet (that will fit in your freezer) with parchment or waxed paper.

Make the first chocolate layer Place half the chocolate in a microwave-safe bowl. Microwave in 15-second bursts, stirring after each, until melted. (You can also do this in a heatproof bowl set over a pan of simmering water.) Pour the chocolate onto the prepared baking sheet and use an offset or silicone spatula to spread the chocolate into an 8 by 12-inch rectangle. Freeze for 10 minutes.

Make the seeded tahini filling In a small bowl, stir together the tahini, flaxseeds, chia seeds, and 2 tablespoons of the hemp seeds. Spread over the frozen chocolate, almost all the way to the edges. Freeze for 10 minutes.

Top with more chocolate Melt the remaining chocolate and pour it over the tahini layer. Use an offset or flexible spatula to spread the melted chocolate to the edges of the bottom chocolate layer. Working quickly before the chocolate sets, sprinkle with the pumpkin seeds, remaining 1 tablespoon hemp seeds, and the flaky sea salt. Freeze for at least 2 hours. Break into chunks to serve.

To Store

Store the bark in a parchment-lined airtight container in the freezer for up to 2 months.

Spread the tahini mixture over the chocolate, chill, then pour the remaining melted chocolate over the top.

Use an offset or flexible spatula to spread the melted chocolate to the edges.

Working quickly before the chocolate sets, sprinkle with the pumpkin and hemp seeds, plus some flaky sea salt.

Scorecard

Checking off your goals as you achieve them can be a powerful motivator. Think of the scorecard as a way to track the foods that are important to eat from the perspective of your microbes. (It doesn't mean that you can't eat other foods that aren't on the scorecard, just that it doesn't matter to score them.) The goal isn't perfection or sticking to this every day, but rather a way to see incremental progress over time. Some days it'll be easy to stay on track; others, it won't. That's normal. Even two servings of vegetables a day makes a difference for your gut microbes.

 You can photocopy the scorecards on the following page or print a downloadable version at LMH.how/scorecard.

HERE'S HOW TO USE IT Each color represents a level, and each box counts for one serving. You're aiming to check the boxes at the level you're at. If you are going for the Beginner level, then check off all the yellow boxes. At Intermediate, check the yellow *and* the orange. Pro, yellow, orange, and green. Boot-camp level, go for all the colored boxes. Anything you get beyond that is great!

SERVING SIZES

Leafy green vegetables: ½ cup cooked or 1 cup raw

Other vegetables or fruit: ½ cup cooked or 1 cup raw

Whole grains: ½ cup cooked

Beans and legumes: ½ cup cooked

Nuts and seeds: ¼ cup nuts, 2 tablespoons nut butter, or 1 tablespoon seeds

Fermented foods: No minimum serving size; better to eat frequently than go for large portions

BEGINNER LEVEL

(Check off yellow boxes)
1 serving leafy green vegetables
1 serving other vegetables or fruit

INTERMEDIATE LEVEL

(Check off the yellow and orange boxes)
2 servings leafy green vegetables
1 serving other vegetables or fruit
1 serving whole grains
1 serving beans and legumes
1 serving nuts and seeds
No ultraprocessed foods

PRO LEVEL

(Check off yellow, orange and green boxes)
2 servings leafy green vegetables
2 servings other vegetables or fruit
2 servings whole grains
2 servings beans and legumes
2 servings nuts and seeds
No added sugar
No ultraprocessed foods

BOOT-CAMP LEVEL

(Check off yellow, orange, green and blue boxes)
2 to 3 servings leafy green vegetables
2 to 3 servings other vegetables or fruit
2 servings whole grains
2 servings beans and legumes
2 servings nuts and seeds
2 servings fermented foods
No added sugar
No ultraprocessed foods

CUT

No Added Sugar			
Leafy Green Vegetables			
Other Vegetables or Fruit			
Whole Grains			
Beans and Legumes			
Nuts and Seeds			
Fermented Foods			
No Ultraprocessed Foods			

No Added Sugar			
Leafy Green Vegetables			
Other Vegetables or Fruit			
Whole Grains			
Beans and Legumes			
Nuts and Seeds			
Fermented Foods			
No Ultraprocessed Foods			

No Added Sugar			
Leafy Green Vegetables			
Other Vegetables or Fruit			
Whole Grains			
Beans and Legumes			
Nuts and Seeds			
Fermented Foods			
No Ultraprocessed Foods			

No Added Sugar			
Leafy Green Vegetables			
Other Vegetables or Fruit			
Whole Grains			
Beans and Legumes			
Nuts and Seeds			
Fermented Foods			
No Ultraprocessed Foods			

No Added Sugar			
Leafy Green Vegetables			
Other Vegetables or Fruit			
Whole Grains			
Beans and Legumes			
Nuts and Seeds			
Fermented Foods			
No Ultraprocessed Foods			

No Added Sugar			
Leafy Green Vegetables			
Other Vegetables or Fruit			
Whole Grains			
Beans and Legumes			
Nuts and Seeds			
Fermented Foods			
No Ultraprocessed Foods			

No Added Sugar			
Leafy Green Vegetables			
Other Vegetables or Fruit			
Whole Grains			
Beans and Legumes			
Nuts and Seeds			
Fermented Foods			
No Ultraprocessed Foods			

No Added Sugar			
Leafy Green Vegetables			
Other Vegetables or Fruit			
Whole Grains			
Beans and Legumes			
Nuts and Seeds			
Fermented Foods			
No Ultraprocessed Foods			

APPENDIX

Recipes by Slug

🥘 ONE POT/ONE PAN

Nutritional Index

While I don't use nutritional numbers to chart my eating, I recognize that many people do use these numbers to plan what they eat. Please do note, however, that nutritional analysis is an imperfect process and based on an average of any given ingredient, so these numbers are at best an approximation, and at worst, a distraction from the essence of the food. The two numbers that I do personally take into account are grams of fiber and added sugar, as they are the most important for eating with your microbes in mind, so those figures are shown in blue so you can see them easily at a glance. (Values are rounded to the nearest tenth decimal, except calories and sodium, which are rounded to nearest whole integer.)

Crispy Roasted Chickpeas 100
Serving Size: ¼ cup
Calories: 107 Protein: 3.6g Carbohydrates: 11.9g Total Dietary Fiber: 2.6g Total Sugars: 0.1g Added Sugar: 0g Fat: 5.1g Saturated Fat: 0.6g Cholesterol: 0mg Vitamin A: 0.5 IU Vitamin C: 0mg Calcium: 3.8mg Iron: 1mg Potassium: 137.1mg Sodium: 86mg

Pickled Shallots 101
Serving Size: ¼ cup
Calories: 35 Protein: 1.1g Carbohydrates: 6.9g Total Dietary Fiber: 1.32g Total Sugars: 3.14g Added Sugar: 0.1g Fat: 0g Saturated Fat: 0g Cholesterol: 0mg Vitamin A: 3.0 IU Vitamin C: 3.3mg Calcium: 19.9mg Iron: 0.7mg Potassium: 142.7mg Sodium: 231mg

Cauliflower "Bread Crumbs" 102
Serving Size: 2 tablespoons
Calories: 48 Protein: 1.4g Carbohydrates: 3.6g Total Dietary Fiber: 1.5g Total Sugars: 1.4g Added Sugar: 0g Fat: 3.6g Saturated Fat: 0.6g Cholesterol: 0mg Vitamin A: 0.8 IU Vitamin C: 34.2mg Calcium: 16.3mg Iron: 0.3mg Potassium: 213.9mg Sodium: 161mg

Smoky Roasted Fennel 104
Serving Size: ¼ recipe
Calories: 115 Protein: 2.2g Carbohydrates: 12.9g Total Dietary Fiber: 5.6g Total Sugars: 6.7g Added Sugar: 0g Fat: 7.4g Saturated Fat: 0g Cholesterol: 0mg Vitamin A: 1,781.6 IU Vitamin C: 20.5mg Calcium: 88.3mg Iron: 1.4mg Potassium: 718.8mg Sodium: 229mg

Roasted White Turnips 105
Serving Size: ¼ recipe
Calories: 92 Protein: 1.1g Carbohydrates: 7.3g Total Dietary Fiber: 2.1g Total Sugars: 4.3g Added Sugar: 0g Fat: 7.2g Saturated Fat: 0.8g Cholesterol: 0mg Vitamin A: 0.4 IU Vitamin C: 23.4mg Calcium: 24.5mg Iron: 0.3mg Potassium: 1mg Sodium: 140mg

Roasted Celery Root 105
Serving Size: ¼ recipe
Calories: 134 Protein: 2.7g Carbohydrates: 16.3g Total Dietary Fiber: 3.4g Total Sugars: 2.7g Added Sugar: 0g Fat: 7.6g Saturated Fat: 0.9g Cholesterol: 0mg Vitamin A: 79.1 IU Vitamin C: 16.2mg Calcium: 81mg Iron: 1.5mg Potassium: 524.1mg Sodium: 310mg

Roasted Mushrooms 107
Serving Size: ¼ recipe
Calories: 116 Protein: 5.7g Carbohydrates: 10.5g Total Dietary Fiber: 4g Total Sugars: 1.9g Added Sugar: 0g Fat: 7.5g Saturated Fat: 1g Cholesterol: 0mg Vitamin A: 82.3 IU Vitamin C: 0mg Calcium: 5.8mg Iron: 2.3mg Potassium: 716.4mg Sodium: 241mg

Roasted Romanesco 108
Serving Size: ¼ recipe
Calories: 164 Protein: 7g Carbohydrates: 14.4g Total Dietary Fiber: 7.5g Total Sugars: 0g Added Sugar: 0g Fat: 11.2g Saturated Fat: 1.1g Cholesterol: 0mg Vitamin A: 0.8 IU Vitamin C: 246.9mg Calcium: 74.4mg Iron: 1.7mg Potassium: 632.9mg Sodium: 287mg

Slow-Roasted Shallots 109
Serving Size: ⅛ recipe
Calories: 176 Protein: 3.3g Carbohydrates: 22.4g Total Dietary Fiber: 4.3g Total Sugars: 10.5g Added Sugar: 0g Fat: 9.5g Saturated Fat: 1g Cholesterol: 0mg Vitamin A: 5.9 IU Vitamin C: 10.6mg Calcium: 49.7mg Iron: 1.6mg Potassium: 445.7mg Sodium: 63mg

Lemony Roasted Broccoli Rabe 110
Serving Size: ¼ recipe
Calories: 134 Protein: 5.7g Carbohydrates: 6.4g Total Dietary Fiber: 0.5g Total Sugars: 1.1g Added Sugar: 0g Fat: 11.3g Saturated Fat: 1.2g Cholesterol: 0mg Vitamin A: 0.8 IU Vitamin C: 41.9mg Calcium: 189.3mg Iron: 3.7mg Potassium: 335.3mg Sodium: 336mg

Garlicky Sautéed Chard 113
Serving Size: ¼ recipe
Calories: 95 Protein: 2.9g Carbohydrates: 7.3g Total Dietary Fiber: 2.5g Total Sugars: 1.8g Added Sugar: 0g Fat: 7.1g Saturated Fat: 1g Cholesterol: 0mg Vitamin A: 8,764.5 IU Vitamin C: 46.8mg Calcium: 80.6mg Iron: 2.7mg Potassium: 566.6mg Sodium: 583mg

Blanched Haricots Verts or Green Beans 114
Serving Size: ¼ recipe
Calories: 42 Protein: 2.4g Carbohydrates: 8.4g Total Dietary Fiber: 2.4g Total Sugars: 2.4g Added Sugar: 0g Fat: 0g Saturated Fat: 0g Cholesterol: 0mg Vitamin A: 358.1 IU Vitamin C: 10.7mg Calcium: 47.8mg Iron: 0.9mg Potassium: 0mg Sodium: 70mg

Perfectly Steamed Broccoli 116
Serving Size: ¼ recipe
Calories: 48 Protein: 5.1g Carbohydrates: 8.6g Total Dietary Fiber: 3.9g Total Sugars: 2.5g Added Sugar: 0g Fat: 0.6g Saturated Fat: 0.1g Cholesterol: 0mg Vitamin A: 5,102.9 IU Vitamin C: 0mg Calcium: 152.5mg Iron: 1.5mg Potassium: 552.8mg Sodium: 46mg

Grilled Romaine 116
Serving Size: ½ romaine head
Calories: 62 Protein: 0.1g Carbohydrates: 0.4g Total Dietary Fiber: 0.1g Total Sugars: 0.2g Added Sugar: 0g Fat: 6.8g Saturated Fat: 0.9g Cholesterol: 0mg Vitamin A: 84.4 IU Vitamin C: 0.2mg Calcium: 2.6mg Iron: 0.1mg Potassium: 14.3mg Sodium: 94mg

Extra-Crispy Roasted Asparagus 117
Serving Size: ½ recipe
Calories: 174 Protein: 4.3g Carbohydrates: 8.7g Total Dietary Fiber: 4.3g Total Sugars: 4.3g Added Sugar: 0g Fat: 14g Saturated Fat: 1.5g Cholesterol: 0mg Vitamin A: 1,068.5 IU Vitamin C: 19.2mg Calcium: 44mg Iron: 0.8mg Potassium: 3.8mg Sodium: 420mg

Melted Onions 119
Serving Size: 3 onion halves
Calories: 138 Protein: 2g Carbohydrates: 16.5g Total Dietary Fiber: 3.2g Total Sugars: 7g Added Sugar: 0g Fat: 7.7g Saturated Fat: 4.6g Cholesterol: 15mg Vitamin A: 312.7 IU Vitamin C: 12.2mg Calcium: 45.6mg Iron: 0.5mg Potassium: 263.8mg Sodium: 147mg

Resistant Starch Potatoes— Fingerlings 120
Serving Size: ¼ recipe
Calories: 87 Protein: 2g Carbohydrates: 20g Total Dietary Fiber: 2.7g Total Sugars: 0.7g Added Sugar: 0g Fat: 0g Saturated Fat: 0g Cholesterol: 0mg Vitamin A: 0 IU Vitamin C: 22.4mg Calcium: 13.3mg Iron: 0.8mg Potassium: 0mg Sodium: 7mg

Resistant Starch Potatoes—New Potatoes 120
Serving Size: ¼ recipe
Calories: 93 Protein: 2.7g Carbohydrates: 18.7g Total Dietary Fiber: 1.3g Total Sugars: 2.7g Added Sugar: 0g Fat: 0g Saturated Fat: 0g Cholesterol: 0mg Vitamin A: 0 IU Vitamin C: 24mg Calcium: 26.7mg Iron: 1.4mg Potassium: 0mg Sodium: 7mg

Resistant Starch Potatoes—Yukon Gold 120
Serving Size: ¼ recipe
Calories: 82 Protein: 2.1g Carbohydrates: 20.6g Total Dietary Fiber: 2.1g Total Sugars: 1g Added Sugar: 0g Fat: 0g Saturated Fat: 0g Cholesterol: 0mg Vitamin A: 0 IU Vitamin C: 3.7mg Calcium: 82.5mg Iron: 1.1mg Potassium: 0mg Sodium: 36mg

Chickpea Flatbread 123
Serving Size: ¼ flatbread
Calories: 471 Protein: 16.9g Carbohydrates: 43.7g Total Dietary Fiber: 8.3g Total Sugars: 8.14g Added Sugar: 0g Fat: 25.3g Saturated Fat: 3.3g Cholesterol: 0mg Vitamin A: 33.9 IU Vitamin C: 0mg Calcium: 57.2mg Iron: 3.8mg Potassium: 642.3mg Sodium: 613mg

Brown Rice 124
Serving Size: ½ cup
Calories: 120 Protein: 2.4g Carbohydrates: 28g Total Dietary Fiber: 2.4g Total Sugars: 0g Added Sugar: 0g Fat: 1.2g Saturated Fat: 0g Cholesterol: 0mg Vitamin A: 0 IU Vitamin C: 0mg Calcium: 0mg Iron: 0.6mg Potassium: 0mg Sodium: 224mg

Oat Groats 124
Serving Size: ½ cup
Calories: 90 Protein: 0g Carbohydrates: 17g Total Dietary Fiber: 2.5g Total Sugars: 0g Added Sugar: 0g Fat: 0g Saturated Fat: 1.25g Cholesterol: 0mg Vitamin A: 0 IU Vitamin C: 0mg Calcium: 13mg Iron: 0.9mg Potassium: 94mg Sodium: 187mg

Lentils 124
Serving Size: ½ cup
Calories: 69 Protein: 5.1g Carbohydrates: 10.9g Total Dietary Fiber: 2.3g Total Sugars: 1.1g Added Sugar: 0g Fat: 0g Saturated Fat: 0g Cholesterol: 0mg Vitamin A: 0 IU Vitamin C: 1.4mg Calcium: 11.4mg Iron: 1.5mg Potassium: 0mg Sodium: 160mg

Pinto Beans 124
Serving Size: ½ cup
Calories: 123 Protein: 7.8g Carbohydrates: 22.6g Total Dietary Fiber: 7.7g Total Sugars: 0.3g Added Sugar: 0g Fat: 0.6g Saturated Fat: 0.1g Cholesterol: 0mg Vitamin A: 0 IU Vitamin C: 0.7mg Calcium: 39.8mg Iron: 1.8mg Potassium: 375.4mg Sodium: 382mg

Chickpeas 124
Serving Size: ½ cup
Calories: 107 Protein: 6g Carbohydrates: 18g Total Dietary Fiber: 5.3g Total Sugars: 3.3g Added Sugar: 0g Fat: 1.7g Saturated Fat: 0g Cholesterol: 0mg Vitamin A: 0 IU Vitamin C: 1.6mg Calcium: 26.7mg Iron: 1.8mg Potassium: 0mg Sodium: 193mg

Quinoa 124
Serving Size: ½ cup
Calories: 97 Protein: 3.6g Carbohydrates: 18g Total Dietary Fiber: 1.8g Total Sugars: 0g Added Sugar: 0g Fat: 1.52g Saturated Fat: 0g Cholesterol: 0mg Vitamin A: 0 IU Vitamin C: 0mg Calcium: 12mg Iron: 2mg Potassium: 0mg Sodium: 230mg

Buckwheat 124
Serving Size: ½ cup
Calories: 160 Protein: 6g Carbohydrates: 32g Total Dietary Fiber: 1g Total Sugars: 1g Added Sugar: 0g Fat: 1g Saturated Fat: 0g Cholesterol: 0mg Vitamin A: 0 IU Vitamin C: 0mg Calcium: 4.7mg Iron: 1.3mg Potassium: 0mg Sodium: 280mg

Millet 124
Serving Size: ½ cup
Calories: 133 Protein: 4.7g Carbohydrates: 26.7g Total Dietary Fiber: 6g Total Sugars: 0g Added Sugar: 0g Fat: 0g Saturated Fat: 1.3g Cholesterol: 0mg Vitamin A: 0 IU Vitamin C: 0mg Calcium: 0mg Iron: 1mg Potassium: 0mg Sodium: 187mg

Trash or Treasure Broth 129
Serving Size: 1 quart
Calories: 0 Protein: 0g Carbohydrates: 0g Total Dietary Fiber: 0g Total Sugars: 0g Added Sugar: 0g Fat: 0g Saturated Fat: 0g Cholesterol: 0mg Vitamin A: 0 IU Vitamin C: 0mg Calcium: 91mg Iron: 0mg Potassium: 0mg Sodium: 18mg

Parsley, Kale, and Pumpkin Seed Pesto 132
Serving Size: ¼ cup
Calories: 238 Protein: 5.2g Carbohydrates: 4g Total Dietary Fiber: 1.4g Total Sugars: 0.2g Added Sugar: 0g Fat: 22.8g Saturated Fat: 3.6g Cholesterol: 0mg Vitamin A: 2,187.4 IU Vitamin C: 26.8mg Calcium: 37.2mg Iron: 2.4mg Potassium: 140.2mg Sodium: 178mg

Cheater's Romesco 133
Serving Size: ¼ cup
Calories: 124 Protein: 2.4g Carbohydrates: 5.6g Total Dietary Fiber: 2.6g Total Sugars: 0.8g Added Sugar: 0g Fat: 10.43g Saturated Fat: 1.3g Cholesterol: 0mg

Vitamin A: 333.2 IU Calcium: 66.5mg Iron: 1mg Potassium: 87mg Sodium: 295mg

White Tahini Sauce 134
Serving Size: 2 tablespoons
Calories: 112 Protein: 2.5g Carbohydrates: 4.1g Total Dietary Fiber: 1.6g Total Sugars: 0.2g Added Sugar: 0g Fat: 10.4g Saturated Fat: 1.5g Cholesterol: 0mg Vitamin A: 47.3 IU Vitamin C: 3.1mg Calcium: 151.6mg Iron: 2.3mg Potassium: 10.2mg Sodium: 210mg

Faux Caesar 135
Serving Size: 2 tablespoons
Calories: 140 Protein: 1g Carbohydrates: 0.4g Total Dietary Fiber: 0g Total Sugars: 0.1g Added Sugar: 0g Fat: 15g Saturated Fat: 1.5g Cholesterol: 0mg Vitamin A: 0.7 IU Vitamin C: 1.6mg Calcium: 1.2mg Iron: 0.6mg Potassium: 6.4mg Sodium: 513mg

Spicy Miso Mayo 136
Serving Size: 2 tablespoons
Calories: 107 Protein: 0.7g Carbohydrates: 3g Total Dietary Fiber: 0.1g Total Sugars: 1.5g Added Sugar: 0g Fat: 10.2g Saturated Fat: 1g Cholesterol: 0mg Vitamin A: 0 IU Vitamin C: 0.3mg Calcium: 0.7mg Iron: 0.4mg Potassium: 7.2mg Sodium: 351mg

Kimchi Dressing 137
Serving Size: 2 tablespoons
Calories: 62 Protein: 0.3g Carbohydrates: 0.2g Total Dietary Fiber: 0g Total Sugars: 0.1g Added Sugar: 0g Fat: 6.7g Saturated Fat: 0.7g Cholesterol: 0mg Vitamin A: 7.8 IU Vitamin C: 0mg Calcium: 3.4mg Iron: 0.5mg Potassium: 12.6mg Sodium: 186mg

Nine-Minute Eggs with Steamed Greens and Kimchi Dressing 141
For a single serving
Calories: 312 Protein: 15.2g Carbohydrates: 10.3g Total Dietary Fiber: 1.6g Total Sugars: 0.2g Added Sugar: 0g Fat: 24.42g Saturated Fat: 4.4g Cholesterol: 430mg Vitamin A: 11,513 IU Vitamin C: 85.1mg Calcium: 150.1mg Iron: 3.6mg Potassium: 29mg Sodium: 606mg

Egg, Bacon, and Kale Breakfast Tacos 142
For a single serving
Calories: 386 Protein: 19.7g Carbohydrates: 29.5g Total Dietary Fiber: 4.3g Total Sugars: 1.8g Added Sugar: 0g Fat: 21.3g Saturated Fat: 8.5g Cholesterol: 450mg Vitamin A: 4,098.8 IU Vitamin C: 39.8mg Calcium: 169.8mg Iron: 3.5mg Potassium: 195.5mg Sodium: 435mg

Refried Beans and Fried Eggs with Avocado, Spinach, and Pico de Gallo 145
For a single serving
Calories: 698 Protein: 31.7g Carbohydrates: 53.8g Total Dietary Fiber: 19.5g Total Sugars: 5.7g Added Sugar: 0g Fat: 37.2g Saturated Fat: 7g Cholesterol: 430mg Vitamin A: 8,085.8 IU Vitamin C: 42.1mg Calcium: 235.2mg Iron: 9mg Potassium: 1,361.4mg Sodium: 1,039mg

Salty-Sweet Kefir and Olive Oil Fruit Bowl 148
For a single serving
Calories: 572 Protein: 21.1g Carbohydrates: 40.4g Total Dietary Fiber: 8.4g Total Sugars: 24.8g Added Sugar: 0g Fat: 39g Saturated Fat: 5.2g Cholesterol: 12.2mg Vitamin A: 174.4 IU Vitamin C: 33.2mg Calcium: 438.1mg Iron: 3.5mg Potassium: 843.6mg Sodium: 95mg

Almond, Date, and Chia Waffles 151
Serving Size: ½ Belgian-style waffle
Calories: 346 Protein: 9.9g Carbohydrates: 27.3g Total Dietary Fiber: 8.4g Total Sugars: 9.9g Added Sugar: 0.1g Fat: 23.4g Saturated Fat: 6.4g Cholesterol: 73.8mg Vitamin A: 361.3 IU Vitamin C: 3.9mg Calcium: 242.7mg Iron: 2mg Potassium: 201.3mg Sodium: 178mg

Salted Smashed Sweet Potatoes with Miso-Date Butterscotchy Sauce 152
For a single serving
Calories: 536 Protein: 8.9g Carbohydrates: 92.3g Total Dietary Fiber: 13g Total Sugars: 32.3g Added Sugar: 0g Fat: 19.1g Saturated Fat: 11.5g Cholesterol: 0mg Vitamin A: 43,222.2 IU Vitamin C: 36.9mg Calcium: 76.1mg Iron: 2mg Potassium: 162.7mg Sodium: 269mg

Caramelized Baked Apples with Yogurt and Granola 155
For a single serving
Calories: 572 Protein: 21.4g Carbohydrates: 64.4g Total Dietary Fiber: 8.3g Total Sugars: 29.9g Added Sugar: 7.5g Fat: 27.1g Saturated Fat: 16.5g Cholesterol: 27.5mg Vitamin A: 199.3 IU Vitamin C: 8.4mg Calcium: 159.9mg Iron: 2.9mg Potassium: 363.1mg Sodium: 214mg

Coconut, Pumpkin Seed, and Buckwheat Granola 156
Serving Size: ½ cup
Calories: 326 Protein: 8.4g Carbohydrates: 31.4g Total Dietary Fiber: 3.8g Total Sugars: 6.4g Added Sugar: 5.4g Fat: 19.5g

Saturated Fat: 11.7g Cholesterol: 0mg Vitamin A: 0.6 IU Vitamin C: 0mg Calcium: 22.2mg Iron: 2.6mg Potassium: 143.1mg Sodium: 86mg

Jicama, Avocado, and Grapefruit Breakfast Salad 159
For a single serving
Calories: 432 Protein: 5g Carbohydrates: 46g Total Dietary Fiber: 16.3g Total Sugars: 26g Added Sugar: 0g Fat: 28.7g Saturated Fat: 4.1g Cholesterol: 0mg Vitamin A: 3,253.8 IU Vitamin C: 148.5mg Calcium: 66.7mg Iron: 1.7mg Potassium: 1,129.6mg Sodium: 302mg

Creamy Coconut and Millet Porridge 162
For a single serving
Calories: 317 Protein: 9.1g Carbohydrates: 52.8g Total Dietary Fiber: 10.1g Total Sugars: 8.4g Added Sugar: 6.1g Fat: 8.8g Saturated Fat: 5.2g Cholesterol: 0mg Vitamin A: 18.7 IU Vitamin C: 0.4mg Calcium: 37.4mg Iron: 2.1mg Potassium: 22mg Sodium: 94mg

Peanut Butter and Amaranth Porridge with Saucy Strawberries 163
Serving Size: ⅛ recipe
Calories: 358 Protein: 14g Carbohydrates: 42.3g Total Dietary Fiber: 8.3g Total Sugars: 9.9g Added Sugar: 4.8g Fat: 17g Saturated Fat: 2.6g Cholesterol: 0mg Vitamin A: 10.5 IU Vitamin C: 45.9mg Calcium: 137.7mg Iron: 4.5mg Potassium: 320.5mg Sodium: 164mg

Broccoli and Quinoa Congee 164
For a single serving
Calories: 248 Protein: 5.6g Carbohydrates: 33.9g Total Dietary Fiber: 5.6g Total Sugars: 2.9g Added Sugar: 0g Fat: 11.3g Saturated Fat: 6.1g Cholesterol: 20g Vitamin A: 1,069.6 IU Vitamin C: 106.8 mg Calcium: 129.4mg Iron: 1.8mg Potassium: 93.7mg Sodium: 523

Mango, Mint, and Kale Smoothie 168
For a single serving
Calories: 349 Protein: 9.5g Carbohydrates: 35.8g Total Dietary Fiber: 7g Total Sugars: 25.9g Added Sugar: 0g Fat: 18.7g Saturated Fat: 8.5g Cholesterol: 0mg Vitamin A: 9,009.6 IU Vitamin C: 78.6mg Calcium: 252.8mg Iron: 3.4mg Potassium: 35.1mg Sodium: 102mg

Spiced Pumpkin Shake 169
For a single serving
Calories: 326 Protein: 13.7g Carbohydrates: 54.7g Total Dietary Fiber: 10.2g Total Sugars: 39.8g Added Sugar: 0.1g Fat: 7.2g Saturated Fat: 1.1g Cholesterol: 6.1mg Vitamin A: 22,516 IU Vitamin C: 4.3mg Calcium: 298.7mg Iron: 3.7mg Potassium: 268mg Sodium: 114mg

Turmeric Pineapple Smoothie 170
For a single serving
Calories: 289 Protein: 7.5g Carbohydrates: 44.8g Total Dietary Fiber: 7g Total Sugars: 14.8g Added Sugar: 0g Fat: 10.2g Saturated Fat: 1g Cholesterol: 0mg Vitamin A: 1.6 IU Vitamin C: 37.7mg Calcium: 117.9mg Iron: 2.7mg Potassium: 238.9mg Sodium: 61mg

Blueberry, Chia, and Beet Smoothie 171
For a single serving
Calories: 227 Protein: 5.8g Carbohydrates: 29.5g Total Dietary Fiber: 10.3g Total Sugars: 17.5g Added Sugar: 0g Fat: 9.5g Saturated Fat: 0.4g Cholesterol: 0mg Vitamin A: 0 IU Vitamin C: 5mg Calcium: 188.5mg Iron: 1.2mg Potassium: 12.5mg Sodium: 90mg

Immune-Boosting Super Smoothie 172
For a single serving
Calories: 360 Protein: 9.6g Carbohydrates: 39.9g Total Dietary Fiber: 10.7g Total Sugars: 18.4g Added Sugar: 0g Fat: 19.4g Saturated Fat: 7g Cholesterol: 0mg Vitamin A: 18,092.4 IU Vitamin C: 65.8mg Calcium: 300.7mg Iron: 3.3mg Potassium: 194.7mg Sodium: 121mg

Spinach and Squash Smoothie 173
For a single serving
Calories: 334 Protein: 8.9g Carbohydrates: 40.6g Total Dietary Fiber: 8.8g Total Sugars: 17.8g Added Sugar: 0g Fat: 17g Saturated Fat: 6.7g Cholesterol: 0mg Vitamin A: 28,653.7 IU Vitamin C: 19.9mg Calcium: 261.2mg Iron: 2.9mg Potassium: 304.7mg Sodium: 173mg

Magic Seed-and-Nut Bread 177
Serving Size: 1 slice
Calories: 265 Protein: 8.9g Carbohydrates: 15.7g Total Dietary Fiber: 8.1g Total Sugars: 1.8g Added Sugar: 1g Fat: 19.6g Saturated Fat: 2.4g Cholesterol: 0mg Vitamin A: 0 IU Vitamin C: 0.1mg Calcium: 61.9mg Iron: 2.4mg Potassium: 115.8mg Sodium: 142mg

Hemp, Chia, and Flax Seed Shaker 180
Serving Size: 1 tablespoon
Calories: 54 Protein: 2.8g Carbohydrates: 3g Total Dietary Fiber: 2.7g Sugars: 0.1g Added Sugar: 0g Fat: 3.9g Saturated Fat: 0.4g Cholesterol: 0mg Vitamin A: 0 IU Vitamin C: 0.1mg Calcium: 14.4mg Iron: 0.6mg Potassium: 0mg Sodium: 0mg

Five-Seed Shaker 180
Serving Size: 1 tablespoon
Calories: 50 Protein: 2.5g Carbohydrates: 2.1g Total Dietary Fiber: 1.7g Total Sugars: 0.1g Added Sugar: 0g Fat: 3.8g Saturated Fat: 0.5g Cholesterol: 0mg Vitamin A: 0 IU Vitamin C: 0mg Calcium: 8.9mg Iron: 0.7mg Potassium: 15.2mg Sodium: 0mg

Dates, Seeds, and Peanut Butter 182
For a single serving
Calories: 529 Protein: 19.8g Carbohydrates: 43.1g Total Dietary Fiber: 11.3g Total Sugars: 28.6g Added Sugar: 0g Fat: 36g Saturated Fat: 4.6g Cholesterol: 0mg Vitamin A: 59.6 IU Vitamin C: 0.1mg Calcium: 94.8mg Iron: 3.5mg Potassium: 707.4mg Sodium: 98mg

Sesame Matcha Shakes 183
For a single serving
Calories: 390 Protein: 9.6g Carbohydrates: 32g Total Dietary Fiber: 5.1g Total Sugars: 21.2g Added Sugar: 0.1g Fat: 26.9g Saturated Fat: 11.8g Cholesterol: 0mg Vitamin A: 29.8 IU Vitamin C: 0mg Calcium: 112mg Iron: 2.1mg Potassium: 140mg Sodium: 100mg

Papaya and Mango Snack Salad 187
For a single serving
Calories: 239 Protein: 4.6g Carbohydrates: 37.8g Total Dietary Fiber: 4.7g Total Sugars: 24.3g Added Sugar: 0g Fat: 9.4g Saturated Fat: 3g Cholesterol: 0mg Vitamin A: 1,666.8 IU Vitamin C: 120mg Calcium: 55.1mg Iron: 1.9mg Potassium: 244.5mg Sodium: 151mg

Matcha-Raspberry Energy Bites 189
Serving Size: One bite
Calories: 148 Protein: 4.4g Carbohydrates: 16.1g Total Dietary Fiber: 3.7g Total Sugars: 6.8g Added Sugar: 0g Fat: 8.4g Saturated Fat: 3.7g Cholesterol: 0g Vitamin A: 18.8 IU Vitamin C: 1mg Calcium: 18.3mg Iron: 0.8mg Potassium: 125.6mg Sodium: 15mg

Double Oat and Almond Banana Bread 190
Serving Size: 1 slice
Calories: 338 Protein: 8.4g Carbohydrates: 39.2g Total Dietary Fiber: 5.4g Total Sugars: 11.7g Added Sugar: 0.1g Fat: 18g Saturated Fat: 1.8g Cholesterol: 53.8mg Vitamin A: 88.2 IU Vitamin C: 3.7mg Calcium: 124mg Iron: 2mg Potassium: 258.4mg Sodium: 114mg

Chickpea Hush Puppies with Herb Dip 197
Serving Size: 3 hush puppies with dip
Calories: 317 Protein: 6.7g Carbohydrates: 25.4g Total Dietary Fiber: 4.3g Total Sugars: 3.4g Added Sugar: 0g Fat: 21.5g Saturated Fat: 2.2g Cholesterol: 25.2g Vitamin A: 217.3 IU Vitamin C: 2.23mg Calcium: 213.4mg Iron: 1.7mg Potassium: 116.6mg Sodium: 351mg

Le Petit Aioli 198
Serving Size: ⅛ recipe
Calories: 465 Protein: 4.7g Carbohydrates: 24.3g Total Dietary Fiber: 4.7g Total Sugars: 3.9g Added Sugar: 0g Fat: 40.8g Saturated Fat: 5.5g Cholesterol: 61.5mg Vitamin A: 5,654 IU Vitamin C: 59.9mg Calcium: 64.4mg Iron: 1.5mg Potassium: 414.4mg Sodium: 386mg

Roasted Pepper and Aioli Flatbread 201
Serving Size: ⅒ recipe
Calories: 382 Protein: 8.3g Carbohydrates: 24.7g Total Dietary Fiber: 5.4g Total Sugars: 7.1g Added Sugar: 0g Fat: 28.4g Saturated Fat: 3.7g Cholesterol: 24.6mg Vitamin A: 2,951.8 IU Vitamin C: 118.7mg Calcium: 41.1mg Iron: 2.2mg Potassium: 480.8mg Sodium: 457mg

Fork-and-Knife Wedge Salad with Crispy Mushrooms and Faux Caesar 202
For a single serving
Calories: 307 Protein: 7.6g Carbohydrates: 12.2g Total Dietary Fiber: 5g Total Sugars: 3g Added Sugar: 0g Fat: 27.6g Saturated Fat: 2.6g Cholesterol: 0mg Vitamin A: 70.5 IU Vitamin C: 8.8mg Calcium: 43mg Iron: 3.8mg Potassium: 858mg Sodium: 835mg

Baked Smoked Trout, Chive, and Artichoke Dip 207
Serving Size: ⅟₁₂ dip
Calories: 241 Protein: 9.5g Carbohydrates: 6.6g Total Dietary Fiber: 1.5g Total Sugars: 2.1g Added Sugar: 0g Fat: 20.2g Saturated Fat: 9.2g Cholesterol: 58.6mg Vitamin A: 184.8 IU Vitamin C: 3.9mg

Calcium: **81.9mg** Iron: **0.2mg** Potassium: **136mg** Sodium: **301mg**

Caramelized Onion Dip 208
Serving Size: **1/10 dip**
Calories: **152** Protein: **1.6g** Carbohydrates: **13.1g Total Dietary Fiber: 2.4g** Total Sugars: **5.9g Added Sugar: 0g** Fat: **11g** Saturated Fat: **1.1g** Cholesterol: **0g** Vitamin A: **65.5 IU** Vitamin C: **12mg** Calcium: **34mg** Iron: **0.6mg** Potassium: **208.1mg** Sodium: **266mg**

Kabocha Squash and Tahini Dip 209
Serving Size: **1/8 dip**
Calories: **148** Protein: **2.1g** Carbohydrates: **6.6g Total Dietary Fiber: 2.7g** Total Sugars: **2.1g Added Sugar: 0g** Fat: **13.5g** Saturated Fat: **1.8g** Cholesterol: **0mg** Vitamin A: **47 IU** Vitamin C: **7.3mg** Calcium: **24.6mg** Iron: **0.6mg** Potassium: **150.3mg** Sodium: **320mg**

Beet, Avocado, and Pistachio Dip 210
Serving Size: **1/8 dip**
Calories: **146** Protein: **2.7g** Carbohydrates: **8.2g Total Dietary Fiber: 3.5g** Total Sugars: **3.3g Added Sugar: 0g** Fat: **12.3g** Saturated Fat: **1.7g** Cholesterol: **0mg** Vitamin A: **60 IU** Vitamin C: **6.2mg** Calcium: **17.9mg** Iron: **0.8mg** Potassium: **321.1mg** Sodium: **100mg**

Roasted Garlic Aioli 211
Serving Size: **1/6 aioli**
Calories: **352** Protein: **1.5g** Carbohydrates: **3.5g Total Dietary Fiber: 0.2g** Total Sugars: **0.2g Added Sugar: 0g** Fat: **38.2g** Saturated Fat: **5g** Cholesterol: **61.5mg** Vitamin A: **83.1 IU** Vitamin C: **4.7mg** Calcium: **23.8mg** Iron: **0.4mg** Potassium: **47.1mg** Sodium: **238mg**

Whipped Cauliflower and Harissa Dip with Herb Oil and Sesame Seeds 212
Serving Size: **1/6 dip**
Calories: **202** Protein: **4.8g** Carbohydrates: **10.5g Total Dietary Fiber: 4.2g** Total Sugars: **2.9g Added Sugar: 0g** Fat: **17.3g** Saturated Fat: **2.6g** Cholesterol: **0mg** Vitamin A: **0.9 IU** Vitamin C: **69.7mg** Calcium: **137.7mg** Iron: **2.4mg** Potassium: **416.8mg** Sodium: **328mg**

Vegetarian Chili with Poblanos and Hominy 216
Serving Size: **1/6 soup**
Calories: **290** Protein: **8.8g** Carbohydrates: **42.9g Total Dietary Fiber: 9.8g** Total Sugars: **6.2g Added Sugar: 0g** Fat: **8.9g** Saturated Fat: **1.1g** Cholesterol: **0mg** Vitamin A: **383.7 IU** Vitamin C: **47.1mg** Calcium: **140.4mg** Iron: **3.4mg** Potassium: **539.6mg** Sodium: **780mg**

Spiced Carrot Soup with Coconut Cream 218
Serving Size: **1/6 soup**
Calories: **299** Protein: **5.8g** Carbohydrates: **28.8g Total Dietary Fiber: 5.9g** Total Sugars: **16.8g Added Sugar: 0g** Fat: **17.8g** Saturated Fat: **14.1g** Cholesterol: **0mg** Vitamin A: **26,233.3 IU** Vitamin C: **17.2mg** Calcium: **95.7mg** Iron: **2.5mg** Potassium: **213.5mg** Sodium: **355mg**

Spiced Lamb Meatball and Escarole Soup 221
Serving Size: **1/6 soup**
Calories: **400** Protein: **21.7g** Carbohydrates: **23.1g Total Dietary Fiber: 9.1g** Total Sugars: **4.2g Added Sugar: 0g** Fat: **24.9g** Saturated Fat: **10.1g** Cholesterol: **69mg** Vitamin A: **2,091.9 IU** Vitamin C: **12.5mg** Calcium: **180.6mg** Iron: **4.8mg** Potassium: **544mg** Sodium: **646mg**

Fennel, Parsnip, and Apple Soup 223
Serving Size: **1/6 soup**
Calories: **210** Protein: **2.9g** Carbohydrates: **36.7g Total Dietary Fiber: 10.3g** Total Sugars: **17g Added Sugar: 0g** Fat: **7.5g** Saturated Fat: **1.1g** Cholesterol: **0mg** Vitamin A: **1,149 IU** Vitamin C: **33.5mg** Calcium: **137.1mg** Iron: **1.6mg** Potassium: **928mg** Sodium: **450mg**

Cauliflower and Sunchoke Soup 224
Serving Size: **1/6 soup**
Calories: **169** Protein: **5g** Carbohydrates: **29.5g Total Dietary Fiber: 5.2g** Total Sugars: **14.2g Added Sugar: 0g** Fat: **5g** Saturated Fat: **0.8g** Cholesterol: **0mg** Vitamin A: **93.7 IU** Vitamin C: **66.8mg** Calcium: **95.3mg** Iron: **4mg** Potassium: **900.3mg** Sodium: **343mg**

Lemony Chicken and Quinoa Soup with Pesto 227
Serving Size: **1/6 soup**
Calories: **291** Protein: **27g** Carbohydrates: **16.1g Total Dietary Fiber: 2.3g** Total Sugars: **2.1g Added Sugar: 0g** Fat: **12.7g** Saturated Fat: **2.9g** Cholesterol: **74mg** Vitamin A: **1,408.6 IU** Vitamin C: **17.7mg** Calcium: **142.1mg** Iron: **2.5mg** Potassium: **521.1mg** Sodium: **558mg**

Brothy Tomatoes, Spinach, and Chickpeas with Herbs 228
Serving Size: **1/4 soup**
Calories: **393** Protein: **11.1g** Carbohydrates: **37g Total Dietary Fiber: 14.5g** Total Sugars: **4.5g Added Sugar: 0g** Fat: **22.3g** Saturated Fat: **3.1g** Cholesterol: **0mg** Vitamin A: **7,626.7 IU** Vitamin C: **67.2mg** Calcium: **114.7mg** Iron: **5.8mg** Potassium: **1,117.2mg** Sodium: **254mg**

Coconut Chicken and Rice Stew 231
Serving Size: **1/8 soup**
Calories: **344** Protein: **19.6g** Carbohydrates: **41.2g Total Dietary Fiber: 5.5g** Total Sugars: **3.5g Added Sugar: 0g** Fat: **10.6g** Saturated Fat: **6.8g** Cholesterol: **45.2mg** Vitamin A: **1,559.6 IU** Vitamin C: **63.1mg** Calcium: **96mg** Iron: **2.1mg** Potassium: **5.2mg** Sodium: **1,164mg**

Olive Tapenade and Onion Quinoa Quiche 235
Serving Size: **1/8 quiche**
Calories: **232** Protein: **12.1g** Carbohydrates: **18.6g Total Dietary Fiber: 2.5g** Total Sugars: **2.1g Added Sugar: 0g** Fat: **12g** Saturated Fat: **2.9g** Cholesterol: **322.5mg** Vitamin A: **663.5 IU** Vitamin C: **3.7mg** Calcium: **52.9mg** Iron: **2.3mg** Potassium: **169.7mg** Sodium: **495mg**

Toasted Corn, Mushroom, and Kale Quiche with a Millet Crust (with parm) 236
Serving Size: **1/8 quiche**
Calories: **353** Protein: **17.4g** Carbohydrates: **31.1g Total Dietary Fiber: 6g** Total Sugars: **1.4g Added Sugar: 0g** Fat: **17.1g** Saturated Fat: **4.8g** Cholesterol: **330mg** Vitamin A: **5,945.9 IU** Vitamin C: **44mg** Calcium: **179.7mg** Iron: **2.5mg** Potassium: **256mg** Sodium: **541mg**

Millet and Black Bean Cakes 239
Serving Size: **1 cake**
Calories: **205** Protein: **8.1g** Carbohydrates: **27.2g Total Dietary Fiber: 2.1g** Total Sugars: **0.4g Added Sugar: 0g** Fat: **7.3g** Saturated Fat: **0.8g** Cholesterol: **0mg** Vitamin A: **128.5 IU** Vitamin C: **3.3mg** Calcium: **87.9mg** Iron: **2.6mg** Potassium: **91.1mg** Sodium: **228mg**

Lentil and Chard Cakes 240
Serving Size: **1 cake**
Calories: **211** Protein: **9g** Carbohydrates: **31g Total Dietary Fiber: 4.6g** Total Sugars: **2.8g Added Sugar: 0g** Fat: **6g** Saturated Fat: **0.9g** Cholesterol: **53.8mg** Vitamin A: **3,543.9 IU** Vitamin C: **19.8mg** Calcium: **50.8mg** Iron: **3.4mg** Potassium: **244.3mg** Sodium: **419mg**

Brown Rice Burrito Bowls with Spicy Black Beans and Onions 242
For a single serving
Calories: 594 Protein: 15.6g
Carbohydrates: 84.9g Total Dietary Fiber: 18.6g Total Sugars: 6g Added Sugar: 0g Fat: 23.9g Saturated Fat: 3.6 g Cholesterol: 0g Vitamin A: 827 IU Vitamin C: 20.9mg Calcium: 92.2mg Iron: 3.8mg Potassium: 1,203.4mg Sodium: 266mg

Saucy Coconut Collards with Crispy Sweet Potato Rounds and Millet 245
Serving Size: ⅙ recipe
Calories: 624 Protein: 16.6g
Carbohydrates: 81.4g Total Dietary Fiber: 17.6g Total Sugars: 10.9g Added Sugar: 0g Fat: 27.6g Saturated Fat: 15.3g Cholesterol: 0mg Vitamin A: 16,429.2 IU Vitamin C: 37.2mg Calcium: 190.5mg Iron: 4.1mg Potassium: 467.8mg Sodium: 795mg

Crispy Tofu Steaks with Broccoli Rabe and Romesco 246
For a single serving
Calories: 542 Protein: 32.9g
Carbohydrates: 14.6g Total Dietary Fiber: 7.8g Total Sugars: 1.8g Added Sugar: 0g Fat: 41g Saturated Fat: 4.8g Cholesterol: 0mg Vitamin A: 4,793.2 IU Vitamin C: 43.8mg Calcium: 623mg Iron: 9.2mg Potassium: 482mg Sodium: 686mg

Brussels Sprout and Peanut Butter Curry Bowl 249
For a single serving
Calories: 882 Protein: 20.7g
Carbohydrates: 80g Total Dietary Fiber: 14.3g Total Sugars: 9.8g Added Sugar: 0g Fat: 57.5g Saturated Fat: 28.6g Cholesterol: 0mg Vitamin A: 1,394.6 IU Vitamin C: 134.8mg Calcium: 126.3mg Iron: 6.9mg Potassium: 898.6mg Sodium: 441mg

Trumpet Mushroom "Scallops" with Cauliflower, Red Pepper, and Miso Puree 250
For a single serving
Calories: 364 Protein: 11.6g Carbohydrates: 41.9g Total Dietary Fiber: 10g Total Sugars: 6.3g Added Sugar: 0g Fat: 18.7g Saturated Fat: 2.6g Cholesterol: 0mg Vitamin A: 852 IU Vitamin C: 78.4mg Calcium: 98.3mg Iron: 4.8mg Potassium: 1,077.8mg Sodium: 763mg

Roasted Eggplant and Chickpeas with Herbed Oat Pilaf 253
For a single serving
Calories: 664 Protein: 22.3g
Carbohydrates: 82.1g Total Dietary Fiber:

12.5g Total Sugars: 7.9g Added Sugar: 0g Fat: 29.3g Saturated Fat: 3.7g Cholesterol: 0mg Vitamin A: 792.9 IU Vitamin C: 17.1mg Calcium: 199.2mg Iron: 7.2mg Potassium: 895.8mg Sodium: 542mg

Loaded Baked Potatoes with Tomatoey Swiss Chard, White Beans, and Arctic Char 256
For a single serving
Calories: 607 Protein: 36.6g
Carbohydrates: 64.7g Total Dietary Fiber: 11.6g Total Sugars: 5.4g Added Sugar: 0g Fat: 22.3g Saturated Fat: 3.9g Cholesterol: 71.4mg Vitamin A: 7,128.1 IU Vitamin C: 58.3mg Calcium: 179.2mg Iron: 5.9mg Potassium: 1,615.4mg Sodium: 576mg

Summer Swordfish with Grilled Pineapple Salsa 259
For a single serving
Calories: 439 Protein: 34.8g
Carbohydrates: 27.9g Total Dietary Fiber: 3.4g Total Sugars: 19.2g Added Sugar: 0g Fat: 21.8g Saturated Fat: 4.2g Cholesterol: 112.3mg Vitamin A: 335.7 IU Vitamin C: 97.5mg Calcium: 44.1mg Iron: 1.4mg Potassium: 965.5mg Sodium: 631mg

Shrimp, Black Bean, and Kimchi Tacos with Romaine Salad 260
For a single serving
Calories: 365 Protein: 26.5g
Carbohydrates: 43.5g Total Dietary Fiber: 10.9g Total Sugars: 2.8g Added Sugar: 0g Fat: 10.6g Saturated Fat: 1.3g Cholesterol: 142.9mg Vitamin A: 415.9 IU Vitamin C: 5.6mg Calcium: 193.4mg Iron: 4.4mg Potassium: 663.4mg Sodium: 1,819mg

Oven-Poached Salmon with Roasted Cauliflower Salad 263
Serving Size: ⅙ recipe
Calories: 356 Protein: 28.5g
Carbohydrates: 20g Total Dietary Fiber: 6.4g Total Sugars: 9.9g Added Sugar: 0g Fat: 18.6g Saturated Fat: 2.7g Cholesterol: 62.4mg Vitamin A: 265.4 IU Vitamin C: 165.7mg Calcium: 85.2mg Iron: 2.4mg Potassium: 1,370.8mg Sodium: 668mg

Garlicky Shrimp and Quinoa "Grits" 264
For a single serving
Calories: 341 Protein: 19.9g Carbohydrates: 25.8g Total Dietary Fiber: 3.6g Total Sugars: 3.5g Added Sugar: 0g Fat: 17.7g Saturated Fat: 9.5g Cholesterol: 172.9mg Vitamin A: 1,106.7 IU Vitamin C: 12.7mg Calcium: 156.4mg Iron: 1.7mg Potassium: 411.6mg Sodium: 1,223mg

Salmon with Broccoli-Pea Puree and Cucumber-Grape-Dill Salsa 267
For a single serving
Calories: 360 Protein: 31.4g
Carbohydrates: 33.3g Total Dietary Fiber: 8.9g Total Sugars: 18.5g Added Sugar: 0g Fat: 14.6g Saturated Fat: 2.1g Cholesterol: 62.4mg Vitamin A: 1,173 IU Vitamin C: 24.7mg Calcium: 98.3mg Iron: 2.3mg Potassium: 746.1mg Sodium: 445mg

Poached Shrimp Caesar Salad 268
For a single serving
Calories: 356 Protein: 22.3g Carbohydrates: 18.6g Total Dietary Fiber: 4.4g Total Sugars: 2.8g Added Sugar: 0g Fat: 21.4g Saturated Fat: 2.5g Cholesterol: 142.9mg Vitamin A: 1,314.4 IU Vitamin C: 17.7mg Calcium: 160.4mg Iron: 2.7mg Potassium: 513mg Sodium: 1,322mg

Five-Minute Tuna and Kimchi Bowl 271
For a single serving
Calories: 535 Protein: 32.6g
Carbohydrates: 22.9g Total Dietary Fiber: 16.7g Total Sugars: 3.6g Added Sugar: 0g Fat: 38.9g Saturated Fat: 5.8g Cholesterol: 33.9mg Vitamin A: 667.4 IU Vitamin C: 29.3mg Calcium: 99.7mg Iron: 3.9mg Potassium: 1,583.2mg Sodium: 826mg

Special Occasion Short Ribs with Olive Oil-Kefir Mashed Potatoes 274
Serving Size: ⅒ recipe
Calories: 1,183 Protein: 34.5g
Carbohydrates: 47.1g Total Dietary Fiber: 7.2g Total Sugars: 5.7g Added Sugar: 0g Fat: 90.7g Saturated Fat: 34.3g Cholesterol: 154mg Vitamin A: 5,346.2 IU Vitamin C: 54.2mg Calcium: 147.4mg Iron: 5.5mg Potassium: 635.7mg Sodium: 904mg

Slow-Roasted Chicken with Extra-Crispy Skin 276
Serving Size: ⅛ chicken
Calories: 485 Protein: 38.2g
Carbohydrates: 1.1g Total Dietary Fiber: 0.4g Total Sugars: 0.3g Added Sugar: 0g Fat: 34g Saturated Fat: 0g Cholesterol: 190mg Vitamin A: 2,056.9 IU Vitamin C: 9.3mg Calcium: 6.1mg Iron: 3mg Potassium: 10mg Sodium: 360mg

Crispy Chicken Thighs with Kale and Black-Eyed Peas 279
For a single serving
Calories: 364 Protein: 40.6g
Carbohydrates: 32.9g Total Dietary Fiber: 8.1g Total Sugars: 1.9g Added Sugar: 0g Fat: 9.1g Saturated Fat: 2.3g Cholesterol: 131.7mg Vitamin A: 11,316.6 IU Vitamin

C: 90.1mg Calcium: 174mg Iron: 5.1mg Potassium: 699.7mg Sodium: 911mg

Southwestern Chicken Burgers with Sweet Potato Fries 280

Serving Size: ⅙ recipe (including bun and toppings)
Calories: 874 Protein: 25.5g Carbohydrates: 129g Total Dietary Fiber: 14.6g Total Sugars: 16.9g Added Sugar: 0g Fat: 31.8g Saturated Fat: 7.8g Cholesterol: 112.5g Vitamin A: 39,217.3 IU Vitamin C: 59.1mg Calcium: 102.4mg Iron: 6.7mg Potassium: 645.1mg Sodium: 965mg

Stuffed Zucchini with Ground Turkey and Millet 283

Serving Size: 1 stuffed zucchini
Calories: 295 Protein: 20.6g Carbohydrates: 25.7g Total Dietary Fiber: 6.2g Total Sugars: 8.1g Added Sugar: 0g Fat: 12.9g Saturated Fat: 3.8g Cholesterol: 44.2mg Vitamin A: 275.1 IU Vitamin C: 63.4mg Calcium: 187.7mg Iron: 2.6mg Potassium: 918.5mg Sodium: 798mg

Long-Braised Lamb with Greens and Spicy Schmear 285

Serving Size: ⅒ recipe
Calories: 789 Protein: 41g Carbohydrates: 59.5g Total Dietary Fiber: 10g Total Sugars: 5.7g Added Sugar: 0g Fat: 44.4g Saturated Fat: 15.8g Cholesterol: 113.9g Vitamin A: 19,371.7 IU Vitamin C: 169.6mg Calcium: 321.7mg Iron: 6.8mg Potassium: 907.6mg Sodium: 1,236mg

White Wine-Braised Endive with Mustardy Pan Sauce 292

For a single serving
Calories: 136 Protein: 1.1g Carbohydrates: 5.7g Total Dietary Fiber: 3.6g Total Sugars: 0.4g Added Sugar: 0g Fat: 8.4g Saturated Fat: 5.3g Cholesterol: 22.5mg Vitamin A: 361.1 IU Vitamin C: 3.6mg Calcium: 27.5mg Iron: 0.4mg Potassium: 276.6mg Sodium: 235mg

Tikka Masala-Inspired Cauliflower with Kefir Raita 293

Serving Size: ⅛ recipe
Calories: 150 Protein: 5g Carbohydrates: 14.1g Total Dietary Fiber: 5g Total Sugars: 6.3g Added Sugar: 0g Fat: 9.5g Saturated Fat: 2.4g Cholesterol: 4.9mg Vitamin A: 378.9 IU Vitamin C: 86.4mg Calcium: 83.9mg Iron: 1.5mg Potassium: 694.3mg Sodium: 368mg

Cauliflower and Quinoa "Tabbouleh" with White Beans and Herbs 294

Serving Size: ¼ recipe
Calories: 235 Protein: 8.7g Carbohydrates: 29.1g Total Dietary Fiber: 8.8g Total Sugars: 1.5g Added Sugar: 0g Fat: 7.9g Saturated Fat: 1.1g Cholesterol: 0mg Vitamin A: 54.3 IU Vitamin C: 94.2mg Calcium: 158.7mg Iron: 3.3mg Potassium: 423.4mg Sodium: 373mg

Crispy Roasted Broccoli with Toasted Sunflower Seeds 297

Serving Size: ⅛ recipe
Calories: 222 Protein: 7g Carbohydrates: 12.5g Total Dietary Fiber: 5.2g Total Sugars: 3.1g Added Sugar: 0g Fat: 18.2g Saturated Fat: 2.5g Cholesterol: 0mg Vitamin A: 5,184.3 IU Vitamin C: 165mg Calcium: 98.8mg Iron: 2.2mg Potassium: 586.8mg Sodium: 328mg

Fingerling Potato Salad with Sauerkraut and Warm Chive-Bacon Vinaigrette 301

For a single serving
Calories: 125 Protein: 4.6g Carbohydrates: 21.6g Total Dietary Fiber: 3.8g Total Sugars: 0.7g Added Sugar: 0g Fat: 2.1g Saturated Fat: 0.8g Cholesterol: 4.2mg Vitamin A: 174.6 IU Vitamin C: 27.9mg Calcium: 17.9mg Iron: 0.9mg Potassium: 26.9mg Sodium: 293mg

Smoky White Beans and Brussels Sprouts 302

For a single serving
Calories: 197 Protein: 7.8g Carbohydrates: 26.6g Total Dietary Fiber: 10.6g Total Sugars: 3.5g Added Sugar: 0g Fat: 7.2g Saturated Fat: 1g Cholesterol: 0mg Vitamin A: 944.7 IU Vitamin C: 100.7mg Calcium: 136.1mg Iron: 2.9mg Potassium: 673.9mg Sodium: 344mg

Marinated Cucumber-Tomato Salad 303

For a single serving
Calories: 114 Protein: 3g Carbohydrates: 10g Total Dietary Fiber: 2.5g Total Sugars: 2g Added Sugar: 0g Fat: 9.3g Saturated Fat: 1.4g Cholesterol: 0mg Vitamin A: 653.8 IU Vitamin C: 16.6mg Calcium: 20mg Iron: 0.8mg Potassium: 118.6mg Sodium: 298mg

Beets with Scallions and Creamy Dill Dressing 304

Serving Size: ¼ recipe
Calories: 291 Protein: 9.3g Carbohydrates: 24.2g Total Dietary Fiber: 7g Total Sugars: 14.7g Added Sugar: 0g Fat: 19.1g Saturated Fat: 3.1g Cholesterol: 4.1mg Vitamin A: 73.7 IU Vitamin C: 16.3mg Calcium: 93.6mg Iron: 2.4mg Potassium: 827mg Sodium: 289mg

Shaved Turnip, Celery, and Kohlrabi Salad 306

Serving Size: ¼ recipe
Calories: 162 Protein: 3.6g Carbohydrates: 12.9g Total Dietary Fiber: 6g Total Sugars: 6g Added Sugar: 0g Fat: 11.8g Saturated Fat: 1.8g Cholesterol: 1.9mg Vitamin A: 210.9 IU Vitamin C: 83mg Calcium: 100.6mg Iron: 1mg Potassium: 488.7mg Sodium: 336mg

Roasted Brussels Sprouts with Toasted Hazelnuts and Pomegranate 307

Serving Size: ⅛ recipe
Calories: 150 Protein: 5.2g Carbohydrates: 14.1g Total Dietary Fiber: 5.5g Total Sugars: 4.5g Added Sugar: 0g Fat: 9.9g Saturated Fat: 1.1g Cholesterol: 0mg Vitamin A: 857.3 IU Vitamin C: 103.4mg Calcium: 60.3mg Iron: 2.1mg Potassium: 534.9mg Sodium: 205mg

Roasted Kabocha Squash with Gochujang and Cilantro 308

Serving Size: ⅙ recipe
Calories: 282 Protein: 7g Carbohydrates: 25.2g Total Dietary Fiber: 4g Total Sugars: 10.3g Added Sugar: 0g Fat: 17.9g Saturated Fat: 2.9g Cholesterol: 0mg Vitamin A: 10,897.6 IU Vitamin C: 29.7mg Calcium: 66.2mg Iron: 2.6mg Potassium: 90.5mg Sodium: 292mg

Delicata Rings with Kefir-Ranch Dip 309

Serving Size: ¼ recipe
Calories: 233 Protein: 5.5g Carbohydrates: 31.9g Total Dietary Fiber: 4.52g Total Sugars: 2.3g Added Sugar: 0g Fat: 10.5g Saturated Fat: 1.6g Cholesterol: 1.5mg Vitamin A: 14,294.6 IU Vitamin C: 40.3mg Calcium: 131.9mg Iron: 1.9mg Potassium: 89.8mg Sodium: 573mg

Brown Rice, Roasted Carrot, and Avocado Salad 310

For a single serving
Calories: 263 Protein: 4.4g Carbohydrates: 29.1g Total Dietary Fiber: 7.1g Total Sugars: 3.5g Added Sugar: 0g Fat: 16.5g Saturated Fat: 2.2g Cholesterol: 0g Vitamin A: 9,805 IU Vitamin C: 12.2mg Calcium: 33.7mg Iron: 1.7mg Potassium: 473.8mg Sodium: 429mg

APPENDIX

Salt-Massaged Napa Cabbage and Kimchi Slaw 311
Serving Size: **⅙ recipe**
Calories: **39** Protein: **2.6g** Carbohydrates: **4.3g Total Dietary Fiber: 2g** Total Sugars: **2g Added Sugar: 0g** Fat: **0.9g** Saturated Fat: **0g** Cholesterol: **0mg** Vitamin A: **1,511.7 IU** Vitamin C: **32.8mg** Calcium: **72.2mg** Iron: **0.6mg** Potassium: **38mg** Sodium: **549mg**

Quick-Braised Coconut Collard Greens 313
Serving Size: **¼ recipe**
Calories: **307** Protein: **5.6g** Carbohydrates: **18.5g Total Dietary Fiber: 6.23g** Total Sugars: **10.2g Added Sugar: 0g** Fat: **24.3g** Saturated Fat: **21.1g** Cholesterol: **0mg** Vitamin A: **5,450.3 IU** Vitamin C: **40.1mg** Calcium: **265.6mg** Iron: **2.1mg** Potassium: **319mg** Sodium: **337mg**

Ginger, Lemongrass, and Fennel Infusion 317
For a single serving
Calories: **0** Protein: **0g** Carbohydrates: **0g Total Dietary Fiber: 0g** Total Sugars: **0g Added Sugar: 0g** Fat: **0g** Saturated Fat: **0g** Cholesterol: **0mg** Vitamin A: **0 U** Vitamin C: **0mg** Calcium: **47.4mg** Iron: **0mg** Potassium: **0mg** Sodium: **9.48mg**

Turmeric-Coconut-Ginger Latte 318
Serving Size: **1 latte**
Calories: **295** Protein: **3.7g** Carbohydrates: **21.4g Total Dietary Fiber: 2.25g** Total Sugars: **15.6g Added Sugar: 0g** Fat: **20.9g** Saturated Fat: **15.6g** Cholesterol: **0mg** Vitamin A: **3.8 IU** Vitamin C: **4.2mg** Calcium: **63.8mg** Iron: **3.8mg** Potassium: **131.7mg** Sodium: **80mg**

Hibiscus and Mezcal Sparklers (without honey) 321
Serving Size: **⅙ recipe**
Calories: **71** Protein: **0.1g** Carbohydrates: **2.3g Total Dietary Fiber: 0.1g** Total Sugars: **0.5g Added Sugar: 0g** Fat: **0g** Saturated Fat: **0g** Cholesterol: **0mg** Vitamin A: **13.4 IU** Vitamin C: **8.1mg** Calcium: **16.6mg** Iron: **0.2mg** Potassium: **64mg** Sodium: **7mg**

Hibiscus and Mezcal Sparklers (with honey) 321
For a single serving
Calories: **94** Protein: **0.1g** Carbohydrates: **7.9g Total Dietary Fiber: 0.1g** Total Sugars: **5.8g Added Sugar: 5.3g** Fat: **0g** Saturated Fat: **0g** Cholesterol: **0g** Vitamin A: **13.4IU** Vitamin C: **8.1mg** Calcium: **16.6mg** Iron: **0.2mg** Potassium: **64mg** Sodium: **8mg**

Miso-Date Butterscotchy Sauce 325
Serving Size: **2 tablespoons**
Calories: **61** Protein: **0.7g** Carbohydrates: **11.2g Total Dietary Fiber: 0.9g** Total Sugars: **9.4g Added Sugar: 0g** Fat: **1.7g** Saturated Fat: **1.4g** Cholesterol: **0g** Vitamin A: **18.7 IU** Vitamin C: **0.7mg** Calcium: **9.4mg** Iron: **0.2mg** Potassium: **88.8mg** Sodium: **139mg**

Coconut Whipped Cream 326
Serving Size: **¼ cup**
Calories: **176** Protein: **2g** Carbohydrates: **3.8g Total Dietary Fiber: 1.2g** Total Sugars: **0.2g Added Sugar: 0.1g** Fat: **18.2g** Saturated Fat: **16.2g** Cholesterol: **0mg** Vitamin A: **0 IU** Vitamin C: **1.6mg** Calcium: **7.2mg** Iron: **1.2mg** Potassium: **185.5mg** Sodium: **26mg**

Chocolate-Chunk Peanut Butter-Banana "Nice" Cream 327
Serving Size: **⅛ recipe**
Calories: **468** Protein: **8.8g** Carbohydrates: **62.9g Total Dietary Fiber: 8g** Total Sugars: **32.1g Added Sugar: 0.1g** Fat: **23.8g** Saturated Fat: **10.7g** Cholesterol: **0mg** Vitamin A: **0 IU** Vitamin C: **20.8mg** Calcium: **44.9mg** Iron: **3.8mg** Potassium: **1,002mg** Sodium: **108mg**

Roasted Pineapple Parfaits 331
For a single serving
Calories: **364** Protein: **9.3g** Carbohydrates: **50.3g Total Dietary Fiber: 6.2g** Total Sugars: **37.1g Added Sugar: 0g** Fat: **16.9g** Saturated Fat: **8.6g** Cholesterol: **7.1g** Vitamin A: **267.8 IU** Vitamin C: **119.3mg** Calcium: **106.9mg** Iron: **1.5mg** Potassium: **436mg** Sodium: **304mg**

Pistachio Butter Thumbprints with Raspberry-Chia Filling 332
Serving Size: **One cookie**
Calories: **107** Protein: **3.5g** Carbohydrates: **11.3g Total Dietary Fiber: 2.8g** Total Sugars: **2.5g Added Sugar: 1.5g** Fat: **6.1g** Saturated Fat: **0.8g** Cholesterol: **0mg** Vitamin A: **31.1 IU** Vitamin C: **0.5mg** Calcium: **20.2mg** Iron: **0.9mg** Potassium: **156.7mg** Sodium: **72mg**

Sweet Potato, Squash, and Carrot Pie 334
Serving Size: **One slice (1/10th pie)**
Calories: **388** Protein: **8.8g** Carbohydrates: **45.9g Total Dietary Fiber: 6.8g** Total Sugars: **23.8g Added Sugar: 0.2g** Fat: **20.3g** Saturated Fat: **14.4g** Cholesterol: **86mg** Vitamin A: **14,187.5 IU** Vitamin C: **11.4mg** Calcium: **90.1mg** Iron: **2.5mg** Potassium: **265.7mg** Sodium: **237mg**

Chocolate-Dipped Peanut Butter, Miso, and Date Caramels 337
Serving Size: **One caramel**
Calories: **81** Protein: **1.7g** Carbohydrates: **10.7g Total Dietary Fiber: 1.6g** Total Sugars: **8g Added Sugar: 0g** Fat: **4.1g** Saturated Fat: **1.5g** Cholesterol: **0mg** Vitamin A: **16.8 IU** Vitamin C: **0mg** Calcium: **15.1mg** Iron: **0.8mg** Potassium: **102mg** Sodium: **97mg**

Spiced Vanilla Pear Crumble 338
Serving Size: **1/12 recipe**
Calories: **517** Protein: **7.9g** Carbohydrates: **51.1g Total Dietary Fiber: 10g** Total Sugars: **19.8g Added Sugar: 5.3g** Fat: **33.4g** Saturated Fat: **24.9g** Cholesterol: **0mg** Vitamin A: **2 IU** Vitamin C: **5.2mg** Calcium: **84.8mg** Iron: **2.6mg** Potassium: **234.4mg** Sodium: **217mg**

Seeded Chocolate-Tahini Bark 340
Serving Size: **1/12 recipe**
Calories: **377** Protein: **8.8g** Carbohydrates: **17.5g Total Dietary Fiber: 3.7g** Total Sugars: **5.7g Added Sugar: 0g** Fat: **30.6g** Saturated Fat: **13.8g** Cholesterol: **0mg** Vitamin A: **0 IU** Vitamin C: **0.1mg** Calcium: **62.2mg** Iron: **8.3mg** Potassium: **40.5mg** Sodium: **193mg**

Acknowledgments

I want to extend special thanks to the scientists, researchers, and writers who generously lent their time and shared their expertise with me as I wrote the book: Colleen Webb, MS, RDN; Emily Nagoski, PhD; Graham Rook, MD; Gyorgy Scrinis, PhD; Jenny Passione, RD, CC; Julia Plevin; Rob Knight, PhD; Sarah DiGregorio; Sarkis Mazmanian, PhD; Ted Dinan, MD, PhD.

Thank you is only the barest of words on which to hang my feelings of gratitude for the people who offered encouragement, ideas, and comfort throughout the process of creating this book. A whole world of support came together in ways big and small to make *Help Yourself* possible.

Thank you to my editor, Stephanie Fletcher, for believing in my vision and for championing the book from the start, and to everyone at Houghton Mifflin Harcourt for shepherding *Help Yourself* from proposal to publication. To my agent, Sarah Smith, I couldn't have done it without you. Thank you also to the whole team at David Black Agency. To art director Allison Chi and designer Laura Palese for designing this book so beautifully.

To the photo shoot team, thank you: Linda Pugliese for the gorgeous photographs. Monica Pierini, stylist extraordinaire, for making my food look so beautiful. Krystal Rack for the best attitude ever on set. To Precycle for letting us shoot in your space.

To my parents, Jim and Maggie—this book would not exist without your love and support. To Charlotte Hunt, Vanessa Magro, Annie Daly, and Blake MacKay—thank you for being the scaffolding around me during this process.

To Annie Boardman, Abby Delgoffe, Ali Eastman and Zane Aukee, Ben Mims, Cat Emil, Dawn Perry and Matt Duckor, Felicia Resor, Greg Oke, Jess Thomas and Hagan Hinshaw, Jordana Rothman, Joy Jorgensen, Natasha Bunzl, Ned Rosenman and Audrey Banks, Stacy Fisher, and Steve Harvey, thank you for your friendship while I wrote this book.

To the people who have taught me and guided me over the years, in particular Dawn Perry, Lygeia Grace, and Sarah Copeland.

To Colleen Webb and Jenny Passione for their expertise in nutrition. To Syd Schwarz for connecting me with Colleen Webb.

To Maggie Hunt, Darla Jackson, Casey Elsass, and Chrissy Tkac for testing recipes.

To the people who housed me as I wrote this book (mostly) as a nomad—Lauren and Mike Bogorad, Jamie Fellner, Jess and Hagan Hinshaw, Joy Jorgensen and Raphael Langenscheidt, Lily Calaway and Lenny Langenscheidt, and Maggie and Jim Hunt.

Resources

This is an inexhaustive list of books that I recommend for exploring beyond the pages of *Help Yourself*.

My Favorite Vegetable-Focused Cookbooks

At Home in the Whole Food Kitchen and *Whole Food Cooking Every Day* by Amy Chaplin

Food for a Happy Gut by Naomi Devlin

Be Good to Your Gut by Eve Kalinik

Six Seasons by Joshua McFadden

Plenty and *Plenty More* by Yotam Ottolenghi

Fermentation Books

The Art of Fermentation by Sandor Ellix Katz

The Noma Guide to Fermentation by René Redzepi and David Zilber

Books Referenced

Anderson, Scott C., John F. Cryan, and Timothy G. Dinan. *The Psychobiotic Revolution: Mood, Food, and the New Science of the Gut-Brain Connection*. Washington, DC: National Geographic Partners, 2017.

Chutkan, Robynne. *The Microbiome Solution: A Radical New Way to Heal Your Body From the Inside Out*. New York: Avery, 2015.

Clear, James. *Atomic Habits: An Easy & Proven Way to Build Good Habits and Break Bad Ones*. New York: Avery, 2018.

Collen, Alanna. *10% Human: How Your Body's Microbes Hold the Key to Health and Happiness*. New York: HarperCollins Publishers, 2015.

Dweck, Carol S. Mindset: *The New Psychology of Success*. New York: Ballantine Books, 2006.

Enders, Giulia. *Gut: The Inside Story of Our Body's Most Underrated Organ*. Translated by David Shaw. Vancouver: Greystone Books, 2015.

Gilbert, Jack, and Rob Knight. *Dirt Is Good: The Advantage of Germs for Your Child's Developing Immune System*. New York: St. Martin's Press, 2017.

Knight, Rob and Brendan Buhler. *Follow Your Gut: The Enormous Impact of Tiny Microbes*. New York: Simon & Schuster, 2015.

Lawless, Kristin. *Formerly Known As Food: How the Industrial Food System Is Changing Our Minds, Bodies, and Culture*. New York: St. Martin's Press, 2018.

Mayer, Emeran. *The Mind-Gut Connection: How the Hidden Conversation Within Our Bodies Impacts Our Mood, Our Choices, and Our Overall Health*. New York: Harper Wave, 2016.

Rubin, Gretchen. *Better than Before*. New York: Broadway Books, 2015.

Scrinis, Gyorgy. *Nutritionism: The Science and Politics of Dietary Advice*. New York: Columbia University Press, 2013.

Sonnenburg, Justin, and Erica Sonnenburg. *The Good Gut: Taking Control of Your Weight, Your Mood, and Your Long-Term Health*. New York: Penguin Books, 2015.

Taubes, Gary. *The Case Against Sugar*. New York: Alfred A. Knopf, 2016.

Yong, Ed. *I Contain Multitudes: The Microbes Within Us and a Grander View of Life*. New York: Ecco, 2018.

Citations

PAGE

21   *Imbalance in gut microbiota is correlated with:* Jack A. Gilbert et al., "Current Understanding of the Human Microbiome," *Nature Medicine* 24 (2018): 392–400, https://doi.org/10.1038/nm.4517.

24   *a term coined by Dan Buettner:* Dan Buettner and Sam Skemp, "Blue Zones: Lessons from the World's Longest Lived," *American Journal of Lifestyle Medicine* 10, no. 5 (2016): 318–21, https://doi.org/10.1177/1559827616637066.

29   *over 300 million genes:* Andrew Maltez Thomas and Nicola Segata, "Multiple Levels of the Unknown in Microbiome Research," *BMC Biology* 17 (2019): 48, https://doi.org/10.1186/s12915-019-0667-z.

33   *often called the "second brain":* Michael D. Gershon, "The Enteric Nervous System: A Second Brain," *Hospital Practice* 34, no. 7 (1999): 31–52, https://doi.org/10.3810/hp.1999.07.153.

   The ENS influences: Amar Sarkar et al., "Psychobiotics and the Manipulation of Bacteria–Gut–Brain Signals," *Trends in Neurosciences* 39, no. 11 (2016): 763–81, https://doi.org/10.1016/j.tins.2016.09.002.

   the two systems are in close communication: Sigrid Breit et al., "Vagus Nerve as Modulator of the Brain-Gut Axis in Psychiatric and Inflammatory Disorders," *Frontiers in Psychiatry* 9 (2018): 44, https://doi.org/10.3389/fpsyt.2018.00044.

   The stomach's clever shape: Justin Sonnenburg and Erica Sonnenburg, *The Good Gut: Taking Control of Your Weight, Your Mood, and Your Long-Term Health* (New York: Penguin Books, 2015), 12.

34   *which ranges in length:* Sonnenburg and Sonnenburg, *The Good Gut,* 12.

   Fructose is absorbed by the liver: Karen W. Della Corte et al., "Effect of Dietary Sugar Intake on Biomarkers of Subclinical Inflammation: A Systematic Review and Meta-Analysis of Intervention Studies," *Nutrients* 10, no. 5 (2018): 606, https://doi.org/10.3390/nu10050606.

   popularized by Charles Darwin: Alanna Collen, *10% Human: How Your Body's Microbes Hold the Key to Health and Happiness* (New York: HarperCollins Publishers, 2015), 13.

35   *substances like medications and chemicals:* Sonnenburg and Sonnenburg, *The Good Gut,* 70–71.

   That means it's a perfect poo: Sonnenburg and Sonnenburg, *The Good Gut,* 110.

   Constipation can be caused by: Iain J. D. McCallum, Sarah Ong, and Mark Mercer-Jones, "Chronic Constipation in Adults," *BMJ: British Medical Journal* 338, no. 7697 (2009): 763–66, https://doi.org/10.1136/bmj.b831.

36   *gut microbiota can change:* Gabriela K. Fragiadakis et al., "Long-Term Dietary Intervention Reveals Resilience of the Gut Microbiota Despite Changes in Diet and Weight," bioRxiv 729327 (2019), https://doi.org/10.1101/729327.

37   *microbiota determines glucose response:* Tal Korem et al., "Bread Affects Clinical Parameters and Induces Gut Microbiome-Associated Personal Glycemic Responses," *Cell Metabolism* 25, no. 6 (2017) 1243–53.e5, https://doi.org/10.1016/j.cmet.2017.05.002.

38   *Some are experts at synthesizing vitamins:* Sonnenburg and Sonnenburg, *The Good Gut,* 20–21.

   regulating the release of anti-inflammatory immune cells: Christopher A. Lowry et al., "The Microbiota, Immunoregulation, and Mental Health: Implications for Public Health," *Current Environmental Health Reports* 3, no. 3 (2016): 270–86, https://doi.org/10.1007/s40572-016-0100-5.

   butyrate signals the enteric nervous system: Ara Koh et al., "From Dietary Fiber to Host Physiology: Short-Chain Fatty Acids as Key Bacterial Metabolites," *Cell* 165, no. 6 (2016): 1332–45, https://doi.org/10.1016/j.cell.2016.05.041.

39   *gamma aminobutyric acid (GABA):* Philip Strandwitz, "Neurotransmitter Modulation by the Gut Microbiota," *Brain Research* 1693, pt. B (2018): 128–33, https://doi.org/10.1016/j.brainres.2018.03.015.

   like to eat dietary fiber: Joanne Slavin, "Fiber and Prebiotics: Mechanisms and Health Benefits," *Nutrients* 5, no. 4 (2013): 1417–35, https://doi.org/10.3390/nu5041417.

40   *This type of starch:* Sonnenburg and Sonnenburg, *The Good Gut,* 120–21.

41 *lower bacterial richness is associated with:* Lindsey G. Albenberg and Gary D. Wu, "Diet and the Intestinal Microbiome: Associations, Functions, and Implications for Health and Disease," *Gastroenterology* 146, no. 6 (2014): 1564–72, https://doi.org/10.1053/j.gastro.2014.01.058.

42 *With chronic stress comes inflammation:* John F. Cryan and Timothy G. Dinan, "Mind-altering Microorganisms: The Impact of the Gut Microbiota on Brain and Behaviour," *Nature Reviews Neuroscience* 13, no. 10 (2012): 701–12, https://doi.org/10.1038/nrn3346.

    The "old friends" mechanism: Graham A. W. Rook, Christopher A. Lowry, and Charles L. Raison, "Microbial 'Old Friends,' Immunoregulation and Stress Resilience," *Evolution, Medicine, and Public Health* 2013, no. 1 (2013): 46–64, https://doi.org/10.1093/emph/eot004.

43 *like sucking on a pacifier:* Bill Hesselmar et al., "Pacifier Cleaning Practices and Risk of Allergy Development," *Pediatrics* 131, no. 6 (2013): e1829–e1837, https://doi.org/10.1542/peds.2012-3345.

    Decreased exposure to these factors: Thomas Gensollen et al., "How Colonization by Microbiota in Early Life Shapes the Immune System," *Science* 352, no. 6285 (2016): 539–44, https://doi.org/10.1126/science.aad9378.

    A decline in gut microbial diversity: Paul W. O'Toole and Ian B. Jeffery, "Microbiome–health Interactions in Older People," *Cellular and Molecular Life Sciences* 75, no. 1 (2018): 119–28, https://doi.org/10.1007/s00018-017-2673-z.

    When this normally tight barrier is loosened: Michael Camilleri, "Leaky Gut: Mechanisms, Measurement and Clinical Implications in Humans," *Gut* 68, no. 8 (2019): 1516–26, https://doi.org/10.1136/gutjnl-2019-318427.

44 *if healing the lining would improve symptoms:* Camilleri.

    Researchers now suspect: Lukas Niederreiter, Timon E. Adolph, and Herbert Tilg, "Food, Microbiome and Colorectal Cancer," *Digestive and Liver Disease* 50, no. 7 (2018): 647–52, https://doi.org/10.1016/j.dld.2018.03.030.

    a distinct microbial signature: Jakob Wirbel et al., "Meta-analysis of Fecal Metagenomes Reveals Global Microbial Signatures that are Specific for Colorectal Cancer," *Nature Medicine* 25 (2019): 679–89, https://doi.org/10.1038/s41591-019-0406-6.

    Crohn's can affect: Centers for Disease Control and Prevention, "What Is Inflammatory Bowel Disease (IBD)?" https://www.cdc.gov/ibd/what-is-ibd.htm (accessed October 31, 2019).

    IBD develops as a: Jonas Halfvarson et al., "Dynamics of the Human Gut Microbiome in Inflammatory Bowel Disease," *Nature Microbiology* 2 (2017): 17004, https://doi.org/10.1038/nmicrobiol.2017.4.

    It is estimated to affect: Scott Anderson, John F. Cryan, and Ted Dinan, *The Psychobiotic Revolution: Mood, Food, and the New Science of the Gut-Brain Connection* (Washington, DC: National Geographic, 2017), 213.

45 *Probiotics have not been proven:* Cryan, Anderson, and Dinan, 165–66.

46 *diet is increasingly seen as:* Felice N. Jacka, "Nutritional Psychiatry: Where to Next?," *EBioMedicine* 17 (2017): 24–29, https://doi.org/10.1016/j.ebiom.2017.02.020.

    It is known to transmit information: Mary I. Butler, John F. Cryan, and Timothy G. Dinan, "Man and the Microbiome: A New Theory of Everything?," *Annual Review of Clinical Psychology* 15 (2019): 371–98, https://doi.org/10.1146/annurev-clinpsy-050718-095432.

47 *Hormones like ghrelin:* Breit et al.

    Sleep disruption alters gut bacteria: Christian Benedict et al., "Gut Microbiota and Glucometabolic Alterations in Response to Recurrent Partial Sleep Deprivation in Normal-Weight Young Individuals," *Molecular Metabolism* 5, no. 12 (2016): 1175–86, https://doi.org/10.1016/j.molmet.2016.10.003.

50 *Orthorexia is an eating disorder:* Hellas Cena et al., "Definition and Diagnostic Criteria for Orthorexia Nervosa: A Narrative Review of the Literature," *Eating and Weight Disorders—Studies on Anorexia, Bulimia, and Obesity* 24, no. 2 (2019): 209–46, https://doi.org/10.1007/s40519-018-0606-y.

55 *But this leads to the erroneous belief:* Gary Taubes, *The Case Against Sugar* (New York: Alfred A. Knopf, 2016), 109.

    And switching to a high-calorie: Collen, *10% Human,* 69–70.

56   *This is a controversial diet:* Gauree G. Konijeti et al., "Efficacy of the Autoimmune Protocol Diet for Inflammatory Bowel Disease," *Inflammatory Bowel Diseases* 23, no. 11 (2017): 2054–60, https://doi.org/10.1097/MIB.0000000000001221.

   As humans migrated: Erica D. Sonnenburg and Justin L. Sonnenburg, "Starving Our Microbial Self: The Deleterious Consequences of a Diet Deficient in Microbiota-Accessible Carbohydrates," *Cell Metabolism* 20, no. 5 (2014): 779–86, https://doi.org/10.1016/j.cmet.2014.07.003.

57   *Children are likely to experience:* Celiac Disease Foundation, "Symptoms of Celiac Disease," https://celiac.org/about-celiac-disease/symptoms-of-celiac-disease/ (accessed on November 1, 2019).

   In their additive form: Laura J. Dixon et al., "Combinatorial Effects of Diet and Genetics on Inflammatory Bowel Disease Pathogenesis," *Inflammatory Bowel Diseases* 21, no. 4 (2015): 912–22, https://doi.org/10.1097/MIB.0000000000000289.

58   *It's a whole food if:* Gyorgy Scrinis, *Nutritionism: The Science and Politics of Dietary Advice* (New York: Columbia University Press, 2013), 219.

59   *research by the American Gut Project:* Daniel McDonald et al., "American Gut: An Open Platform for Citizen Science Microbiome Research," *mSystems* 3, no. 3 (2018): e00031–18, https://doi.org/10.1128/mSystems.00031-18.

61   *Ultraprocessed products are made from:* C. A. Monteiro et al., "Ultraprocessed Products Are Becoming Dominant in the Global Food System," *Obesity Reviews* 14, no. S2 (2013): 21–28, https://doi.org/10.1111/obr.12107.

63   *from the field of toxicology:* Kristin Lawless, *Formerly Known as Food: How the Industrial Food System Is Changing Our Minds, Bodies, and Culture* (New York: St. Martin's Press, 2018), 144.

65   *Alcohol also seems to encourage:* D. Compare et al., "Gut-Liver Axis: The Impact of Gut Microbiota on Non Alcoholic Fatty Liver Disease," *Nutrition, Metabolism and Cardiovascular Diseases* 22, no. 6 (2012): 471–76, https://doi.org/10.1016/j.numecd.2012.02.007.

74   *One oft-maligned ingredient:* James Hamblin, "The Next Gluten," *The Atlantic,* April 24, 2017. https://www.theatlantic.com/health/archive/2017/04/the-next-gluten/523686/ (accessed on November 1, 2019).

   In fact, one notable study: Victoria Miller et al., "Fruit, Vegetable, and Legume Intake, and Cardiovascular Disease and Deaths in 18 Countries (PURE): A Prospective Cohort Study," *The Lancet* 390, no. 10107 (2017): 2037–49, https://doi.org/10.1016/S0140-6736(17)32253-5.

   Nightshades are routinely called: Cleveland Clinic healthessentials, "Arthritis: Should You Avoid Nightshade Vegetables?" https://health.clevelandclinic.org/arthritis-should-you-avoid-nightshade-vegetables (accessed on November 1, 2019).

77   *This is called* automaticity: James Clear, *Atomic Habits: An Easy & Proven Way to Build Good Habits & Break Bad Ones* (New York: Avery, 2018), 144–45.

78   *Research shows that we view our future selves:* Hal E. Hershfield, "Future Self-Continuity: How Conceptions of the Future Self Transform Intertemporal Choice," *Annals of the New York Academy of Sciences* 1235, no. 1 (2011): 30–43, https://doi.org/10.1111/j.1749-6632.2011.06201.x.

79   *This is called having a growth mindset:* Carol S. Dweck, *Mindset: The New Psychology of Success* (New York: Ballantine Books, 2006), 7.

80   *The problem is not slipping up:* Clear, 201.

143 *glyphosate (the main ingredient in Roundup):* Lola Rueda-Ruzafa et al., "Gut Microbiota and Neurological Effects of Glyphosate," *NeuroToxicology* 75 (2019): 1–8, https://doi.org/10.1016/j.neuro.2019.08.006.

254 *Omega-3s may contribute to:* Lara Costantini et al., "Impact of Omega-3 Fatty Acids on the Gut Microbiota," *International Journal of Molecular Sciences* 18, no. 12 (2017): 2645, https://doi.org/10.3390/ijms18122645.

APPENDIX

Index

"Lindsay has achieved the impossible with *Help Yourself*: a book about health that trades in pleasure and manages to cast gut microbes as guests at a fantastic party that your body gets to host. Through the lens of her own experience, and with a scientific rigor often missing from the fact-averse #wellness canon, Lindsay imagines a world in which food can offer both joy and salvation in the same bite."

—JORDANA ROTHMAN, food writer and co-author of *Tacos: Recipes and Provocations*

"Most cookbooks just focus on how to get food from supermarket to mouth. In *Help Yourself,* Lindsay goes a lot further, examining how our bodies actually process (or don't) what we eat. Lindsay presents a compelling case for how we can all be gentler on our bodies and our guts, without sacrificing big bold flavors."

—CHRIS MOROCCO, deputy food editor, *Bon Appétit*

"As someone who's suffered my fair share of food-related health issues and the joyless diet plans prescribed to treat them, Lindsay's 'taste-first' approach to healthier eating is a revelation. Her recipes rise above soulless science to give you solutions you'll actually enact with recipes you'll crave. This book is an indispensable guide to a better way of treating your body through food, and I'll be cooking from it every week."

—BEN MIMS, cooking columnist for the *Los Angeles Times*

"*Help Yourself* isn't just a provision for hearty eating, it provides us with peace of mind, exploring the links between our personal microbiota and a symbiotic approach towards better gut health. What's doubly impressive is that these restorative recipes are delicious too; they home in on Lindsay's talents as a cook without getting outdone by the edifying science preceding them."

—MICHAEL HARLAN TURKELL, award-winning photographer, author, and podcast host